PROCOPIUS OF CAESAREA:
THE PERSIAN WARS

Procopius was the major historian of the reign of Justinian and one of the most important historians of Late Antiquity. This is the first stand-alone English translation of his work *The Persian Wars*. It offers a new translation, which has at its basis one published fifty years ago by Averil Cameron. *The Persian Wars*, despite the title, is a wide-ranging work that reports the history and geography not only of Mesopotamia and the Caucasus, but also of southern Arabia and Ethiopia, Iran and Central Asia, and Constantinople itself. This book is equipped with notes, maps and plans, an introduction, and a translation of a further Greek text, that of Nonnosus, which overlaps with Procopius'. It will be of interest to specialists and the general reader alike.

GEOFFREY GREATREX is a Professor in the Department of Classics and Religious Studies at the University of Ottawa and President of the Canadian Committee of Byzantinists. He has spent the past thirty years in research on the late Roman eastern frontier, much of it concerned with the work of Procopius, and has published extensively on the subject.

PROCOPIUS OF CAESAREA:
THE PERSIAN WARS

Translation, with Introduction and Notes

EDITED BY

GEOFFREY GREATREX

University of Ottawa

With acknowledgements to

AVERIL CAMERON

University of Oxford

CAMBRIDGE
UNIVERSITY PRESS

Shaftesbury Road, Cambridge CB2 8EA, United Kingdom

One Liberty Plaza, 20th Floor, New York, NY 10006, USA

477 Williamstown Road, Port Melbourne, VIC 3207, Australia

314–321, 3rd Floor, Plot 3, Splendor Forum, Jasola District Centre, New Delhi – 110025, India

103 Penang Road, #05–06/07, Visioncrest Commercial, Singapore 238467

Cambridge University Press is part of Cambridge University Press & Assessment, a department of the University of Cambridge.

We share the University's mission to contribute to society through the pursuit of education, learning and research at the highest international levels of excellence.

www.cambridge.org
Information on this title: www.cambridge.org/9781316617076

DOI: 10.1017/9781316694077

© Geoffrey Greatrex 2022

First published 2022
First paperback edition 2025

A catalogue record for this publication is available from the British Library

ISBN   978-1-107-16570-0   Hardback
ISBN   978-1-316-61707-6   Paperback

Contents

Maps and Battle Plans

Preface

As I note in the Preface to my detailed Commentary to this work, which will be published simultaneously, a publicist could perhaps describe this as the first new translation in English for over a hundred years, since Dewing's Loeb translation (vol. 1) appeared first in 1914. But in fact such an assertion would not be strictly accurate, for two reasons. First, Averil Cameron published in 1967 a paperback translation of significant extracts from the *Persian* and *Gothic Wars*, the *Anecdota* and the *Buildings*. With her kind permission I have used this translation as the basis of my own; it is a great shame that it was never widely available because the press that published it disappeared soon afterwards. Second, Anthony Kaldellis in 2014 brought out a one-volume translation of the *Wars* which, while ostensibly a revision of Dewing's, is almost a new work in itself. I discuss other translations below in the Introduction.

In addition to the translation of Procopius I have included a new translation of Nonnosus' work, so far as it survives in Photius' ninth-century summary. The same translation, with more copious notes, may also be found in my Commentary. It sheds further light on the situation in southern Arabia in the first part of Justinian's reign, complementing what Procopius reports at 1.19–20.

I am grateful to various colleagues and friends who have assisted me with the translation, notably Richard Burgess and Eleanor Dickey. While working on this translation I also made one into Esperanto, on which Saioa Escobar was kind enough to send me comments; these have in turn helped me with the English version. Dariusz Brodka invariably responded quickly to questions I had about his Polish translation, with which Kamilla Twardowska also helped me. Julian and Elizabeth Lock read through the translation with their expert proof-reading eyes, as did my mother at a subsequent stage. Lucas McMahon helped insert the section numbers at an early stage. For the accompanying maps I am grateful to JaShong King, who produced most of them, as also to

Catharine Hof and Grégoire Poccardi for the city plans. Maxime Petitjean kindly gave permission to adapt his battle plans for Dara and Callinicum, while Chris Lillington-Martin did likewise for the maps of the area around Dara. I should also like to thank Scott Winges for his work on the indices and to express my thanks to Barbara Docherty for her attentive copy-editing and to Michael Sharp at Cambridge University Press for his faith in the project over its long duration.

The notes are quite brief: full details are, of course, to be found in my Commentary. While attempting to orientate the reader on basic points, I have tended to give references to basic works such as the *Prosopography of the Later Roman Empire* and the *Oxford Dictionary of Late Antiquity*, alongside a few works devoted to the Roman eastern frontier. I have listed relevant general works in the Further Reading section, pp. 16–17.

Acknowledgements

I am grateful, as noted in the Preface, to Averil Cameron for her permission to adapt and complete her translation of 1967. This was published by the Washington Square Press, which is an imprint of Simon and Schuster, it should be noted, but has long been unavailable.

I should like to express my gratitude also for permission to adapt several plans:

- Elif Keser-Kayaalp and Nihat Erdoğan for the plan of Dara (fig. 28)
- Grégoire Poccardi and Catherine Saliou for the plan of Antioch (fig. 27)
- John Watt and Liverpool University Press for the plan of Edessa, which is based on map IV in J. Watt and F. Trombley, *The Chronicle of Joshua the Stylite* (Liverpool, 1999) (fig. 29)
- Fig. 9 is adapted with permission from Christopher Lillington-Martin
- Fig. 10 is adapted with permission from Andrew Brozyna
- Figs. 11–16 and 20 are adapted with permission from Maxime Petitjean

The work of producing and adapting the maps was carried out for the most part, as noted in the Preface, by JaShong King, but I must also thank Catharine Hof for her adaptation of the city plans of Amida, Antioch, Dara and Edessa. Ross Burns kindly provided fig. 26, which shows the road network in the Roman East, while Jonathan Bardill likewise prepared fig. 22, the map of Constantinople at the time of the Nika riot.

Abbreviations

See also the list of other sources at the end of the Introduction, pp. 16–17.

AEBI	*Arabs and Empires before Islam*, ed. G. Fisher (Oxford, 2015).
ODLA	*The Oxford Dictionary of Late Antiquity*, ed. O. Nicholson (Oxford, 2018).
PLRE	*Prosopography of the Later Roman Empire*, vols. 2–3, ed. J.R. Martindale (Cambridge, 1980–92).
REF	G. Greatrex and S.N.C. Lieu, *The Roman Eastern Frontier and the Persian Wars, A.D. 363–630* (London, 2002).
RPLA	B. Dignas and E. Winter, *Rome and Persia in Late Antiquity: Neighbours and Rivals* (Cambridge, 2007).
RPW	G. Greatrex, *Rome and Persia at War, 502–532* (Leeds, 1998).

Tables of Names

(1) Names of People

Greek name (transliterated)	Name used in this translation	Other versions of the name
Abandanēs	Abandanes	
Abokharabos	Abu Karib	Abū Karib
Abramos	Abramus	Abraha
Akakios	Acacius	
Adergoudounbadēs	Adergudunbades	Ādhargulbād
Adolios	Adolius	
Adonachos	Adonachus	
Aeimachos	Aeimachus	
Aigan	Aigan	
Alamoundaros	al-Mundhir	
Alexandros	Alexander	
Amazaspēs	Amazaspes	Hamazasp
Ambazoukēs	Ambazuces	
Ambros	ʿAmr	
Anastasios	Anastasius	
Anatolios	Anatolius	
Andreas	Andreas	Andrew
Aniabedēs	Aniabedes	? *ayēnbadh*
Antōnina	Antonina	
Apiōn	Apion	
Aratios	Aratius	
Areobindos	Areobindus	

Greek name (transliterated)	Name used in this translation	Other versions of the name
Arethas	al-Harith	al-Ḥārith
Argek	Argek	
Arkadios	Arcadius	
Arsakēs	Arsaces	Aršak, Arshak
Artabanēs	Artabanes	Ardavan
Askan	Ascan	
Aspebedēs	Aspebedes	? *spāhbad*
Augaros	Abgar	
Augoustos	Augustus	
Azarethēs	Azarethes	Exarath, ? *hazārbed*
Baradotos	Baradotus	Bar-Hadad
Baresmanas	Baresmanas	? *marzban*
Basilidēs	Basilides	
Basileios	Basil	
Bassakēs	Bassaces	Vasak
Bassikios	Bassicius	Vasak
Belisarios	Belisarius	
Blasēs	Blases	Balash, Valash
Blēskhamēs	Bleschames	
Boēs	Boes	
Boraïdēs	Boraides	
Bouzēs	Buzes	
Bradoukios	Braducius	
Kabadēs	Kavadh	Cabades, Qubad, Qobad
Kaïsos	Qays	Caisus
Kandidos	Candidus	
Kaosēs	Kaoses	Kāwūs, Kayūs
Keler	Celer	
Khanarangēs	*kanarang*	kanārang, Kanārangīyān
Khosroēs	Khusro	Ḵosrow, Kisra, Xusro

Greek name (transliterated)	Name used in this translation	Other versions of the name
Kōnstantianos	Constantianus	
Koutzēs	Cutzes	
Kyrillos	Cyril	
Kyros	Cyrus	
Dagisthaios	Dagisthaeus	
Diogenēs	Diogenes	
Dioklētianos	Diocletian	
Domnentiolos	Domnentiolus	
Dorotheos	Dorotheus	
Eirenaios	Irenaeus	
Ephraimios	Ephraem	
Esimiphaios	Esimiphaeus	Sumūyafaʿ Ashwaʿ
Euaris	Euaris	Evaris
Eusebios	Eusebius	
Phlorentios	Florentius	
Gabalas	Jabala	Gabala
Geōrgios	George	
Germanos	Germanus	
Glōnēs	Glones	Aglon
Godidisklos	Godidisclus	
Goubazēs	Gubazes	
Gourgenēs	Gurgenes	
Gousanastadēs	Gusanastades	Gushnaspdād
Hellesthaios	Hellesthaeus	Kālēb, ʾElla ʾAṣbeḥa
Hermogenēs	Hermogenes	
Honōrios	Honorius	
Hypatios	Hypatius	

Tables of Names

Greek name (transliterated)	Name used in this translation	Other versions of the name
Iphigeneia	Iphigenia	
Isaakēs	Isaac	
Isdigerdēs	Yazdgerd	
Isdigousnas	Yazdgushnasp	Iesdegousnaph, Iesdek
Iakōbos	Jacob	
Iasōn	Jason	
Iēsous	Jesus	
Iōannēs	John	
Ioulianos	Julian	
Ioustinianos	Justinian	
Ioustinos	Justin	
Ioustos	Justus	
Libelarios	Libelarius	
Longinos	Longinus	
Loukas	Luke	
Markellos	Marcellus	
Martinos	Martin	
Mebodēs	Mebodes	Māhbōdh
Mermeroēs	Mihr-Mihroe	
Mirranēs	Mirranes	Mihran
Molatzēs	Molatzes	
Moundos	Mundus	
Nabedēs	Nabedes	Nabed
Narsēs	Narses	
Nikētas	Nicetas	
Odonathos	Odenathus	
Olybrios	Olybrius	
Orestēs	Orestes	

Greek name (transliterated)	Name used in this translation	Other versions of the name
Origenēs	Origen	
Osroēs	Osrhoes	
Pakourios	Pacurius	
Patrikiolos	Patriciolus	
Patrikios	Patricius	
Paulos	Paul	
Peranios	Peranius	
Perozēs	Peroz	Fīrūz
Petros	Peter	
Phabrizos	Vahriz	
Pharesmanēs	Pharesmanes	Farzman
Pharsansēs	Pharsanses	
Philemouth	Philemuth	
Phokas	Phocas	
Phoubelis	Phubelis	
Pityaxēs	Pityaxes	*bdeashkh, bidaxš*
Pompeios	Pompey	
Probos	Probus	
Proklos	Proculus	Proclus
Prokopios	Procopius	
Pyladēs	Pylades	
Rhekinarios	Rhecinarius	
Rhekithangos	Rhecithangus	
Roufinos	Rufinus	
Senekios	Senecius	
Seosēs	Seoses	Siyāvush
Sergios	Sergius	
Silbanos	Silvanus	
Solomōn	Solomon	
Soummos	Summus	

Greek name (transliterated)	Name used in this translation	Other versions of the name
Sounikas	Sunicas	
Stephanakios	Stephanacius	
Stephanos	Stephanus	
Stratēgios	Strategius	
Symeōn	Symeon	
Tatianos	Tatian	
Theodōra	Theodora	
Theodōros	Theodore	
Theodōsios	Theodosius	
Theoktistos	Theoctistus	
Theuderikhos	Theoderic	
Timostratos	Timostratus	
Traïanos	Trajan	
Tribounianus	Tribonian	
Tribounos	Tribunus	
Balerianos	Valerian	
Ouararanēs	Bahram	Vahram
Ouarramēs	Varrames	Bahram, Vahram
Béros	Verus	
Bitalianos	Vitalian	
Ouittigis	Vitigis	Wittigis
Zaberganēs	Zabergan	
Zamēs	Zames	Zham, Jāmāsp
Zēnōn	Zeno	
Zēnobia	Zenobia	

(2) Names of Places and Peoples

Name in Procopius' Greek	Name used in this translation	Other name(s)
Aborrhas (river)	Khabur	
Ailas	Aela	Aqaba

Name in Procopius' Greek	Name used in this translation	Other name(s)
Aithiopai	Ethiopians	
Amida	Amida	Diyarbakır
Ammodios	Ammodius	Amuda, ʿAmudin
Antinoou (*polis*)	City of Antinous	Antinoë, Antinoöpolis
Antiokheia	Antioch	Antakya
Apameia	Apamea	Afamia
Arkhaiopolis	Archaeopolis	Nokalakevi
Arsinos (river)	Arsinus	Arsanias, Murat Su
Artakē	Artace	Erdek
Arzamōn	Arzamon	Tell Harzem
Arzanēnē	Arzanene	
Attakhas	Attachas	Attachae
Auxōmis	Auxomis	Axum, Aksum, Ethiopia
Auxōmitai	Auxomites	Axumites, Aksumites, Ethiopians
Barbalissos	Barbalissus	Eski Meskene
Batnai	Batnae	Batnan, Serug
Beroia	Beroea	Aleppo, Halab
Blemyes	Blemmyes	? Beja
Bōlon	Bolum	Bołberd
Bosporos	Bosporus	Panticapaeum, Kertch
Boulikas	Bulicas	
Byzantion	Byzantium	Constantinople, Istanbul
Kadisēnoi	Kadiseni	
Kaisareia	Caesarea	
Kallinikon	Callinicum	ar-Raqqa
Kappadokia	Cappadocia	
Karrhai	Carrhae	Harran
Kaspiai Pylai	Caspian Gates	
Kassandreia	Cassandreia	Potidaea
Kaukasos	Caucasus	
Kelesēnē	Kelesene	

Name in Procopius' Greek	Name used in this translation	Other name(s)
Khersōn	Cherson	Sevastopol
Kherronēsos	Chersonese	
Khorzianēnē	Khorzianene	
Kilikia	Cilicia	
Kirkēsion	Circesium	
Kitharizōn	Citharizon	
Kolkhis	Colchis	Lazica, (Western) Georgia
Komana	Comana	
Kommagēnē	Commagene	
Kōnstantina	Constantia	Viranşehir
Ktēsiphōn	Ctesiphon	
Kyzikos	Cyzicus	
Daphnē	Daphne	
Daras	Dara	Anastasiopolis
Doubios	Dubios	Dvin
Elephantinē	Elephantine	
Ephthalitai	Hephthalites	Abdelai
Erouloi	Heruls	
Euphratēsia	Euphratesia	Euphratensis
Europos	Europus	Carchemish, Jerablous
Pontos Euxeinos	Euxine Sea	Black Sea
Gabboulon	Gabbulon	Usually found as Gabboulōn
Gorgō	Gorgo	Gorgān, Gurgān
Hebraioi	Jews	Hebrews
Homeritai	Homerites	Ḥimyarites
Ounnoi	Huns	

Name in Procopius' Greek	Name used in this translation	Other name(s)
Ibēres	Iberians	Georgians
Illyrioi	Illyricum	
Iōtabē	Iotabe	
Isauroi	Isaurians	
Istros	Danube	
Hierosolyma	Jerusalem	
Lazika	Lazica	(Western) Georgia
Libanos	Lebanon	
Libyoi	Libyans	Africans
Ligouroi	Ligurians	
Lykaones	Lycaonians	
Makedōnoi	Macedonians	
Maddēnoi	Maddeni	Ma'add
Massagetai	Massagetae	Huns
Mēdoi	Medes	Persians
Melitēnē	Melitene	Malatya
Mindouos	Minduos	
Mokhērēsis	Mokheresis	? Mourisius
Maurousioi	Moors	
Mopsouestia	Mopsuestia	Yakapınar
Neilos	Nile	
Noubatai	Nobatae	Noubades
Nymphios	Nymphius	Batman-su
Obbanē	Obbane	
Oinokhalakōn	Oenochalakon	
Orokasias	Orocasias	
Orontēs	Orontes	Asi
Osrhoēnē	Osrhoene	

Name in Procopius' Greek	Name used in this translation	Other name(s)
Palaistina	Palestine	
Peloponnēsioi	Peloponnese	
Pelousion	Pelusium	
Persai	Persians	
Petrai	Petra	Al-Batrā
Pharangion	Pharangium	İspir, Sper
Philai	Philae	
Phisōn	Phison	
Phoinikē	Phoenice	Phoinice Libanensis
Phoinikōn	Palm Grove	
Pitious	Pityus	Bichvinta, Pitsunda
Pontos	Pontus	
Potidaia	Potidaea	
Erythra thalassa	Red Sea	
Rhizaion	Rhizaeum	Rize
Rōmaioi	Romans	
Roufinianai	Rufinianae	
Sabeiroi	Sabirs	
Sarakēnoi	Saracens	Arabs
Saros	Sarus	Sarız
Seleukeia	Seleucia	
Sisauranōn	Sisauranon	Sisarbanon
Skanda	Scanda	
Sophanēnē	Sophanene	
Sounitai	Sunitae	Siwnik'
Soura	Sura	Suriya
Sykai	Sycae	
Tauroi	Taurians	
Tauros (mountains)	Taurus	
Theodosioupolis	Theodosiopolis	Erzerum, Erzurum

Name in Procopius' Greek	Name used in this translation	Other name(s)
Thermopylai	Thermopylae	
Thessalia	Thessaly	
Thilasamōn	Thilasamon	
Thrakia	Thrace	
Trapezous	Trapezus	Trebizond, Trabzon
Trētos	Tretus	
Tzanoi	Tzani	
Bandiloi	Vandals	
Leukosyroi	White Syrians	
Zēkhoi	Zekhi	
Zēnobia	Zenobia	Halabiyya

Proper Names and Notes in the Translation

I have used the normal (Latin) versions of Greek/Roman names in the translation. This is not, I realise, a neutral choice: Anthony Kaldellis prefers to use the Greek version of a name, so that he refers to Ioannes rather than John and to Kappadokia rather than Cappadocia, arguing that to use the Latin or English forms is a distortion and a 'redundant affectation'. On the other hand, it has been the norm not only in English, but also in (e.g.) French and German for centuries. As he correctly notes, consistency is almost impossible to maintain in any case, since he is prepared to refer to Justinian rather than Ioustinianos. For non-Roman people I have chosen a simple version of their name in the appropriate language, e.g. Khusro (Chosroes in Greek) and al-Harith (Arethas in Greek); I have deliberately avoided diacritics in these names, preferring (e.g.) Abu Karib to Abū Karib for the Greek Abokharabos. In cases where I am uncertain of the identification of someone with a Greek name, I have preferred to retain it: hence I refer to Seoses, for instance, not Siyavush, unlike Kaldellis, and prefer *mirranes* to Mihran. For place names I use the normal English versions, e.g. Antioch rather than Antiokheia; again, there are exceptions, e.g. Dvin instead of Dubios, a decision dictated partly by the strangeness of the name Dubios (or Dubius, as I would normally have transcribed it) in English. In the case of titles, I have preferred to insert the Latin titles rather than translate the Greek: instead of 'General of the East' I therefore give *magister militum per Orientem*. A Glossary of such titles is to be found on p. xxviii.

In order to avoid confusion, I have provided Tables of Names so that the Greek and non-Greek versions can be compared.

Explanation of the Notes

The notes are deliberately brief and mostly devoid of references to secondary literature. Readers seeking more guidance are encouraged to turn to my Commentary, published simultaneously, where extensive references are given. They do refer to other primary sources, however, and so below I offer a list of these sources and of translations. In many cases translations may also be found in the source books that feature among the Abbreviations on p. xii, *REF* and *RPLA*. I offer at the end of this translation as an Appendix an English translation of the patriarch Photius' summary of Nonnosus' work, a report on diplomatic missions to southern Arabia in the 530s/540s. References without indication of the work are to Procopius' *Wars*.

There are numerous cross-references in the notes. A reference to (e.g.) 7.22 refers to chapter 7, section 22 (of the same book). If there is any doubt as to which book is meant, then that is inserted as well, e.g. 1.7.22, which would refer to Book 1. Any reference where the work is not specified is to Procopius' *Wars*.

Primary Sources

The abbreviation TTH used here refers to the very useful series from Liverpool University Press, Translated Texts for Historians. Page numbers are generally those of the translations with the exception of the *Chronicon Paschale* and Theophanes.

Agath.
: Agathias, *Histories*, tr. J.D. Frendo (Berlin and New York, 1975).

Chr. Pasch.
: *Chronicon Paschale*, tr. M. and M. Whitby, *Chronicon Paschale 284–628 AD*, TTH (Liverpool, 1989).

C.J.
: *Codex Justinianus*, tr. B.W. Frier et al., *The Codex of Justinian*, 3 vols. (Cambridge, 2016).

Ps.-Dion. ii.
: *Pseudo-Dionysius of Tel-Mahre, Chronicle, known also as the Chronicle of Zuqnin. Part III*, tr. W. Witakowski, TTH (Liverpool, 1996). Also available in *The Chronicle of Zuqnin Parts III and IV A.D. 488–775*, tr. A. Harrak (Toronto, 1999). This source reproduces extensively lost sections of the sixth-century church history of John of Ephesus.

Evagr. *HE*
: Evagrius, *The Ecclesiastical History of Evagrius Scholasticus*, tr. M. Whitby, TTH (Liverpool, 2000).

Hdt.
: Herodotus, *Histories*, many translations available.

Joh. Eph.
: John of Ephesus: see Ps.-Dion.

Joh. Lyd.
: *De Mag.* John Lydus, tr. A. Bandy, *On Powers, or The Magistracies of the Roman State* (Philadelphia, 1982).

Jord. *Rom.*
: Jordanes, *Romana*, tr. P. van Nuffelen and L. van Hoof, TTH (Liverpool, 2020).

Ps.-Josh.
: (Pseudo-)Joshua the Stylite, *The Chronicle of Pseudo-Joshua the Stylite*, tr. J. Watt and F. Trombley, TTH (Liverpool, 2000).

Mal.	Malalas, *Chronographia*, tr. E. and M. Jeffreys and R. Scott (Melbourne, 1986).
Marc. *com.*	*The Chronicle of Marcellinus*, tr. B. Croke (Sydney, 1995).
NovJ.	D. Miller and P. Sarris, *The Novels of Justinian*, 2 vols. (Cambridge, 2018).
Proc.	Procopius, *Wars*, tr. H.B. Dewing, 5 vols. (Cambridge, MA, 1914–28). This tr. is revised by A. Kaldellis, *Prokopios: The Wars of Justinian* (Indianapolis, 2014).
Proc. *Aed.*	Procopius, *De Aedificiis/Buildings*, tr. H.B. Dewing (Cambridge, MA, 1940).
Proc. *Anecd.*	Procopius, *Anecdota/Secret History*, tr. H.B. Dewing (Cambridge, MA, 1935); also tr. A. Kaldellis, *The Secret History with Related Texts* (Indianapolis, 2010); also tr. G. Williamson and P. Sarris, *The Secret History* (London, 2007).
Tabari	*The History of al-Tabari*, vol. 5, The *Sāsānids, The Byzantines, The Lakhmids, and Yemen*, tr. C.E. Bosworth (Albany, 1999).
Theoph.	Theophanes, *The Chronicle of Theophanes Confessor*, tr. C. Mango and R. Scott (Oxford, 1997). Page references are to the Greek text (to be found in the translation).
Th. Sim.	Theophylact Simocatta, *The Histories*, tr. M. and M. Whitby (Oxford, 1986).
Thuc.	Thucydides, *History of the Peloponnesian War*, many translations available.
Ps.-Zach.	Pseudo-Zachariah, *The Chronicle of Pseudo-Zachariah of Mytilene: Church and War in Late Antiquity*, tr. G. Greatrex, R. Phenix and C. Horn, TTH (Liverpool, 2011).

Glossary

Further details on these offices or titles (or units of measurement) may be found in *ODLA*.

bucellarii, sing. *bucellarius*	elite soldiers in the service of a particular (Roman) general
centenarion, pl. *centenaria*	unit of weight (100 Roman lbs.), often applied to gold coins
dux, pl. *duces*	duke or military commander attached to a particular province
kanarang	Persian military commander in charge of Abharshahr (the north-eastern frontier of the Persian empire)
magister militum	master of soldiery, high-ranking military official
magister militum per Armeniam	master of soldiery stationed on the north-eastern frontier
magister militum per Orientem	master of soldiery stationed on the eastern frontier
magister militum praesentalis	master of soldiery stationed in the capital
magister officiorum	master of offices, head of the central civil administration of the empire
phylarch	commander of auxiliaries (often Arab) allied to the empire
praepositus (sacri cubiculi)	grand chamberlain of the palace
praetorian prefect	important regional civil functionary
quaestor (sacri palatii)	high-ranking imperial official concerned with legal matters
stade	classical unit of measurement of distance: there were seven stades to one Roman mile; the Roman mile equates to 1.472 km (a little under one mile today).

Introduction

Procopius' *Persian Wars*, a work that was first published in A.D. 550/1, is one of the most important sources on both the eastern Roman empire and Persia in the sixth century. This is the first free-standing English translation of the work. The aim of this short Introduction is to place the work in its context – that is, both the historical context, i.e. the sixth-century world, and the place of the work in the tradition of writing history (historiography). This survey will be only cursory: there are many resources now available for those wanting more detailed information. The reader can find further details on them in the Further Reading section at the end of the Introduction.

Procopius

What little is known of Procopius' life emerges from his own writings. As he tells us at the very start of *The Persian Wars*, he was born in Caesarea, Palestine. A prosperous port city with a sizeable, diverse population, it was also the seat of the governor of Palaestina Prima, parts of whose *praetorium* (headquarters) have been uncovered by archaeologists. The nearby city of Gaza was renowned as a centre of learning, both pagan and Christian, and several of its citizens produced works that still survive – Choricius (of Gaza) and Procopius (of Gaza), to name but two. It is worth noting here that the works of Thucydides were particularly prized at Gaza. Whether our Procopius studied in Gaza, however, is uncertain.

Having trained in the law, perhaps at Berytus (Beirut), he was appointed as the legal adviser or *assessor* (Greek *symboulos*) of the *dux* Belisarius in 527. He remained in the general's entourage for at least the following thirteen years, serving with him first in the East, where he witnessed his commander's victory at Dara in 530 and defeat at Callinicum in 531, then for his remarkable triumphs in the West, first in North Africa against the Vandals (in 533–4), then in Italy against the Ostrogoths (535–40). He may well have accompanied the general subsequently when he returned to the East in 541–2, but he was back in Constantinople later that year, where he witnessed the ravages wrought by the plague, described at *Persian Wars* 2.22–3. For the most part, it is believed that he remained in Constantinople thereafter, working on the (first seven books of the) *Wars* and the *Anecdota* (or *Secret History*), both of which were completed by 550/1. As he composed his history he grew increasingly disenchanted with the way in which the Emperor Justinian conducted his wars, which had led to uprisings and setbacks in Italy and North Africa and to the sacking of Antioch, the most important city near the eastern frontier, in 540. A change of tone is perceptible in later passages, e.g. at 2.30.17, but it does not seem as though he attempted to rewrite sections written earlier; it is therefore difficult to pinpoint Procopius' views, which evidently varied over time.

While the *Anecdota*, Procopius' blazing indictment of the misdeeds of Justinian, Theodora and their ministers, naturally remained concealed, the first seven books of the *Wars*, so the historian tells us, enjoyed considerable success. He therefore produced an eighth book in 552/3 that extended his narrative of events in the East, in Lazica in particular, and in Italy, where he reported Narses' final defeat of the Ostrogothic leaders Totila and Teias. At some point in the 550s, more probably towards the middle of the decade, the *De Aedificiis* or *Buildings* was also published, a work that relates, in glowing terms, the various building projects initiated by the Emperor Justinian throughout the empire (apart from Italy).

Nothing further is known of the historian. A certain Procopius rose to the post of city prefect in 562 and in this role was called upon to investigate a supposed plot by Belisarius against the emperor; but there are no grounds for identifying him with our author.

The Eastern Roman Empire in the Sixth Century

When people talk of the 'decline and fall of the Roman empire' they usually have in mind the collapse of the western empire in the fifth century. The causes of the relentless shrinking of the western empire, which continued steadily from 395 through to the deposition of the last emperor, Romulus, known as 'Augustulus', the little Augustus, in 476, remain a matter of fierce debate. For our purposes, it is best simply to underline that the pensioning off of the last emperor was by no means as dramatic an event as has sometimes been imagined: the Senate in Rome continued to sit, while a series of non-Roman rulers, first Odoacer, then Theoderic the Ostrogoth, ruled in Italy and even somewhat beyond the peninsula. In the East, meanwhile, thanks in part to the massive city walls of Constantinople built in the early fifth century, imperial power survived. There were, to be sure, serious challenges to the stability of the East Roman state – which we call the (remaining) Roman empire, but which is also often referred to now as the Byzantine empire – such as Attila's Huns in the 440s, Gothic peoples in the Balkans in the 460s and 470s, and significant disputes about church doctrine that divided much of the East. The Emperor Zeno was even ousted from power briefly in 475–6, and, despite recovering his throne, struggled to re-establish control. Only under his successor, Anastasius (491–518), did the empire enjoy a period of relative calm, although it took a lengthy war in the 490s to secure Roman control of the highland province of Isauria, which was followed by a conflict with Persia. Nonetheless, notwithstanding continuing doctrinal disputes, Anastasius was able to put the empire on a sound financial footing and to bequeath to his successor, Justin I (518–27), a healthy treasury.

By this point, the contours of the eastern empire were well established (fig.1). The empire itself had been partitioned from 395, having been divided between the two sons of Theodosius I, Arcadius in the East and Honorius in the West. No one had necessarily thought that the division would become permanent, and the empire remained, at least in theory, a unified state, in which legislation passed in one half of the empire applied equally in the other. Eastern emperors made efforts to prop up their western counterparts, but in the end they proved inadequate. So while the Ostrogoths took over Italy – in this case, however, with the sanction of the East – the Vandals overran North Africa, the Franks and others established themselves in Gaul and the Visigoths in Spain, in the East the Balkans, Cyrenaica, Egypt, the Near East and Anatolia remained under Roman control. By the sixth century Constantinople had grown to become one of the largest cities in the eastern Mediterranean. Estimates of its population vary, but it certainly was between half a million and a million; only Antioch and Alexandria could rival it. From the capital, the emperors ruled the provinces and directed the empire's generals: Theodosius I had been the last ruler to take the field in person. The emperor was assisted by an extensive bureaucracy, situated mainly in Constantinople, but also in the provinces, each of which was in the

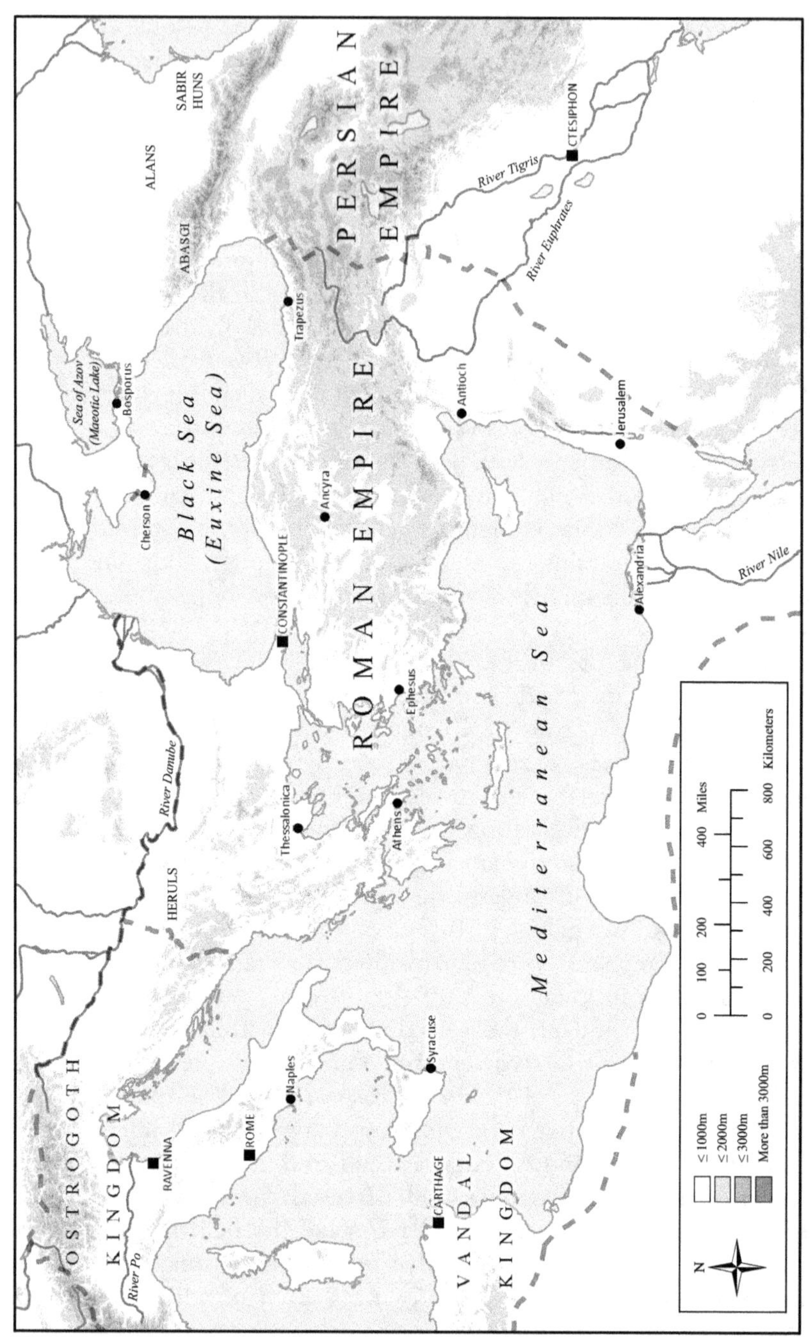

Figure 1 The Eastern Roman Empire in 527

hands of a governor; *duces* or dukes were responsible for military matters, while governors handled civil administration. In the senior bureaucracy *magistri militum*, i.e. 'masters of soldiers', were the highest-ranking generals, while on the civilian side – the two domains were generally kept separate – the praetorian prefect(s) were responsible for the administration of provinces and the raising of taxes from them. The *magister officiorum*, i.e. 'master of offices', straddled the two worlds, commanding troops in the palace and supervising protocol as well as engaging in diplomatic activity with foreign powers.

The reign of Justinian saw a remarkable expansion of the eastern empire: in the 530s eastern armies under Belisarius reconquered first North Africa from the Vandals, then Italy from the Ostrogoths. In both cases it proved difficult to maintain control as the newly conquered peoples resisted corrupt officials and often proved a match for incompetent and greedy Roman commanders. This was particularly true in Italy, where the Ostrogothic ruler Totila (541–52) rolled back nearly all east Roman gains over the 540s. Only with the despatch of substantial Roman reinforcements under Narses in the 550s was Italy finally definitively subdued. Roman forces also gained some footholds in Spain at this time; in the Balkans, meanwhile, they proved less effective at resisting invasions by Gepids, Lombards, Slavs and others.

An increasing proportion of the Roman empire was Christian. The process of Christianisation since the conversion of Constantine in the early fourth century was gradual, but over the fifth century the religion had taken firm root in the eastern Roman empire. Its impact was felt in all spheres of life, whether through the spread of churches and participation in religious rites or through the rhythm of the year's calendar, now punctuated by holy days and commemorations of saints and martyrs, or indeed through contact with monks and holy men. Of course, substantial swathes of the countryside remained pagan; many Romans might never see a holy man, bishop or monk, relying instead just on a local priest. In a Christian empire, the definition of faith took on a greater importance: it was essential that the empire and its ruler be orthodox, that the right faith prevail. Church councils were therefore summoned in order to establish orthodoxy. Over the fifth century controversy raged as to the precise nature of Christ: was he human, was he divine, or did he somehow combine these two natures? The Council of Chalcedon, held in 451, decreed that he was 'in two natures', human and divine. Many parts of the eastern empire were opposed to this definition, preferring to see him as combining the two natures in one: they are known today usually as Miaphysites, though in older works they are called Monophysites. From 451 to 518 it was not clear, despite the Council's decisions, which interpretation would prevail. Under Justin and Justinian, however, the Council's decisions received imperial backing and were enforced through much of the empire (apart from Egypt). Channels of communication nonetheless remained open with anti-Chalcedonians, helped by the support of Justinian's wife Theodora, herself an opponent of the Council.

Not much of this aspect of Roman society is visible in Procopius' work, which is why it is worth mentioning it here. But the attentive reader will notice holy men (such as Jacob, 1.7.5–11), monks (1.7.22) and bishops (such as Megas, bishop of Beroea, 2.6.17, or Baradotus, bishop of Constantia, 2.13.13) in the narrative. Some of his descriptions of these people give the impression that a sixth-century reader would have been unfamiliar with them: Procopius goes out of his way to explain what a monk is, for instance. This is in fact an aspect of the historian's style: he is imitating Thucydides in particular, a writer of the fifth century B.C., in whose time Christianity was unheard of. As a consequence, in order to maintain the style of his predecessor, he explains new features that existed in the sixth century A.D. Some modern scholars have inferred that Procopius, like Thucydides, was a pagan, who was deliberately distancing himself from Christianity. Most, however, see the issue as a stylistic one: Procopius, despite these oblique allusions to Christianity and references to 'fate' and 'destiny', was a conventional Christian, as (e.g.) his interest in the legend of Abgar of Edessa (2.12) indicates.

Two further aspects of urban life in the Roman empire of the sixth century deserve mention. First, the circus factions. By the sixth century gladiatorial games had long been abandoned; beast hunts were also falling out of favour. Interest focused instead on chariot-racing, carried out in huge hippodromes: the one in Constantinople, parts of which are visible today, could accommodate some 100,000 people. At the races various teams competed, each of which represented a colour, whether White, Red, Blue or Green. The last two factions were the largest and most powerful; they were represented in every city of the East. They were involved not just in fielding teams for the horse-races but also in other entertainments. Between the Blues and the Greens there existed a fierce rivalry, which on occasion erupted into all-out violence: the Emperor Anastasius took a tough line in suppressing the periodic riots that broke out. Justinian, an ardent supporter of the Blues before he ascended the throne, had more difficulty in imposing his will. When he did try to impose a crackdown, however, it backfired spectacularly: the result was the 'Nika' riot (the cry 'Nika', 'Win!', was a circus acclamation) in January 532 (1.24) that was only quelled by the intervention of troops after a week of rioting.

Factional strife was not the only scourge of the cities of the eastern empire. In the 520s two earthquakes inflicted extensive damage on cities in the Near East, especially Antioch. Far more devastating was the outbreak of bubonic plague from 541, which started in Egypt but swiftly spread to all parts of the empire and beyond. Procopius witnessed the ravages of the 'Early Medieval Pandemic' in Constantinople (2.22–3) and paints a vivid picture of the situation. Periodic resurgences of the plague would continue to strike the empire for two centuries.

Since *The Persian Wars* deals above all with military affairs, a few words on the sixth-century Roman army would be useful. As already noted, the most senior commanders were the *magistri militum*, of which two were based at Constantinople, another in Mesopotamia and another (from 528) in Armenia. Under them were the *duces* or dukes, generally attached to provinces, although increasingly associated rather with fortresses. The Roman army comprised *limitanei* or 'frontier soldiers', who were the backbone of the provincial forces, and *comitatenses*, mobile forces under the *magistri militum* – although *duces* could also command them. A typical Roman army numbered from 15,000 to 25,000, at least when the *duces*' forces had been mustered and combined with those under one or more *magistri militum*. In the 540s, when Khusro invaded the eastern provinces, it seems as though the Romans struggled to field an army to oppose him, probably because contingents had been shifted to the West for the wars against the Vandals and Goths. Procopius, it is true, does mention a force of 30,000 that invaded Persian Armenia in 542 (2.24.16), although this may be exaggerated, especially since it was decisively defeated by a much smaller Persian army. An important element among the Roman forces was made up of *bucellarii*, 'biscuit-boys', a term used for the personal bodyguards of generals, who might number in the hundreds, or, more rarely, thousands. Procopius refers to them by the Greek terms *doryphoroi* ('spearmen') and *hypaspistai* ('shield-bearers'); we have translated these terms as 'spearmen' and 'guards' for the most part (e.g. at 1.25.7). Cavalry had come to play an increasingly large role on the battlefield, even if infantry units remained in the majority: as noted below, Procopius was particularly impressed by the skill of the Hunnic-style Roman horse-archers.

The Persian Kingdom in the Sixth Century

Just as the Roman empire had struggled to survive in the fifth century, so also had the Persian kingdom. For the most part the Persian state was less bureaucratised than the Roman one, relying more on seven leading families to exercise the great offices of state, which were linked by tradition to these noble houses. Although the rule of the Sasanian dynasty was never challenged until the end of the sixth century, kings could be unseated by rivals from within the royal family, so that the nobility could in such cases wield great power. Procopius, like other Graeco-Roman writers, sometimes confuses names and titles, not surprisingly given the association of certain houses with certain offices. On the whole, he appears to be well-informed on Persian matters and, unlike some other historians of his period, such as Agathias, generally free of prejudice; he does, however, harbour a particular dislike of Justinian's great rival, King Khusro I, known as Anushirvan ('of the immortal soul', 531–79).

In the fifth century the Persians faced continuous threats from the steppes of Central Asia. In order to contain this menace they built a long and imposing wall, stretching eastwards from the Caspian Sea, known as the Gorgan wall. It is only recently that the sheer extent and complexity of this enterprise has become clear. While the precise date of its construction is uncertain, it appears that major work was conducted in the fifth century in order to ward off nomadic invaders. At the same time, the Sasanian kings associated themselves with the mythical Kayanid rulers of ancient Iran, who had similarly engaged in combat with enemies from the steppe. The Roman sources are aware of two groups with whom the Persians fought, first the Kidarite Huns, then the more powerful Hephthalite Huns; coin evidence points to the presence of other groups east of Iran, in modern Afghanistan. King Peroz (459–84), having vanquished the Kidarites, enjoyed much less success against the Hephthalites. Despite several defeats, he continued to campaign against them only to be roundly defeated in 484, perishing in the battle himself. His brother and successor, Balash (484–8), found himself faced with an empty treasury and was swiftly ousted by Peroz's son Kavadh (488–96/7, 498/9–531). He appears to have struggled to master the situation, failing to obtain financial support from the Romans. He may have associated himself with a socially radical group, the Mazdakites, who challenged the nobility's grip on power, but the whole issue is very unclear. He was at any rate expelled from the throne by a discontented nobility and sought refuge with the Hephthalites; with their backing he was able to return and overthrow his brother Jamasp.

Kavadh and his son Khusro I, both strong monarchs, managed to tighten the dynasty's grip on power. Khusro in particular introduced reforms that diminished the influence of the nobles and accorded greater rights to the numerous peasantry of Persia. He likewise made changes to the military structures of the empire, creating a four-fold command for the four sectors of the empire, i.e. in the north, south, east and west. Despite the defeats at the hands of the Hephthalites, the Persian army remained a powerful instrument, being particularly skilled at siege warfare, for instance: Procopius' account describes numerous Persian sieges of Roman cities, many of them successful. The sixth-century military manual the *Strategikon*, attributed to the Emperor Maurice (582–602), notes this skill as well as the discipline of the Persian forces.

The Persian empire, known as Eranshahr ('Empire of the Aryans', i.e. of the Iranian people), comprised, at its core, Iran (Persia) itself, and certain adjoining regions. But at various points it also incorporated a larger territory, including (e.g.) large parts of Armenia (known as Persarmenia), and some parts of modern Pakistan and Afghanistan. It naturally therefore contained adherents of various religions, including the state-sponsored Zoroastrianism, whose priests also played an important role in the administration of justice, Christians, Jews and others. While some persecution of Christians did occur sporadically, the Persian church, established with the support of Yazdgerd I (399–420) in 410, generally managed to collaborate with the court. The strategic location of Persia meant that it was well placed to act as an intermediary in trade between the Mediterranean and the Far East, notably for the import of silk: it was for this reason that Justinian sought, albeit unsuccessfully, to bypass Persia with Ethiopian collaboration (1.20).

Romano-Persian Relations in Late Antiquity

Parthia or Persia had always been Rome's great rival in the East. Once the Sasanian dynasty overthrew the Parthians in the 220s, its first kings launched repeated attacks on Roman territory, sacking Antioch and deporting large numbers of prisoners. The situation stabilised in the fourth century and, after Julian's disastrous invasion of Persia in 363, a durable frontier was established. The Persians took over the important Roman border fortress of Nisibis; a couple of decades later they obtained by far the larger part of Armenia, which became Persarmenia, while the remainder fell under Roman control. Given the troubled situation of both empires in the fifth century, it is not surprising that there was little strife

between them during this period. A devastating Hunnic raid at the end of
the fourth century, passing through the Caucasus, may also have encouraged them to work together. Thus it was that Yazdgerd I agreed to act as
the guardian of the young Theodosius II (408–50), a remarkable develop-
ment that Procopius is the first source to report (1.2.1–10). Tensions did
flare at certain points during the century, most notably in 421–2, when
all-out war occurred, but in general the frontier remained peaceful.

It was therefore all the more of a shock when Kavadh crossed the frontier and invaded Roman territory late in 502; Roman fortifications and
troops were ill-prepared to withstand him. Eager for plunder to reward
his Hephthalite backers and other local allies, Kavadh sacked the city of
Amida (1.7) and tried to make further gains. Massive Roman reinforcements thwarted him, so that he preferred to abandon hostilities, selling
the city back to the Romans (1.8–9). The Emperor Anastasius, in order to
deter future invasions, therefore built a major base close to the frontier, at
the city of Dara (1.10). In the early 520s the Caucasian kingdom of Lazica
(Colchis) defected from Persia to the Romans, renewing its earlier allegiance. Despite this setback, the aged King Kavadh approached the
Emperor Justin to adopt his son Khusro, thereby securing his position
against his brothers and potential rivals. When the negotiations broke
down (1.12), hostilities began soon afterwards; by this point, in 527,
Justinian had inherited the throne from his uncle. The defection of the
Iberian kingdom (modern Georgia) to the Romans at just this time
inflamed the situation further; both the Lazi and the Iberians were
Christian and thus more naturally aligned with Rome. Although negotiations continued, by 530 the Persians decided to launch an all-out offensive into Roman Mesopotamia. At the battle of Dara in June that year
the young *magister militum* Belisarius and the *magister officiorum*
Hermogenes inflicted a decisive defeat on the Persians, while their colleagues Sittas and Dorotheus also beat off a Persian army at Satala in
Roman Armenia (1.13–15). Undeterred, Kavadh ordered a further offensive the following year, which threatened the city of Antioch. Belisarius
intercepted the invasion force and shadowed it during its retreat along
the Euphrates. Just as it was about to reach Persian territory, the Roman
soldiers insisted on giving battle and sustained an embarrassing defeat in
April 531 (1.17–18); in the case of this battle, we are fortunate to have a
detailed alternative description of the course of events provided by the
chronicler John Malalas (18.60), far more critical of Belisarius, which may
well have been produced by an enquiry held to investigate the causes of
the defeat. Kavadh died later the same year and negotiations between his

successor and Justinian led, at last, to the conclusion of the 'Eternal Peace'. In exchange for 11,000 pounds of gold and the moving of the *dux* (duke) from Dara back to Constantia, the Romans regained two forts in eastern Lazica and, more importantly, an enduring peace – at least in theory.

But the peace was to prove far from eternal. Aware of Justinian's conquests in the West and urged on by envoys from the Ostrogoths and the Armenians, Khusro sought a pretext for war. He found it in strife between the Arabs allied to each side. He therefore invaded the Roman eastern provinces in spring 540, sacking the city of Antioch and penetrating as far as the Mediterranean, where he bathed (2.5–13). It is likely that he was seeking to demonstrate by various means his superiority over his rival ruler, Justinian, who desperately tried to come to terms. Khusro nonetheless continued his offensive in the following year, invading Lazica and seizing the newly founded Roman city at Petra. Belisarius meanwhile undertook an invasion of Persian Mesopotamia, where he captured a fort but soon retired to Roman territory (2.15–19). By bluff, Belisarius was able to ward off Khusro's invasion along the Euphrates in 542 – or perhaps the king had heard of the plague that was sweeping through the empire. Justinian decided to exploit the situation by attacking Persian Armenia, but the Roman armies, despite outnumbering their foes, were soundly beaten (2.24–5). In the following year, 543, Khusro retaliated with an attack on the city of Edessa, but it withstood his vigorous attempts to storm it (2.26–7). Having reached this stalemate, the two sides agreed a truce in spring 545, yet fighting persisted in Lazica, where it would continue through to 556 (2.28–30, 8.1–17, Agathias, *Histories*). Only in late 561 was a peace treaty at last concluded which, unlike the 'Eternal Peace', assured the Persians of an annual payment, albeit in instalments for several years at a time. Nevertheless, even this treaty held only until 572.

The next war lasted nearly twenty years and ended only because of instability within Persia; as a result the Romans made considerable gains by the terms of the treaty of 591. When therefore the Roman state in its turn was thrown into disarray by the overthrow of the Emperor Maurice in 602, Khusro II, the grandson of Khusro I, launched an offensive. So began the 'last great war of antiquity' in which the Persians initially took over the entire Near East and Egypt only to see all their gains swept aside by a devastating invasion of the Persian heartlands by the Emperor Heraclius (610–41). Yet his victory in its turn was very quickly nullified by the arrival of the armies of the Islamic rulers who would dominate the whole Near East thereafter.

The Persian Wars

'Now war and imperial power are generally agreed to be the greatest things in the world' (1.24.26). So says an otherwise unknown senator during a debate on how to proceed against Justinian during the Nika riot of 532. These are the themes of Procopius' work: as he says at the very start, he wishes to preserve the memory of remarkable deeds for posterity. His preface (1.1) – which serves as the preface for all seven books of the *Wars* – underlines the importance of the events described and his own competence to write them up, having been an eyewitness of many of them. He then proceeds to insist on the importance of recent achievements, evidently trying to counter a prevailing conservatism among contemporaries, who looked back wistfully in some cases to the famous legions of Rome. Procopius, on the other hand, sings the praises of the new horse-archers, who adopted Hunnic techniques and provided the spearhead for Belisarius' victories, particularly in the West.

The Persian Wars is then above all a work about war: in concentrating on this he is faithfully following his predecessors of the fifth century B.C., Herodotus and Thucydides, and the many writers who had written history in their wake. His work offers a full account of the eastern wars fought under Justinian, from 527 to 549. It includes a quite extensive introduction, however, which covers the fifth century in cursory fashion, often preferring intriguing anecdotes to sober reportage. Strife at the Persian court features throughout the work, e.g. in the deposition of Kavadh (1.5.1–7) or in plots against Khusro (1.23): it is clear that readers were interested in Persian affairs and in exotic tales of the East, e.g. about a shark that loved an oyster (1.4.17–31) or a 'Prison of Oblivion' (1.5.9–40). But Procopius found space to report other events as well, notably the insurrection in Constantinople that almost unseated the emperor, the Nika riot (1.24), as well as the downfall of the praetorian prefect John the Cappadocian, a figure he clearly detested (1.25); internal references show that he was adding these elements in the mid 540s. He further provides a valuable account of the plague in Constantinople, which he had witnessed at first hand (2.22–3). In this he was also following in the footsteps of Thucydides, who had described the impact of the plague in Athens in 430 B.C.

Procopius writes in a dialect of Greek known as Attic, the same as that used by Thucydides, albeit with later refinements and with some traces also of Herodotus' influence. He peppers his account with speeches put into the mouths of leading figures, whether Khusro, Belisarius or diplomatic envoys. Some of them he might have heard himself, others can only be made up. However strange this technique may seem to a modern reader, it was standard practice among historians in antiquity. It allowed the writer to illustrate the character of the speaker, of course, e.g. the good sense and strategic competence of Belisarius, and sometimes also to indicate what was at stake, e.g. in an imminent battle: often there are pairs of speeches from opposing commanders, who explain how they intend to proceed. The speeches can also provide an opportunity for criticism of Roman officials or even the emperor himself, e.g. in the attack on Justinian launched by Armenian envoys to Khusro before the outbreak of war in 540 (2.3.32–53). These speeches often start with a relevant maxim or saying, upon which the speaker then elaborates. Some of them, it is true, can appear to be rather dry exercises in rhetoric of the type that Procopius must have learnt at school.

Procopius' *Persian Wars* forms only part of his account of military campaigns of Justinian's reign: as noted above, the historian accompanied Belisarius to the West and wrote up a vivid account of warfare first in North Africa, *The Vandal Wars* (= *Wars* 3–4), then in Italy (= *Wars* 5–7). His decision to divide his material by theatre of war is an unusual one, for which the only obvious precedent is the second-century (A.D.) historian Appian. When he came to add an eighth book in 552/3 he covered all the theatres of war within it while still keeping them separate. The division of *The Persian Wars* into two books, chapters and sections, does not go back to the author himself. There is nonetheless a difference in tone perceptible between Books I and II: the optimistic tone of Book I – which continues in Book III, relating Belisarius' spectacular victories against the Vandals – contrasts with the more downbeat Book II, in which the Romans are clearly on the defensive. Although some scholars have detected an overarching theme to the *Wars* – a consistent indictment of Justinian and his policies – the tone seems too varied to allow for such a blanket assessment. The work was subsequently abridged by the patriarch Photius in the ninth century, who shows no interest in the later books of the *Wars*, and it was also mined extensively by the compilers of an encyclopaedia in the tenth century: the Emperor Constantine Porphyrogenitus (945–59) commissioned the assembling of extracts from classical and Late Antique historians to provide useful information on a large range of topics, though only a few of the volumes have survived. Procopius' work was appreciated both for its narrative, especially the tactics applied by Belisarius that could be of use subsequently, and for its prose style. This helps to explain why the work has survived in its entirety, while so many other historical works from this period exist only in a fragmentary state.

This Translation

There have been few translations of *The Persian Wars* into English, especially compared with the many versions of the *Anecdota* or *Secret History* that exist. The first was by Sir Henry Holcroft, an M.P. and scholar, which appeared in 1653; the volume, of which I am fortunate to have an original copy in front of me, contains all eight books of *The Wars* albeit in an odd order. I am most grateful to Cyril Mango for having given me his copy of this translation. First come *The Persian Wars*, then the four books of *The Gothic Wars*, then finally *The Vandalic Wars*. It was published posthumously, with a short preface, and had been checked over by a noted scholar, Edmund Chilmead. The next translation into English was by H.B. Dewing in the Loeb series. It first appeared in 1914 with a facing Greek text. This translation furnished the basis of Anthony Kaldellis' one-volume translation of the *Wars*, which was published in 2014.

The present translation takes as its basis one by Averil Cameron that was published in 1967. The press that published her translation of excerpts from several of Procopius' works ceased trading soon afterwards, so that it had little chance to circulate and to become widely known. I have therefore, with her kind permission, made use of it, revising it and filling in the gaps. It follows that I am responsible for any errors that remain. Alongside the indication of chapters and sections I have also included in the margins references to the page numbers in the Teubner edition of Haury and Wirth, published in 1962. This is the Greek text on which the translation is based; in a very few cases, indicated in the notes, I have deviated from this edition.

It is worth noting briefly translations into other modern languages. A French translation by Janick Auberger has just appeared, while the Spanish one by Francisco Antonio García Romero (Madrid, 2000) has a good introduction and notes. I have also taken into account the German translation of Otto Veh (Munich, 1970) and the more recent Polish one by Dariusz Brodka *Prokopiusz z Cezarei. Historia Wojen*, vol.1 (Cracow, 2013). I hope to publish in the near future an Esperanto translation of the work.

Conclusion

Procopius is the author through the lens of whose works the Emperor Justinian – and especially his wife Theodora – are still perceived: his three very different compositions shed a huge amount of light on the sixth-century eastern empire. *The Persian Wars* is perhaps the most varied of the three parts of the *Wars*, providing coverage not only of the war on the eastern front, but also of events in Constantinople, notably the Nika riot and the 'Early Medieval Pandemic', as well as internal Persian affairs. At least one chapter (1.25), which describes the plot hatched by Belisarius' wife Antonina to bring down John the Cappadocian, may well have been destined originally for the *Anecdota* or *Secret History*, but was inserted here instead because it was now safe openly to malign the person who had been Justinian's right-hand man. In short, there is much to recommend this work to the reader.

Further Reading (Mainly in English)

On Procopius

Averil Cameron, *Procopius and the Sixth Century* (London, 1985).
G. Greatrex, 'Perceptions of Procopius in Recent Scholarship', *Histos* 8 (2014), 76–121, available on-line at https://histos.org/Histos82014.html.
G. Greatrex, ed., 'Work on Procopius outside the English-speaking World: A Survey', *Histos Supplementary Volume 9*, available on-line at https:/histos.org/SV09Procopius.html.
G. Greatrex and S. Janniard, eds., *Le monde de Procope/The World of Procopius* (Paris, 2018).
C. Lillington-Martin and E. Turquois, eds., *Procopius of Caesarea: Literary and Historical Interpretations* (Abingdon, 2018).
M. Meier and F. Montinaro, eds., *A Companion to Procopius* (Leiden, 2022).

On the Roman Empire in the Fifth and Sixth Centuries

Averil Cameron, *The Mediterranean World in Late Antiquity, 395–700* (Abingdon, 2012).
H. Elton, *The Roman Empire in Late Antiquity: A Political and Military History* (Cambridge, 2018).
F. Haarer, *Justinian* (Edinburgh, 2022).
M. Kulikowski, *The Tragedy of Empire: From Constantine to the Destruction of Roman Italy* (Cambridge, MA, 2019).
M. Maas, ed., *The Cambridge Companion to the Age of Justinian* (Cambridge, 2005).
M. Maas, ed., *The Cambridge Companion to the Age of Attila* (Cambridge, 2015).
S. Mitchell, *A History of the Later Roman Empire*, 2nd edition (Oxford, 2015).
P. Sarris, *Empires of Faith: The Fall of Rome to the Rise of Islam, 500–700* (Oxford, 2011).
M. Whitby, *The Wars of Justinian* (Barnsley, 2021).

On the Persian Empire in the Fifth and Sixth Centuries

T. Daryaee, *Sasanian Persia: The Rise and Fall of an Empire* (London, 2009).

M. Jackson Bonner, *The Last Empire of Iran* (Piscataway, NJ, 2020).

K. Rezakhani, *Reorienting the Sasanians: East Iran in Late Antiquity* (Edinburgh, 2017).

E. Sauer, with H. Omrani Rekavandi, T.J. Wilkinson and J. Nokandeh, *Persia's Imperial Power in Late Antiquity: The Great Wall of Gorgān and Frontier Landscapes in Sasanian Iran* (Oxford, 2013).

J. Wiesehöfer, *Ancient Persia* (London, 1996).

General Reference Works

Encyclopaedia Iranica, ed., E. Yarshater (London, 1985–), available on-line.

The Oxford Handbook of Late Antiquity, ed., S.F. Johnson (Oxford, 2012).

The Oxford Dictionary of Late Antiquity, ed., O. Nicholson (Oxford, 2018).

The Persian Wars

Book I

Chapter 1

(1) Procopius of Caesarea has written the history of the wars which
Justinian, the Roman emperor, waged against barbarians in the East and
West, as events befell each of them, so that immensely great deeds might
not go unrecorded and that the vast progression of time might not over-
whelm them, consign them to oblivion, and wipe them wholly from
sight – deeds whose record he thought would be something great and
highly beneficial both to the present generation and to those to come, if
ever time should place men in the same kind of crisis again.[1] (2) For the
exposition of a similar story can bestow benefits on those who are
inclined in future to go to war and take part in other kinds of contests,
by revealing how the struggle went for earlier contenders, and by offering
some idea of what outcome the present situation will probably have, at
least for those who plan most wisely. (3) He knew that he was himself
especially capable of recording this for the following reason: it so
happened that he was chosen as adviser by the general Belisarius and was
present with him at nearly everything that happened.[2] (4) He considered
cleverness suitable for rhetoric, the telling of myth for poetry, but for
history, truth. (5) Accordingly, he did not conceal the failings even of any
of his closest associates, but recorded accurately what happened to
everyone, whether they did well or otherwise.[3]

(6) One who really wishes to judge will find nothing greater or more
mighty than what happened in these wars.[4] (7) In them were done the
greatest marvels of any that we know by report, unless any of my readers

---

[1] The opening sentences evoke both Procopius' classical predecessors, Herodotus and Thucydides.
[2] See Introduction, pp. 1–2, on Procopius' career.
[3] Probably an allusion to the *Anecdota* or *Secret History*, which indeed lays bare the faults of
Belisarius and many others.
[4] Some scholars believe this Homeric parallel to be ironic, but it is best taken as a genuine defence of
sixth-century mounted archers.

should award the prize to ancient times and refuse to consider happenings in his own time as marvels. (8) This at least is why some call present-day warriors mere 'bowmen'[5] but give to the men of old names like 'hand-to-hand fighters', 'shield-bearers', and others such. They imagine that this valour has not survived into the present day; but their opinion is superficial and without basis in fact. (9) They have never thought to themselves that Homer's archers, who are even insulted by being named after their art, had no horse, no spear, no shield to defend them, no other protection for their body. They went into battle on foot and had to hide themselves, choosing a comrade's shield or leaning against the stone on some grave[6] (10) from where they could neither save themselves if they were routed nor attack the enemy if the latter were in flight, nor even fight in the open. Instead they always gave the impression of stealing something from those involved in the engagement. (11) And apart from this, their skill was so inferior that they would draw the bowstring to their own breast and then let fly the arrow weakly and naturally with no effect on their target.[7] This is what archery seems to have been like in the old days. (12) But today's archers go into battle with corselets and greaves fitted as far as the knee. Their arrows are slung on their right side and on the other their sword. (13) In addition, some carry a spear and a short shield on the shoulders without a shield strap, capable of covering their face and neck. (14) They are excellent horsemen, and they are able to draw the bow in either direction without difficulty, as the horse gallops, and to hit the enemy whether he is pursuing or fleeing. (15) The string is pulled towards their forehead, beside the right ear, giving the arrow such power that it kills whoever comes in its path, no shield or corselet being likely to withstand its force. (16) But some think nothing of these matters and honour and marvel at times of old and refuse to grant credit to new inventions. Yet this does not mean that great and remarkable achievements did not take place in these wars. (17) What the Romans and the Persians did and experienced in their war will be told first. I shall begin a little way back.

Chapter 2

(1) When Arcadius, the Roman emperor, was near to death in Byzantium he worried about his son and the empire (for his son Theodosius was not

---

⁵ An allusion to Homer, *Il.* 11.385.
⁶ Allusions to Homer, *Il.* 8.267 and 11.371, the latter case involving the Trojan archer Paris.
⁷ Allusions to Homer, *Il.* 4.123 and 11.390.

yet weaned), not knowing how to make the best arrangements for both.[8] (2) He thought that if he gave Theodosius a colleague in the empire, he would in effect be signing his own son's death warrant by introducing to him an enemy who had assumed the imperial power. (3) But if he established him on the throne alone, many would inevitably exploit the boy's isolation and make a bid for the empire, and once they had attained it, they would easily usurp the throne and kill Theodosius, who had no relative in Byzantium to be his guardian. (4) He did not imagine that the divine Honorius would help, for things were now bad in Italy. (5) The news from Persia troubled him no less, and he was afraid that these barbarians would exploit the youth of the emperor and do dreadful damage to Rome. (6) In this bewilderment Arcadius – though not in other respects intelligent – thought of a plan which was certainly strong enough to save his son and the empire, whether after discussing it with some advisers such as usually attend an emperor in large numbers, or at the prompting of a divine inspiration. (7) He made a will in which he proclaimed his son the heir of the royal power and made Yazdgerd, the Persian king, his guardian, laying on him many injunctions in the will to preserve the empire for Theodosius with all his strength and foresight. (8) Arcadius died after making these arrangements for the empire and his domestic affairs. And Yazdgerd, the Persian king, who was even before this extremely famous for the magnanimity of his nature, displayed a remarkable and noteworthy virtue when he had received and read the document. (9) He did not overlook Arcadius' orders in any respect but kept complete peace with Rome for the whole period and preserved the throne for Theodosius. (10) At the time, he sent a letter to the Roman senate, agreeing to be the guardian of the Emperor Theodosius and threatening war if anyone should try to plot against him.[9]

(11) But when Theodosius had grown up and reached maturity, Yazdgerd fell ill and vanished from the world of men, and Bahram, the king of Persia, attacked Roman territory with a large army.[10] He did no harm, however, and returned to his own country in the following manner

---

[8] Arcadius reigned from 395 to 408; his son Theodosius II was born in 401 and raised to the rank of Augustus already in 402. See *PLRE* 2, Theodosius 6, *ODLA*, Theodosius II. The appeal to Persia is likely to have occurred well before Arcadius' death. Agath. 4.26.3–4 is sceptical as to the story's accuracy, a scepticism shared by some modern scholars. See *RPLA*, 94–6.

[9] Theoph. 80 names an official sent by Yazdgerd, a certain Antiochus, who is attested at the Roman court. See *PLRE* 2, Antiochus 5.

[10] Yazdgerd I died in 420 and was succeeded by Bahram V (420–38). There was a war between Rome and Persia in 421–2, cf. *REF*, 38–42, but the incident alluded to here may rather reflect a more minor incursion by Bahram's successor, Yazdgerd II (438–57), which took place in 440 or 441, cf. *REF*, 44–5, *RPLA*, 136–8.

without achieving anything. (12) The Emperor Theodosius had happened to send Anatolius, the *magister militum per Orientem*, by himself as sole ambassador to the Persians. When he came to the Persian army he jumped off his horse and went alone to Bahram on foot. (13) When Bahram saw him he asked those present who the man was who was approaching. They said that it was the Roman general. (14) And the king, overcome by the greatness of the honour, turned his own horse around and rode away; all the Persian host followed him. (15) When he reached his own land he regarded the ambassador with great kindliness and agreed to peace terms just as Anatolius asked. The terms were that neither side should build any new fortress in their own territory adjacent to the other's borders.[11] When they had concluded this, each side attended to its own affairs.

Chapter 3

(1) Later Peroz, the Persian king,[12] was waging a war about land boundaries against the people of the Hephthalite Huns, whom they call 'White'.[13] He mustered a notable army and advanced against them (fig. 2). (2) The Hephthalites are a Hunnic people and are called Huns, but they do not mix with or associate with any of the Huns whom we know, for they have no land bordering on theirs. They do not in fact live near them at all, but next to the Persians towards the north, where the city called Gorgo is situated, on the very border of Persia, and there they often fight against each other over the boundaries (fig. 3).[14] (3) They are not nomads like the other Hunnic peoples, but have lived from of old in a good land. (4) For this reason they have never invaded Roman territory except with the Persian army. These alone of the Huns are white-bodied and not hideous to look at. (5) Nor is their way of life the same as the others', nor do they live the life of a beast like them. They are rather ruled by one king and have a lawful government and deal in an upright and just way with each other and with their neighbours, just like Romans and

---

[11] Probably agreed after the 421–2 war, cf. *REF*, 42–3 with Proc. *Aed.* 2.1.5.

[12] Peroz wrested the throne from his brother Hormizd III in a civil war after the death of Yazdgerd II in 457. He was initially victorious against another central Asian Hunnic people, the Kidarites, as the Roman historian Priscus reports. See *ODLA*, Peroz.

[13] The Hephthalites, referred to also as Abdelai in some sources, were a Hunnic people from the Altai mountains whose rising power challenged the Persian state on its north-eastern frontier. See *RPLA*, 97–8, *ODLA*, Hephthalites.

[14] Gorgo is the Persian Gorgān, east of the Caspian Sea, near which a long and imposing wall was built by the Persians in the late fifth century. See *ODLA*, Gorgan and Walls, defensive, Persian.

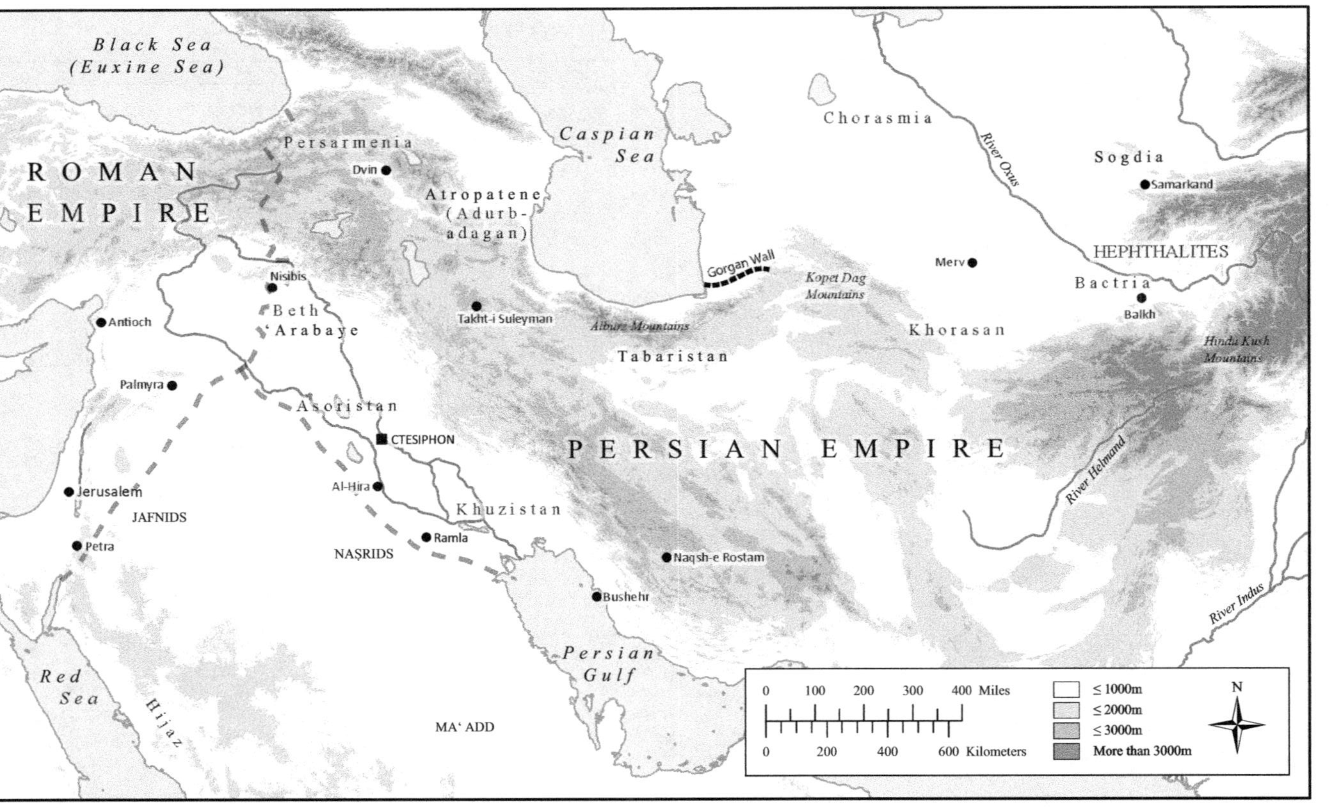

Figure 2   The Persian Empire

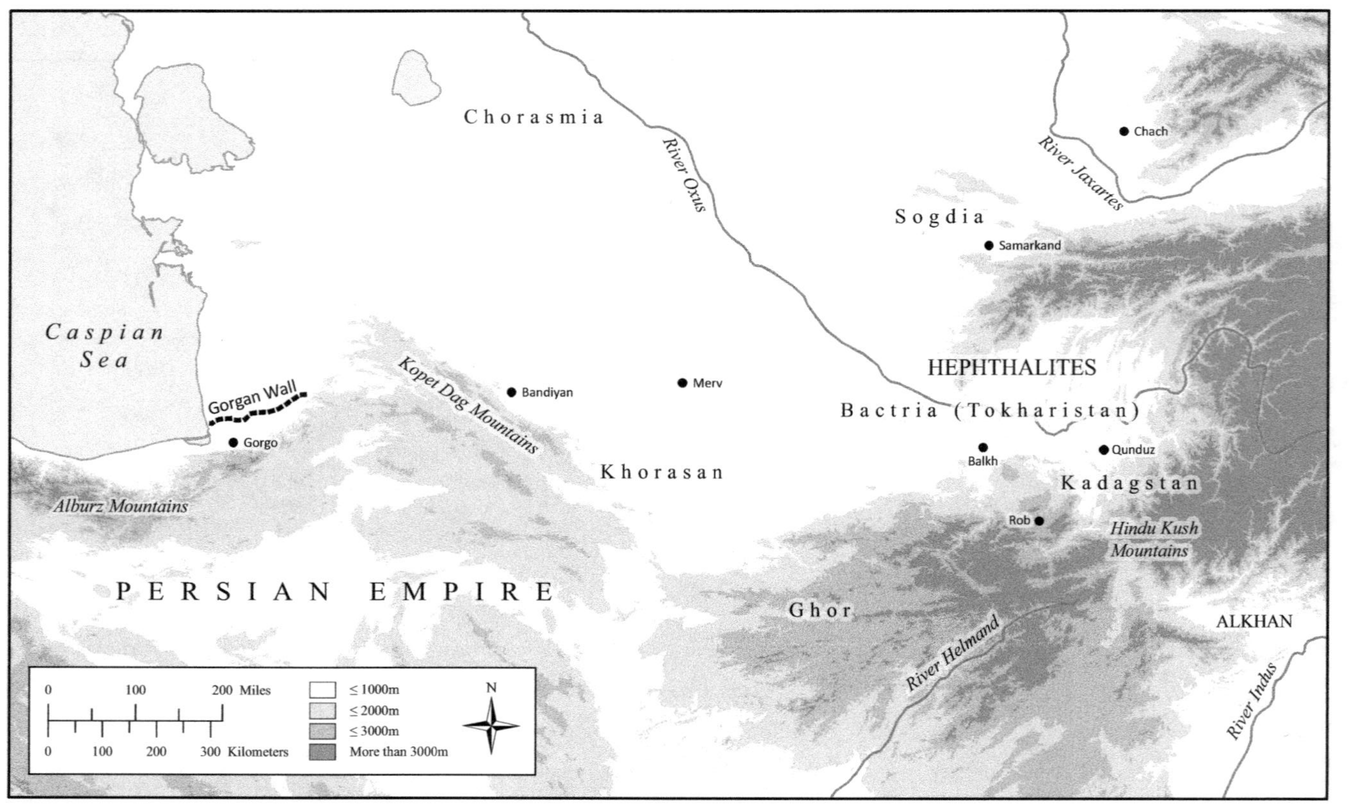

Figure 3   The Persian Northeastern Frontier

Persians. (6) The rich ones choose as many as twenty comrades or more to be their drinking fellows forever and share all their money, with common power over it. (7) When the man who made them his comrades dies, it is the custom for these men to be taken alive with him to his tomb.

(8) On Peroz's expedition against these Hephthalites an ambassador was present who had been sent to him by the Emperor Zeno, Eusebius by name.[15] The Hephthalites, giving the enemy the impression that they were terrified by their approach and were going into flight, made at a run for a place encircled all around by precipitous mountains which were entirely covered by numerous trees with thick foliage. (9) When one proceeded a long way within the mountains, a path could be seen in the middle, very wide, but with no exit at its end, for it stopped at the circle of mountains itself. (10) Peroz, therefore, innocent of all guile and not reflecting that he was in foreign territory, heedlessly pursued them. (11) A few of the Huns were in flight ahead of him, but most of them got behind the enemy army by hiding in the rough ground. As yet they did not wish to be seen by them, so that the Persians would go further into the ambush, come right inside the ring of mountains, and be unable to get out again. (12) The Persians noticed them, however, for they could already perceive some danger, and while keeping quiet themselves about the situation through terror of Peroz they besought Eusebius to advise the king – who was in complete ignorance of the danger – to take care and not to be overbold, and to see whether there might be some means to safety. (13) He came before Peroz, but did not reveal their present plight. Instead, he began with a parable: 'A lion', he said, 'once met a goat bound and bleating on a fairly low hill. The lion, in eagerness for its feast, sprang to snatch it, but fell into a deep pit with a narrow circular and continuous path (it had no outlet) which the goat's keepers had purposely built, placing the goat above the pit as a snare for the lion'. (14) When Peroz heard this, he grew alarmed in case the Persians had pursued the enemy to their own detriment. He advanced no further; he remained there and thought about their position. (15) But now the Hephthalites in pursuit came out into the open and put a guard on the entrance to the place to stop the Persians from retreating. (16) The Persians, realising then clearly what a bad situation they were in, regarded the position as disastrous for them, with no hope that they would escape the danger. (17) But the

---

[15] The date of this campaign is debated; it took place perhaps in 474, the year in which Zeno ascended the throne. The identity of Eusebius is also uncertain.

Hephthalite king[16] sent some of his men to Peroz and reproached him for his foolish rashness, as a result of which he would indeed have destroyed recklessly both himself and the Persian race. He promised, however, that even so the Huns would grant them safety if Peroz was willing to do obeisance to him as his lord and master, and give pledges on his native oaths that the Persians would never campaign against the Hephthalite people. (18) When Peroz heard this, he consulted with the magi who were with him, asking whether he should fulfil the demands of the enemy. (19) The magi answered that as to the oath he could do as he liked, but for the rest he must confound the enemy by guile. (20) For, they said, they had a custom whereby every day they did obeisance to the rising sun. (21) So Peroz should watch carefully for the time and meet the Hephthalite ruler at dawn, and then make his obeisance turning towards the rising sun. This way, they advised, he would be able to evade the dishonour brought by the action. (22) So Peroz gave the pledges for the peace and did obeisance to his enemy as the magi advised him, and gladly retired home with the whole Persian army intact.

Chapter 4

(1) Not long afterwards, however, disregarding the oath he had sworn, he began to wish to exact vengeance on the Hephthalites for their insult to him.[17] (2) He mustered Persians and allies from all his territories and set out on an expedition against the Hephthalites, leaving behind only one of his sons, Kavadh by name, who was just a youth at the time, and taking all the rest with him, some thirty in number. (3) When the Hephthalites heard of the expedition they were angry at being deceived by the enemy and reproached the king for abandoning everything to the Persians. (4) But he laughed and asked them what it was of theirs that he had abandoned – their land, their arms, or any other of their possessions. (5) They answered that he had abandoned the opportune moment on which everything else depends. (6) They eagerly advocated meeting the invaders, but he restrained them for the moment, maintaining that as yet the invasion was not certain, since the Persians were still in their own territory. But as he waited there, he did this. (7) In the plain where the Persians were likely to invade the land of the Hephthalites, he marked off a large and extensive space, making a broad, deep trench, and left a

---

[16] The Hephthalite king is called Akhshunwār by Tabari, 113, and Khushnawāz by Firdausi.
[17] This disastrous campaign of Peroz took place in 484 and is widely reported, e.g. in Ps.-Josh., 11 and Tabari, 110–19 (three versions).

narrow piece in the middle untouched, just wide enough for ten horses. (8) He laid reeds over the trench and concealed the real surface by scattering earth on top of the reeds. Then he told the Hunnic troops that when they were about to retire behind this trench, they were to draw themselves together into a narrow column and go carefully along this solid piece of land, taking care not to fall into the trench. (9) And he hung from the top of the royal standard the salt upon which Peroz had earlier sworn the oath that he was breaking in making war on the Huns. (10) As long as he heard that the enemy were in their own territory he kept his peace, but when he learnt from the scouts that they had reached the city of Gorgo, which is on the furthermost boundary of Persia, and had now left there and were advancing upon his own army, remaining himself with the greater part of his troops on his side of the trench, he ordered a few men to advance and show themselves to the enemy some distance away in the plain. And once they had merely been seen, they were to flee back again with all their might, remembering his instructions about the trench when they came near to it. (11) The detachment did this, and when they came near the trench, they all crossed it, a few at a time, and rejoined the rest of the army. (12) The Persians, filled with martial zeal against the enemy and with no inkling of the plot, came in full pursuit across the flat plain, and fell into the trench – not merely the leaders, (13) but those behind as well. For they were hot in pursuit, as has been said, and had no suspicion of the disaster which had befallen the vanguard. They fell on top of them with their horses and spears and, of course, killed them and perished equally themselves. (14) Among them was Peroz with all his sons. They say that just as he was about to fall into this trench, he realised the danger, and took the pearl that hung from his right ear, a jewel of dazzling whiteness and valuable for its great size, and flung it away, so that no one might wear it after him, it being exceedingly beautiful, such as no other king had possessed before.[18] (15) But their report does not seem credible to me, for in such a perilous situation he would not have thought of anything but the danger. I suppose that in fact his ear was crushed in the disaster and the pearl disappeared somewhere. (16) The Roman Emperor then sought eagerly to buy the pearl from the Hephthalites, but with absolutely no success, for the barbarians could not find it, even after a very careful search. They say, however, that the Hephthalites found it later and gave it to Kavadh. (17) But it is worth

16

17

---

[18] Peroz's pearl became a byword for a treasured item in the later Byzantine tradition. Cedrenus, writing in the eleventh century, adds a few details to Procopius' account.

recounting what the Persians say about this pearl, for perhaps the story may not seem wholly incredible to some.

(18) The Persians, then, say that when this pearl was in its oyster in the sea that borders the Persian coast,[19] the oyster was swimming not far from the shore, and that its shell was open, in the interior of which lay the pearl, a wonderful sight, for no other anywhere could be likened to it in the whole of history either for size or for beauty. (19) A shark of great size and fierceness became enamoured of this sight and followed in its tracks, relaxing neither by night nor by day. When it was forced to look for food, it would look around for something edible where it was, and when it had found something it would snatch at it and devour it as quickly as possible, and then catch up with the oyster and again satisfy itself with the beloved sight. (20) And they say that a fisherman once saw what was going on, but shrank from the danger in fear of the beast, and took the whole story to Peroz the king. (21) They say that when Peroz had heard it, he conceived a great longing for the pearl and urged this fisherman on with flattery and hope of gain. (22) The other, they say, was unable to resist his lord's request and said this to Peroz: 'My lord, riches are dear to men, but life is dearer, and children are most precious of all. (23) Being naturally impelled by love for them a man might perhaps even dare all. I intend to make trial of the beast, and I hope to make you master of the pearl. (24) If I succeed in this struggle, it is easy to see that henceforth I shall be ranked among those called blessed. For it is not unlikely that you, the king of kings, will reward me with all good things, and it will be enough for me, even if it should happen that I gain no reward, that I have been the benefactor of my master. (25) But if it is my fate to be caught by this beast, it shall be your task, O King, to requite my sons for their father's death. (26) For in this way even after my death I shall be earning for my family, and you will win greater fame for your virtue. By helping my children you will reward me, though I shall have no power to thank you for your kindness. For the only generosity that cannot be counterfeited is that which is shown to the dead.' (27) With these words he left. And when he reached the place where the oyster was accustomed to swim and the shark to follow, he sat down on a rock, waiting for a time when he might be able to catch the pearl abandoned by its lover. (28) As soon as the shark had come upon something that would serve him for food, and was delaying over it, the fisherman left those who were with him on the beach to help with his task. Eagerly he made for the

[19] Cedrenus specifies that it was the Persian Gulf, a region well known for its pearls in Antiquity.

oyster and, seizing it, made haste to get clear of danger. But the shark noticed and came to the rescue. (29) The fisherman saw it, and, since he was not far from the beach at the point it caught up with him, he flung his prize with all his might onto the land and was himself not long afterwards caught and killed. (30) The men left on the shore retrieved the pearl, took it to the king and told him what had happened. (31) This story, as narrated, is the Persian account of the pearl. But I return to my former narrative.

(32) In this way Peroz and all the Persian army were destroyed. For anyone who happened not to have fallen into the trench came into the hands of the enemy. (33) And after this a law was made in Persia that while advancing in enemy territory they should never engage in pursuit, even if it should happen that the enemy had been totally routed. (34) Those who had not gone on the expedition but remained in their own country chose as king Kavadh, the youngest son of Peroz, who alone survived. (35) And then the Persians became tribute-paying subjects of the Hephthalites, until Kavadh strengthened his rule and would no longer pay the yearly tribute. The barbarians ruled the Persians for two years.[20]

Chapter 5

(1) Later, however, Kavadh became more autocratic in his government and introduced among other innovations in the constitution a law providing that the Persians should be able to have intercourse with any of their women without distinction – which by no means pleased the people.[21] (2) For this reason they rose against him, deposed him, threw him in prison, and kept him under guard. They made Peroz's brother Blases their king,[22] since no male issue of Peroz survived, as has been told, and since the Persians cannot lawfully make king a private citizen unless the royal house is utterly extinguished. (3) Blases, when he became king, called together the highest of the Persians and held a council about

---

[20] It is more likely that the Hephthalites exercised some sort of hegemony over the Persians until the 510s.

[21] This is generally interpreted as an allusion to the king's support for the reforming Mazdakite movement, which is reported by numerous other sources. The holding of women in common threatened the aristocracy's blood-lines. See *ODLA*, Mazdak and Mazdakism.

[22] Blases appears to be a garbling of the name Balash (or Valash), Peroz's brother, who succeeded to the throne after the defeat of 484. He was overthrown by his nephew Kavadh in 488, but the new king was himself ousted briefly between 496/7 and 498/9 by his own brother Zamasp (or Jamasf). Procopius has conflated Balash and Zamasp. See *RPLA*, 98–9, on this passage.

Kavadh, for the people did not wish to put him to death. (4) Many views favouring different conclusions were expressed. But a man of high standing among the Persians came forward, by name Gusanastades, a *kanarang* by rank (that is, a Persian general),[23] who ruled on the very frontiers of Persian territory in the land which borders that of the Hephthalites. Showing the knife which the Persians use to cut their nails, a knife the length of a man's finger, but not a third of a finger in breadth, he said: (5) 'You see this knife, a very short one. Yet at this moment this knife can perform the task which very soon, rest assured, my dear Persians, twice ten thousand armoured men will not be able to do.' (6) By this he meant to show that if they did not kill Kavadh, by surviving he would soon make trouble for the Persians. (7) But they would not decide actually to put to death a man of royal blood, but only to keep him in the prison called 'Oblivion'. (8) For if a man is thrown into that prison, the law allows no mention of him henceforth, death being the penalty for whoever names him. For this reason it has received this name from the Persians. (9) Yet the history of the Armenians relates that the force of the law concerning the prison of Oblivion was once relaxed by the Persians in the following way.[24]

(10) There was once a truceless war of thirty-two years between the Persians and Armenians during the reign of Pacurius of the Persians and Arsaces, a man of the Arsacid (dynasty), of the Armenians.[25] It happened that as the war dragged on, both sides suffered greatly, and especially the Armenians. (11) But because both sides felt such distrust of each other, neither could send a herald to their adversary. Meanwhile, it happened that the Persians waged a war against certain other barbarians, who lived not far from the Armenians. (12) The Armenians were keen to make a show to the Persians of their goodwill towards them and of their peaceful intent, so they decided to invade the barbarians' territory after giving prior notice to the Persians. (13) They fell on them unexpectedly and killed nearly all of them, from the youngest to the oldest. Pacurius was overjoyed at the events and sent some of his courtiers to Arsaces, who gave him pledges and summoned him to the court. (14) When Arsaces

---

[23] The post of *kanārang* is attested in Bactrian documents; it has been interpreted as meaning 'he who defends the frontiers', but the word might also be a proper name, referring to the Kanārangīyān family. Procopius' Gusanastades probably renders the Persian name Gushnaspdād.

[24] There are many parallels between this story and one to be found in a fifth-century Armenian work, the *Epic Histories*, tr. N. Garsoïan (Cambridge, MA, 1989), 4.20, 4.54 and 5.7. See *ODLA*, *Buzandaran Patmut'iwnk'* (*Epic Histories*). The prison was situated in Khuzestan.

[25] In the *Epic Histories* the Persian king is Shapur II (309–79); there was an Armenian king called Arsaces who reigned between c. 338 and 368.

reached him, he treated him as worthy of every kindness and even held him as a brother on an equal and level footing. (15) He then bound Arsaces by the most terrible oaths and himself swore just as solemnly that the Persians and Armenians would henceforth be friends and allies. He then immediately allowed him to return to his native land.

(16) A little later, certain people slandered Arsaces, alleging that he wished to undertake a revolution. Convinced by them, Pacurius again summoned Arsaces to him, hinting that it was his intention to consult him about general affairs. (17) Without hesitation, he went to Pacurius. He brought with him the fiercest among the Armenians, including Bassicius, who was his general and adviser, for he had attained the greatest courage and good sense. (18) Immediately Pacurius blamed them both, Arsaces and Bassicius, reproaching them because they had disregarded their oaths and so quickly envisaged seceding. But they denied this and constantly insisted that they had planned nothing of the sort. (19) Pacurius therefore had them guarded in disgrace. Then he enquired of the magi as to what should be done with them. (20) The magi thought it by no means just to condemn those who denied the allegations and had not been explicitly caught out, but they offered him a suggestion as to how Arsaces could be compelled to accuse himself. (21) They bade him cover over the floor of the royal tent with soil, half of it from the land of the Persians, the other half from Armenia. And the king acted accordingly. (22) Then the magi, after enveloping the whole tent in magic spells, bade the king pace up and down there with Arsaces and accuse him of violating their agreements and oaths. (23) It was necessary also for them to be present at the conversation, for thus they would be witnesses to all his words. Immediately then Pacurius summoned Arsaces and walked up and down with him in the tent while the magi were present. He asked Arsaces why he had spurned his oaths and was trying again to wear down Persians and Armenians alike with unbearable sufferings. (24) Arsaces, as long as he spoke on the spot where earth from Persian territory was placed, denied the accusations and, invoking the most terrible oaths, insisted that he was a faithful slave of Pacurius. (25) But when, in the middle of his speech, he arrived at the centre of the tent, where they trod on Armenian soil, then he was somehow compelled suddenly to shift to bolder words and did not stop threatening Pacurius and the Persians. He declared that he would avenge himself for this insult as soon as he became master of his own destiny. (26) He made the whole circuit, speaking and boasting thus, until he arrived once again on the way back on the soil from Persia. Then, as

though he were reciting some recantation, he was a suppliant and poured forth pitiful words to Pacurius. (27) When he came again to Armenian earth he went back to his threats. Thus, by frequently shifting from one view to another, he could not hide any of his secrets. (28) Then the magi condemned him for having broken the treaty and oaths. Pacurius stripped the skin from Bassicius, made it into a sack, filled it with chaff, and hung the whole thing from a very tall tree.[26] (29) Arsaces, however, he imprisoned in the prison of Oblivion, since he could not kill a man of royal blood. (30) At a later point, a certain Armenian,[27] who was among the closest associates of Arsaces and had followed him to the lands of the Persians, participated in a campaign of the Persians against a barbarian people. This man was courageous in this struggle and became the chief architect of the Persian victory, as Pacurius observed. (31) For that reason Pacurius asked him to request whatever he wanted, insisting that there was nothing that he would not obtain from him. (32) He asked for nothing other than to serve Arsaces as he wanted for one day. (33) This proposal greatly vexed the king, in that it would oblige him to break an ancient law. So that he might nonetheless continue to speak completely truthfully, he agreed to fulfil the request. (34) When, at the king's order, he found himself at the prison of Oblivion, he greeted Arsaces. They threw their arms around each other and sang a sweet lament, and it was only with difficulty that each released his arms from the other. (35) When they had had their fill and had ceased weeping, the Armenian washed Arsaces and dressed him, neglecting nothing. He clothed him in a royal robe and had him recline on a bed of straw. (36) Then Arsaces entertained those present in royal fashion, as had been his custom previously. (37) At this banquet many words were spoken around the cups that greatly pleased Arsaces, and many other things were revealed that were delightful to him. The drinking extended until night, and they enjoyed conversing with one another exceedingly. Only with difficulty did they leave one another and separate, overcome with happiness. (38) Then they say that Arsaces declared that he had passed the sweetest day of his life there, in the company of the dearest of all men to him, and that he could no longer willingly put up with the miseries of life. (39) So saying, he killed himself with a dagger, which he happened deliberately to have stolen during the banquet, and thus was taken from the world of men.

---

[26] Cf. Agath. 4.23.1–7 on such flayings, well attested as a Persian punishment.
[27] *Epic Histories* 5.7 calls him Drastamat.

(40) The account of the Armenians reports that matters concerning Arsaces took place in the manner in which the story has been told. Then it was that the law on the prison of Oblivion was broken. Now I must return to the point from which I set out.

Chapter 6

(1) Kavadh's wife looked after him while he was in prison, visiting him and bringing him provisions. The jailer began to try to seduce her, for she was remarkably attractive to behold. (2) When Kavadh heard this from his wife, he told her to submit to the man's demands. And so the jailer slept with the woman and fell very passionately in love with her. (3) As a result he allowed her to visit her husband whenever she pleased and to leave again without interference from anyone. There was a man of high standing among the Persians called Seoses,[28] a great friend of Kavadh, (4) who spent all his time near this prison, watching for an opportunity to get Kavadh out. (5) Through Kavadh's wife he told him that horses and men were in readiness for him not far from the prison, giving details of their position. (6) One night Kavadh persuaded his wife to give him her own clothing and to put on his cloak and sit in the prison instead of him where he used to sit. (7) And so Kavadh escaped from the prison. When the guards saw him, they thought it was his wife, and did not restrain him or in any way molest him. (8) At daybreak they saw the woman in the room in her husband's clothes and imagined – which was very far from the truth – that Kavadh was there. This pretence lasted for many days, until Kavadh was far on his way. (9) What happened to the woman when the plot was revealed, and how they punished her, I cannot tell for certain, for the Persians do not agree about it. For this reason I do not recount the versions.[29]

(10) Kavadh escaped all detection, and with Seoses reached the Hephthalite Huns. The king gave him his daughter in marriage and then, since Kavadh was now his son-in-law, put under his command a considerable army against the Persians. (11) This army the Persians did not dare to meet, but dispersed in all directions in flight. (12) But when Kavadh came to the land where Gusanastades had his domain, he told some of his attendants that he would appoint *kanarang* whichever Persian on that

28

29

---

[28] Often identified with Siyāvush in the eastern tradition, although there Kavadh's helper is called Zarmihr.

[29] The story of Kavadh's wife is found also in the eastern tradition, where she is described as his sister, cf. (e.g.) Tabari, 128, 135.

day first came into sight and offered his allegiance. (13) But as he spoke
he regretted his words, since he remembered a law that forbids offices
among the Persians to be conferred on others than those to whom each
belongs by descent. (14) He was afraid of someone coming to him first
who was not related to the *kanarang* and forcing him to break the law, so
as to keep his word. (15) But as he considered this, there came to him a
chance of keeping his word without dishonouring the law. For the first to
come to him chanced to be Adergudunbades, a young man related
to Gusanastades, and particularly good at warfare. (16) He was the first to
call Kavadh his master and do obeisance to him as king and to ask him to
use him like a slave for whatever he wished. (17) So Kavadh reached the
royal palace without difficulty, seized Blases, abandoned by his defenders,
and blinded him in the way in which the Persians customarily blind
criminals – they boil oil and pour it, bubbling, onto their open eyes, or
heat an iron needle in the fire and with this touch the inside of their eyes
– and kept him afterwards under guard. His reign lasted for two years.
(18) Kavadh put Gusanastades to death and appointed Adergudunbades
to the office of *kanarang* in his place, and immediately proclaimed Seoses
adrastadaran salanes.[30] This means the man who is in charge of all offices
and the entire soldiery. (19) Seoses was the first and only man among the
Persians to hold this office. No one had it before or after him. And
Kavadh strengthened his rule and maintained it in safety, for he was
second to none in ingenuity and energy.

Chapter 7

(1) Not long afterwards Kavadh owed money to the king of the
Hephthalites, and since he was unable to pay it, he asked Anastasius, the
Roman emperor, to lend it to him. Anastasius consulted with some of his
courtiers and asked them whether he should do so.[31] (2) They would not
agree to his making the loan. They told him that it would not be in his
interest to strengthen their enemy's friendship with the Hephthalites with
Roman money – it would be better to stir them up against each other as
much as possible. (3) So Kavadh decided, without reason, to make war
on the Romans (fig. 4). First he invaded Armenia without prior warning,

---

[30] Adergudunbades may be Procopius' version of the Persian Ādhargulbād. The office referred to
corresponds to the Persian *artēshtārān sālār*, 'head of the warriors'; Tabari, 104, confirms that it was
one of the highest ranks in Iran, although, contrary to what Procopius says, others are attested as
holding it.
[31] Procopius has moved forward to 502; the Roman Emperor Anastasius had succeeded Zeno in 491.

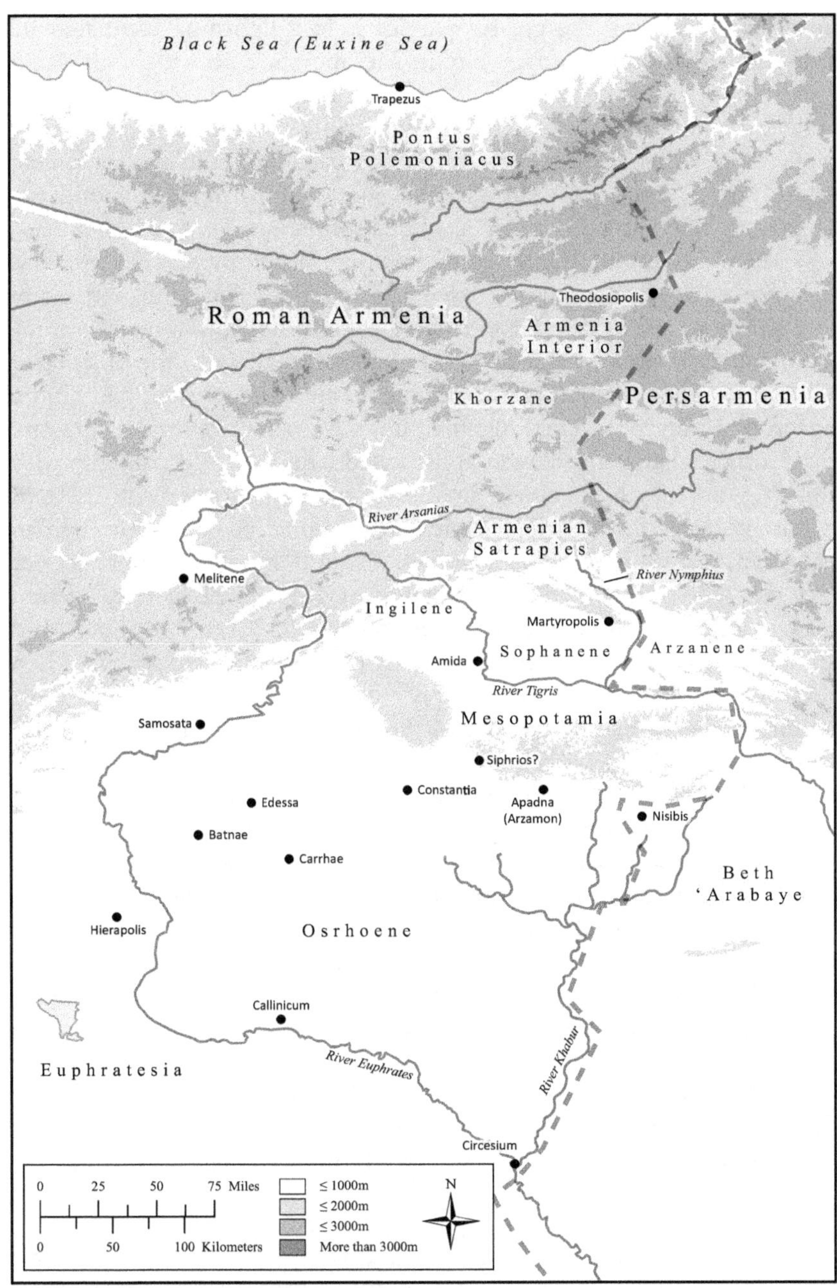

Figure 4   The Roman East During the Anastasian War

and after plundering the greater part of it in a lightning campaign he came suddenly upon Amida, a city in Mesopotamia, to which, although it was winter, he laid siege (fig. 5).[32] (4) The people of Amida had no soldiers present to aid them, for it was a time of peace and prosperity, and were in other respects totally unprepared. Nonetheless, they were certainly not willing to defect to the enemy, and they withstood the danger and hardship with unexpected determination.

(5) There was among the Syrians a just man, Jacob by name,[33] who was far advanced in religious knowledge and practice. This man had many years before confined himself in a place called Endielon, a day's journey from Amida, so as to be able to devote himself in safety to the practice of holiness. (6) The inhabitants thereabouts, to aid his intention, had built a fence round him, not joined together, but with posts fixed independently of one other, so that those who approached could see and converse with him. (7) And they had made a small roof over him to keep off the rain and snow. Here this man had sat for a long time, giving no thought to heat or cold, and living off seeds which he ate only at long intervals, not every day. (8) Certain of the Hephthalites saw this Jacob as they overran that part of the country, and they eagerly drew their bows to shoot him. But all their hands were fixed and could not work their bows. (9) When this story, repeated among the troops, reached Kavadh, he wished to see for himself, and when he had seen it he, together with the Persians who were there, was filled with great wonder and besought Jacob to forgive the barbarians their wrongdoing. And he forgave them in one word, and they were released from their plight. (10) Kavadh then told the man to ask for whatever he wanted, thinking that he would ask for a large sum of money, and actually rashly promised that he would be refused nothing. (11) But he asked him to give him all who should come to him in this war as fugitives. This request Kavadh granted, and gave him a written guarantee of safety. Many came flocking to him from all sides and found safety there, for the affair became very famous. These things occurred thus.

(12) While Kavadh was besieging Amida, he brought against every part of the circuit wall the machine called the ram. The people of Amida each time repelled the attack with transverse beams, but he did not give in

---

[32] The king arrived at Amida (modern Diyarbakır in eastern Turkey), after capturing Theodosiopolis in Armenia (Erzurum) and receiving the surrender of Martyropolis, on 5 October. Ps.-Josh. offers further details, 50, 53, while Ps.-Zach. vii.3–4 provides a full account, sometimes overlapping with Procopius'. See *RPW*, 79–94, *REF*, 63–7.

[33] Not otherwise known; his feast day is on 6 August.

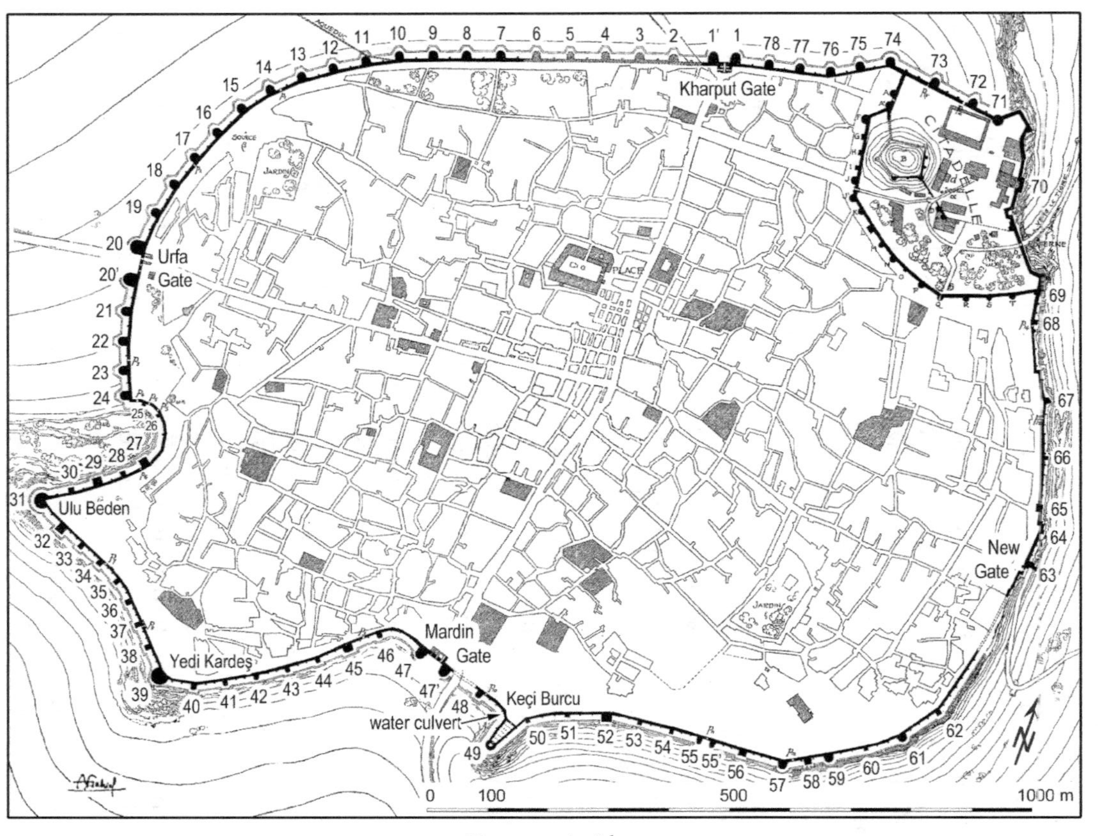

Figure 5   Amida

until he realised that the wall could not be taken by this means.[34] (13) For though he attacked it many times he was unable to destroy or to shake any part of the wall, so securely had the edifice been fashioned long ago by its builders. (14) Meeting with no success here, Kavadh made an artificial hill as a fortress against the city, far higher than the wall; and the besieged within the wall began to tunnel under the hill, secretly removing the earth from there and hollowing out the greater part of the inside of the hill. The outside remained in the shape in which it was built, giving no hint of what was happening. (15) Many Persians climbed up to the top as if in safety, meaning to shoot down onto the heads of those inside the walls from there. But as the crowd climbed up it at a run, the hill suddenly collapsed and killed nearly all of them. (16) Kavadh, at a loss as to how to deal with the situation, decided to raise the siege and ordered the army to retreat on the next day. (17) Then the besieged, paying no heed to the danger, greatly mocked and laughed at the barbarians from the circuit walls. (18) Some prostitutes shamelessly lifted up their skirts and displayed to Kavadh, who was standing very near, the parts of a woman's body that men should not see uncovered. (19) When the magi saw this, they came before the king and forbade the retreat, insisting that they inferred from what had happened that it would come to pass that the people of Amida would soon show to Kavadh all their secret and hidden possessions. And so the Persian army remained there.

(20) But not many days later one of the Persians saw near the towers the exit of an old tunnel, badly concealed with small stones, and only a few at that.[35] (21) He went there alone at night, tested this means of entry, and found himself inside the circuit walls. At dawn he told the whole story to Kavadh. The following night Kavadh made ladders ready and went to the place with a few men. A lucky chance befell him in the following way: (22) the guarding of the tower which was nearest to the tunnel had fallen to the lot of those of the Christians who are the most strict, whom they call monks. It chanced that on that day they were celebrating an annual festival to God.[36] (23) When night fell, all of them, tired out by the festival, and more than usually sated with food and

---

[34] Here and elsewhere in the account of the siege there are echoes of Thucydides, in this case of 2.76.4, the siege of Plataea. Since the details are confirmed by Ps.-Zach., however, there is no reason to doubt his account.

[35] Ps.-Zach. 7.4a identifies the Persian as a certain Kanarak the Lame and situates this weak point at the Tripyrgion ('three towers', cf. 2.27.41), perhaps on the south side of the city near the Mardin gate.

[36] The monks belonged to the monastery of John of the Urtāyē, as Ps.-Zach. 7.4a reports; their abbot was a Persian, which led to rumours of treachery subsequently.

drink, were sleeping a sweet and peaceful sleep, and as a result heard nothing of what was going on. (24) The Persians got within the walls through the tunnel a few at a time, climbed the tower, and, finding the monks still asleep, killed them all. (25) When Kavadh heard of this, he brought the ladders up to the wall very near to this tower. (26) Already it was day. The citizens of Amida on guard in the next tower realised the danger and quickly came up to the rescue. (27) For a long time there was a great pushing and shoving from both sides, and the citizens of Amida, getting the upper hand, killed many of those who had climbed up. They pushed back the men on the ladders and came very near to beating off the danger. (28) But Kavadh himself drew his sabre, rushed to the ladders, and kept terrifying the Persians with it; and death was the punishment for those who dared to retreat from there. (29) And so the Persians got the better of their enemies by sheer numbers and conquered them in the battle. The city was taken by storm on the eightieth day from the beginning of the siege.[37] (30) There was a great slaughter of the Amidenes until an old man from among them, a priest, came up to Kavadh as he was entering the town and said that it did not befit a king to slaughter captives.[38] (31) Kavadh, still gripped by anger, answered, 'Why did you resolve to fight me?' And the other said in answer, 'Because it was God's will to give Amida to you not by our decision, but because of your prowess.' (32) Kavadh was pleased with this reply and allowed them to kill no one after this, but told the Persians to plunder the riches and make slaves of the survivors, and to choose out for himself all those of high rank.

(33) A little later, after leaving a thousand men to garrison the place, and putting Glones in charge, a Persian, and leaving also a few poor wretches from the Amidenes to wait on the Persians, he made for home with all the rest of the army and the prisoners. (34) But to these captives he displayed a kindness worthy of a king. For in a short time he allowed them all to go home, though the official version was that they had escaped from him. (35) And the Roman Emperor Anastasius also treated them in a manner worthy of their bravery, for he remitted the city of all its yearly taxes for seven years and gave them many gifts, both communally and individually, so much so that they forgot for the most part what had happened. But this took place later.[39]

---

[37] The city fell on (or rather shortly after) 10 January, so Ps.-Josh. 54; the Syriac sources mostly put the length of the siege rather at 97 days.

[38] Ps.-Zach. 7.4e and Ps.-Josh. put the casualties at 80,000.

[39] Ps.-Josh. 66, 99 and Ps.-Zach. 7.5e also report Anastasius' generosity.

Chapter 8

(1) At the time of which I was speaking, however, the Emperor Anastasius, learning that Amida was under siege, sent a considerable army with all speed. There were officers in charge of every company, but the supreme commanders were four in number: Areobindus, at that time *magister militum per Orientem*, the son-in-law of Olybrius, who had not long before been emperor of the West; (2) Celer, the chief of the palace guard (the Romans call this office *magister*); and in addition, the *magistri militum praesentales* Patricius the Phrygian and Hypatius, the emperor's nephew. These were the four generals.[40] (3) Justin, who later became emperor on the death of Anastasius, was with them too; Patriciolus with his son Vitalian, who took up arms against the Emperor Anastasius not long afterwards as a usurper; Pharesmanes, a Colchian by birth and particularly good at warfare; and Godidisclus and Bessas, both Goths from among those who did not follow Theoderic when he went to Italy from Thrace, both very noble and experienced in military matters; and many other men of great worth.[41] (4) It is said that the Romans never mustered such an army against the Persians either before or afterwards.[42] But all these leaders did not join together, or make one army for their expedition; each one led his own troops individually against the enemy. (5) The Egyptian Apion was sent as treasurer for the expenses of the army, a man conspicuous among the patricians and full of energy.[43] The emperor in a written statement declared him partner in the imperial power so that he might have the authority to direct the finances as he wished.

(6) This army was mustered with some delay and advanced but slowly. Accordingly, they did not come upon the barbarians in Roman territory, since the Persians had only made a sudden incursion and had immediately afterwards retreated to their own country with all the plunder. (7) None of the generals wanted to start a siege against those who had been left in Amida for the moment, for they heard that they had brought in large quantities of provisions. Instead, they were eager to invade the

---

[40] On these four senior commanders see *PLRE* 2, Areobindus 1, Celer 2, Patricius 14, Hypatius 6. None had much, if any, military experience. Celer was *magister officiorum* or 'master of offices'.

[41] See *PLRE* 2, Iustinus 4, Patriciolus, Vitalianus 2, Pharesmanes 3, Godidisclus, Bessas. Vitalian had rebelled against Anastasius with some success in Thrace in 514. The Theoderic referred to here is the Ostrogothic king, who moved with his followers into Italy at the prompting of the Emperor Zeno, as Procopius describes at *Wars* 5.1.

[42] Ps.-Josh. 54 puts the total at 52,000 men.

[43] On Apion see *PLRE* 2, Apion 2.

enemy territory. (8) Even so, they did not go together against the barbarians; as they advanced, they camped separately from each other. When Kavadh heard this (for he was actually very close), he made with all haste for the Roman frontier and went to meet them. (9) But the Romans did not know that Kavadh was advancing towards them with his whole army: they thought that there was a small detachment of Persians there. (10) Areobindus' force was encamped in a place called Arzamon, two days' journey from Constantia, and Patricius' and Hypatius' in a place called Siphrios, no less than 350 stades from Amida. For Celer had not yet arrived.[44]

(11) When Areobindus realised that Kavadh was advancing against them with the whole of his army, he abandoned the camp and fled with all his troops as fast as he could to Constantia. (12) And when the enemy came up shortly afterwards, they took the camp, money and all, without a man in it. From there they advanced with all speed against the rest of the Roman army. (13) Patricius' and Hypatius' men met with eight hundred Hephthalites, who were ahead of the Persian army, and killed nearly all of them. (14) But knowing nothing of Kavadh and the Persian army, they thought themselves victorious and relaxed their habits. They put down their arms and prepared their lunch, for it was now that time of day. (15) A mountain stream flowed in this place, where the Romans began to wash the meat which was to form their meal. (16) Some, finding the heat oppressive, decided to bathe. Because of this the water in the stream was disturbed in its flow. When Kavadh heard what had happened to the Hephthalites, he advanced with speed against the enemy. (17) But when he saw that the water of the stream was muddied, he guessed what was going on, realised that the enemy were off their guard, and ordered his army to advance against them with all speed. They fell upon them at once as they ate, unarmed. (18) The Romans could not withstand the attack, nor did they think of defence; each fled as best he could. Some of them were caught and killed; others, who had climbed the mountain which stretches up there, flung themselves down the cliff in much panic and confusion. (19) They say that no one was saved from this, but Patricius and Hypatius managed to escape at the beginning of the attack.[45] Then Kavadh retired homewards with all his army, for enemy

39

40

---

[44] Areobindus led an invasion of Persian territory near Nisibis that had some success but was then forced back; meanwhile Patricius and Hypatius had besieged Amida but then moved rather late to come to Areobindus' aid. See Ps.-Josh. 55–6, Ps.-Zach. 7.5a, Theoph. 145–7, with *RPW*, 96–101.

[45] Parallel accounts of these debacles may be found in Ps.-Josh. and Ps.-Zach. See *RPW*, 94–101, *REF*, 71–3.

Huns had invaded his land, and he began to wage a long war against this people in the northern part of the country.[46] (20) In the meantime the rest of the Roman army arrived, but did nothing worthy of note because there was no one in full command of the war; the generals were of equal rank and opposed each other's wishes and would not agree. (21) Celer crossed the river Nymphius with his men and made an incursion into Arzanene. (22) This river is very near Martyropolis, about 300 stades from Amida. But after plundering the villages there they returned soon afterwards, and this attack was a short one.[47]

Chapter 9

(1) Later Areobindus was summoned by the emperor and went to Byzantium.[48] The rest arrived at Amida and laid siege to it in the winter season. They could not manage to take the place by storm, even after many attempts; but they might have done so by famine, for all the besieged's provisions had given out. (2) But the generals knew nothing of their enemies' plight; and seeing that the soldiers were distressed by the siege and by the winter weather, and at the same time suspecting that a Persian army was soon going to advance against them, they were eager to depart from there by any means. (3) And the Persians, not knowing what was to become of them in this peril, concealed their shortage of provisions very carefully, keeping up an appearance of having an abundance of supplies; for they wanted to retire home with some honourable excuse. (4) So both sides held talks, the condition being that the Persians would surrender the city to the Romans on receipt of a thousand pounds of gold. Each side gladly fulfilled its undertaking and the son of Glones surrendered Amida to the Romans, for Glones had already died in the following way.[49]

(5) Before the Romans had encamped at Amida, but when they were not far away from the city, a peasant, who used to go secretly into the city and sell fowl and loaves and many delicacies to this Glones at high prices, came before Patricius the general and promised that he would deliver Glones to him with two hundred Persians, if there was hope of some reward from him.[50] (6) Patricius sent the man off, promising him

---

[46] A reference to a raid by Sabir Huns through the Caucasus passes probably (on which see 10.4).

[47] Celer arrived later than the other commanders, in September 504.

[48] A mistake on Procopius' part: it was Anastasius' nephew, Hypatius, who was recalled.

[49] Ps.-Zach. 7.5d puts the sum handed over at 1100 pounds of gold.

[50] Ps.-Zach. 7.5b names the peasant as Gadana; his source claims to have known him personally. He recounts the same story with a few variations and calls Glones Aglon.

everything that he wanted. The man tore his clothes and entered the city   **42**
looking as though he had been weeping. (7) He came before Glones,
tearing his hair, and said, 'My lord, I was bringing to you all the good
things of the countryside when some Roman soldiers met me (for they
go around the countryside in bands and oppress the poor farmers) and
beat me terribly and went off with everything like thieves,[51] they whose
long-established custom it is to fear the Persians and oppress the farmers.
(8) Defend yourself, my lord, and us and the Persians. If you go hunting
to the outskirts of the city, you shall have a prey by no means to be
despised, for the accursed men go about robbing in fours or fives.' (9)
These were his words.

Glones believed him and asked him how many Persians he thought
would be sufficient for the task. (10) He said that fifty would be enough,
for they would not meet with more than five of them at a time on the
way. But so that they should not be taken unawares by anything, there
would be no harm in taking even a hundred for the task. And if he took
double this, so much the better. For no harm could come to a man from
the larger number. (11) Glones therefore selected two hundred cavalry and
told the man to lead the way. (12) But the peasant assured him that it   **43**
would be better that he should be sent on ahead to spy, and if he reported
that he had seen Romans still going about in the same areas, the Persians
could then sally out at the right time. He seemed to Glones to speak well,
and so was sent forth after Glones dismissed him. (13) He went to the
general Patricius and told him everything. Patricius sent with him two of
his own bodyguard and a thousand soldiers. (14) He concealed them near
the village of Thilasamon, forty stades from Amida, in glens and wooded
places, and told them to stay in this ambush, and set off at a run for the
town. (15) Telling Glones that his prey was ready, he led him and his two
hundred men to the enemy trap. When they had crossed the place where
the Romans lay in ambuscade, without Glones and the Persians seeing, he
roused the Romans from their ambush and showed them the enemy. (16)
When the Persians saw them bearing down upon them, they were
confounded by the surprise attack and did not know what to do. They
could not retreat since the enemy were at their backs, nor could they flee
in any other direction in hostile territory. (17) They ranged themselves for
battle as well as they could in the circumstances and defended themselves
against their attackers, but being far outnumbered they were defeated and
all killed, along with Glones. (18) When Glones' son heard of this, he was   **44**

---

[51] Reading *hoia* rather than *hoi*.

greatly upset and, raging with anger that he could not help his father, burnt the church of the holy Symeon where his father lodged. (19) Neither Glones nor Kavadh nor any other Persian deliberately destroyed or razed any other building by any other method either inside or outside Amida. But I will return to my former narrative.

(20) Thus the Romans paid the money and recaptured Amida two years after it had been taken by the enemy. When they were in the city, their own negligence and the hardihood of the Persians were recognised. (21) After reckoning up the amount of grain left there and the number of barbarians who had left, they discovered that about seven days' rations were left in the city, although Glones and his son had been giving grain to the Persians in quantities insufficient for their needs for a long time. (22) For to the Romans who remained with them, as I mentioned before, they had decided to give nothing at all, ever since the time when the enemy had established the siege. These men had at first resorted to unaccustomed foods and then turned to every kind of unlawful thing, finally even to cannibalism.[52] (23) So the generals realised that they had been deceived by the barbarians, and they reproached the soldiers for their weakness in showing themselves unruly when they could have taken so great a number of Persian prisoners with the city, including Glones' son, whereas the Romans had incurred great disgrace by giving money to their enemy and had only bought Amida from the Persians. (24) But later the Persians made a truce with the Romans, for the Hunnic war was dragging on. The truce was made by Celer, the Roman, and Aspebedes,[53] the Persian, and was for seven years. Both sides retreated to their own country and kept the peace. (25) Thus, as I have narrated, the war began between Rome and Persia and thus it ended. I come now to recount events that concern the Caspian Gates.

Chapter 10

(1) The Taurus mountains of Cilicia traverse first Cappadocia and Armenia and the territory called Persarmenia, then Albania and Iberia and the regions where other independent nations and those subject to the Persians live (fig. 6).[54] (2) The mountain range extends over a large area, and, to

---

[52] Ps.-Zach. 7.5c also reports that cannibalism was practised in the city.

[53] The name may be a rendering of the Persian title *spāhbad*, 'general', but it might also be a personal name.

[54] Albania is situated west of the Caspian, where modern Azerbaijan lies. Iberia is in the central Caucasus and corresponds to eastern Georgia today.

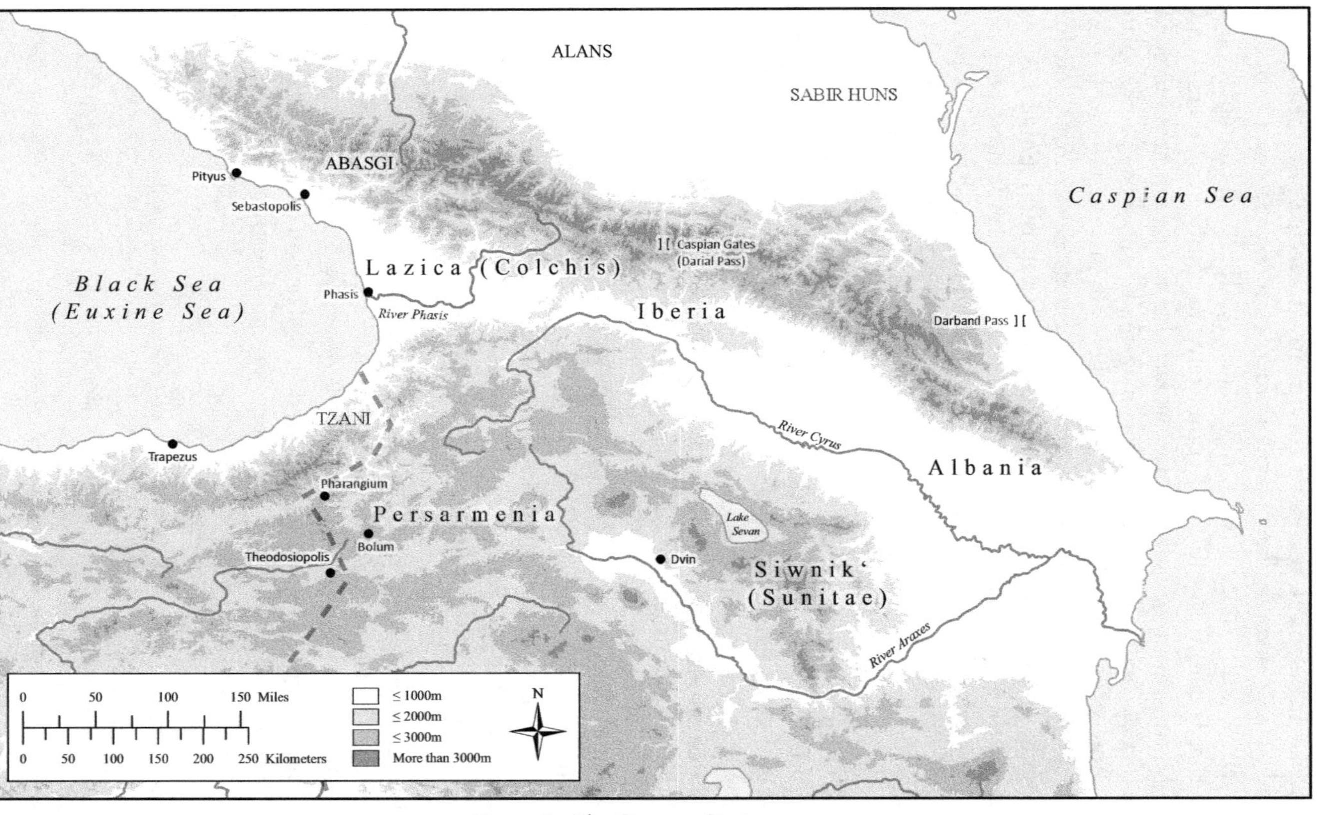

Figure 6   The Caucasus Region, c.510

one advancing along it, it appears consistently to reach a great height and breadth. (3) As one goes beyond the borders of Iberia there is a path in a very narrow pass that extends for fifty stades. (4) This path culminates at a place that is cut off by cliffs and completely inaccessible. For there seems to be no way through at all, save for the fact that nature has here provided some sort of small gate, which appears man-made, known as 'the Caspian Gate' from of old.[55] (5) From this point there are plains suited to horses, remarkably full of sources of water, and an extensive territory good for horse-grazing and generally flat. (6) Here almost all the Hunnic nations are established, reaching as far as the Maeotic lake.[56] (7) If these peoples, whom I just mentioned, go forth through the small gate against the lands of the Persians and Romans, they come with horses fresh, without undertaking the slightest detour or encountering any mountainous regions – save that they pass through those fifty stades to the Iberian borders, as I said. (8) But if they go forth from any other exits, they arrive only with great effort and no longer able to use their own horses, for they are obliged to take many detours, which are also mountainous.

(9) When Alexander, the son of Philip, realised this, he built gates at the aforementioned place and established a fortress there.[57] Many people held the gates as time went on, among whom was Ambazuces, a Hun by birth, and a friend of the Romans and the Emperor Anastasius. (10) When this Ambazuces had reached the depths of old age and was on the point of death he sent a message to Anastasius, asking the emperor to give him money on the condition that he would cede the fortress and the Caspian Gates to the Romans. (11) But the Emperor Anastasius, who did not know how to act without due consideration and was unused to doing so, reckoned that it would be impossible for him to provision the soldiers stationed there; for the place was bereft of any supplies and no people subject to the Romans was to be found in the vicinity. So he acknowledged with great gratitude the goodwill displayed by the man towards him, but categorically refused his offer. (12) When therefore Ambazuces died not long afterwards of a disease, Kavadh overthrew his sons and gained control of the Gates.[58]

---

[55] The pass here described is the Darial or Dariali, now in Georgia close to the Russian border, where recent excavations have uncovered traces of a Late Antique fort and a coin of Kavadh dated to 529. See *RPLA*, 188–95, *ODLA*, Caucasus Passes.

[56] Procopius refers to the steppes of the Ukraine from the Caucasus westwards towards the Crimea and Sea of Azov (the Maeotic Lake).

[57] References to Alexander the Great (356–323 B.C.) and to his father, Philip II of Macedon (382–336 B.C.).

[58] The date of Ambazuces' death is unknown. His offer to Anastasius is generally placed around 505.

(13) The Emperor Anastasius, when he had concluded the truce with Kavadh, built a city in the district of Dara, which was exceedingly strong and worthy of note; it bore the name of the emperor himself.[59] (14) It is ninety-eight stades distant from the city of Nisibis and approximately twenty-eight from the place that divides the territories of the Romans and the Persians. (15) The Persians were keen to prevent the building, but they proved completely incapable of doing so because of the pressure of the Hunnic war.[60] (16) As soon as Kavadh had brought the war to an end, he sent a message to the Romans to accuse them of having built a city right on the Persian borderlands, even though this had been prohibited in the earlier treaties between the Persians and Romans.[61] (17) At this point therefore Anastasius wanted to deflect him and to clear himself of the accusation, which he did by a mixture of threats and the prospect of friendship with him, as well as the gift of not inconsiderable sums of money. (18) This emperor also built another city like this very close to the frontiers of Persarmenia. It had of old been a village, but it received the rank at least of city from the Emperor Theodosius and was even named for him.[62] (19) But Anastasius encircled it with a very stout wall and thus caused no less trouble for the Persians than by the construction of the other city, for both places were bulwarks directed against their territory.

Chapter 11

(1) Anastasius died shortly after this, and Justin took over the empire, beating off all Anastasius' relatives from the imperial power, although they were many and very distinguished.[63] (2) At this, the thought came to Kavadh that the Persians might revolt against his house after his death, since it did not seem likely that he would be able to hand on the throne to any of his sons without opposition. (3) The law destined his eldest son, Kaoses, for the throne, because of his birth, but he did not meet with Kavadh's approval: the father's attitude conflicted both with nature and the law of succession.[64] (4) Zames, who was the second son, was kept by

---

[59] It was also known as Anastasiopolis. Ps.-Josh. 90, Ps.-Zach. 7.6, Marc. *com.* a.518, Proc. *Aed.* 2.1.4–10, all describe its construction, cf. *RPW*, 120–1, *REF*, 74–7, *RPLA*, 100–4.

[60] The war against the Sabir Huns mentioned at 8.19.

[61] As noted at 2.15.

[62] This is Theodosiopolis in Armenia, Erzurum today. Procopius describes Anastasius' work also at *Aed.* 3.5.4–8. See *ODLA*, Theodosiopolis.

[63] Though Anastasius had no legitimate sons, he had three prominent nephews, Hypatius, Pompey and Probus.

[64] The Greek Kaoses probably represents the Persian Kāwūs or Kayūs. He may also be the Phthasouarsan of Theoph. 169–70, who led the Mazdakites and was eliminated by Kavadh before

law from the throne because he had lost one of his eyes, for the Persians cannot lawfully make king a man who has only one eye or any other disability.[65] (5) The father was passionately devoted to Khusro, who had been born to him by Aspebedes' sister, but seeing that the Persians were, one might almost say, all besotted with Zames' bravery (for he was good at warfare), and honoured him for his prowess in other respects, he was afraid that they might rise against Khusro and do irreparable harm to the dynasty and to the monarchy. (6) He thought it best therefore to put a stop to the war against Rome and to its causes on condition that Khusro should become the adopted son of the Emperor Justin, for only in this way could he preserve stability for the throne. So he sent envoys with a letter concerning this to the Emperor Justin in Byzantium. (7) The letter was as follows: 'You know yourself that we have suffered injustices from the Romans, but I have firmly resolved to forgive you all these wrongs, knowing well that the most victorious tend to be those who, with right on their side, are still willing to yield and give way to their friends. (8) Yet I ask of you a favour for this, which, by linking in ties of kinship and in the goodwill that would naturally follow not only ourselves but the whole of each of our peoples, will be capable of bringing about an abundance of the blessings of peace. (9) I mean that you should make my son Khusro, who will be the heir to my throne, your adopted son.'[66]

(10) When the Emperor Justin had received and read this, he and Justinian, the emperor's nephew, who was expected to succeed him on the throne, were overjoyed. (11) And they would have made all haste to comply, and to set down the adoption in writing according to Roman law, had not Proculus prevented them. He was then one of the emperor's attendants with the office of *quaestor*, an upright man, notoriously inaccessible to bribery.[67] (12) He did not, therefore, readily propose any law, nor would he make any change in the established order. This was what he said at that time in opposition:

(13) 'I am not accustomed to undertake innovations, and, moreover, I fear them above all else, knowing that security cannot be preserved in the midst of change. (14) I think that even if a person was very daring in such matters, he would shrink from this particular action and dread the

the end of his reign. Despite Procopius' insistence, primogeniture was not invariably practised at the Persian court.

[65] Zames is probably the Persian Zham, a shortened form of the name Jāmāsp.

[66] Cf. 1.2.1–10, the guardianship of Yazdgerd I for the young Theodosius, with *RPLA*, 104–5.

[67] Proculus (or Proclus) is attested as *quaestor sacri palatii* in the 520s, cf. *PLRE* 2, Proculus 5. The legal arguments he puts forward here are of dubious value.

upheaval that will result from it. (15) For I think that at the present moment the real issue under consideration is simply how, under a specious pretext, to hand over the Roman empire to the Persians. They make no attempts to conceal or to veil their intentions; they admit their plan openly and see fit by this means to deprive us of our sovereignty altogether, presenting manifest deceit under the guise of straightforwardness and covering their shameful design with apparent unconcern. (16) Each of you ought to try with all your might to shake off this attempt by the barbarians – you, O Emperor, that you might not be the last emperor of Rome, and you, General, that you might not damage your prospects of gaining the throne. (17) Other sophistic utterances, wrapped up in pretentious verbiage, might perhaps need an interpreter for the masses, but this embassy aims right from the outset to make this Khusro, whoever he may be, the adopted heir of the Roman Emperor. (18) Think of it in this way: a father's property is naturally due to his sons, and although the laws among all men are perpetually in conflict because of their variation, in this matter they are at one and in harmony with each other in Rome and among all barbarian nations in declaring that the sons are the possessors of their father's estate. And so if you embrace this first step, it will remain for you to agree to all the consequences.'

(19) These were Proculus' words. The emperor and his nephew heard it through and deliberated on their course of action. (20) But in the meantime Kavadh had sent another letter to the Emperor Justin, asking him to send some men of high rank to make peace with him and to tell him by letter how he wished to arrange the boy's adoption. (21) At that Proculus argued against the Persian initiative even more than before, claiming that their real objective was to make quite sure of gaining control of the Roman empire. (22) He put forward a plan to make peace with them forthwith and to send important men from the emperor for this purpose, who, when asked by Kavadh how the adoption of Khusro was to take place, would reply explicitly that it must be in a way appropriate to a barbarian. He reminded them that barbarians do not adopt children by written enactments but by the panoply of arms.[68] (23) So the Emperor Justin despatched the envoys in accordance with this, promising that high-ranking Romans would follow very soon to settle satisfactorily the question of the peace and the matter concerning Khusro. (24) He made the same reply to Kavadh in a letter. So the Roman delegation was

---

[68] Such adoptions were practised with western barbarians: thus had Zeno adopted the Gothic leader Theoderic and Justin himself Theoderic's grandson Eutharic in 519.

53 despatched, consisting of Hypatius, the nephew of the former Emperor
Anastasius, a patrician and holder of the office of *magister militum per
Orientem*, and Rufinus, the son of Silvanus, a leading patrician and
known to Kavadh through their fathers.[69] (25) On the Persian side was a
man of great power and authority called Seoses, *adrastadaran salanes* in
rank, and with him Mebodes, holding the office of *magister*.[70] (26) These
men met in a place which forms the boundary between Rome and Persia,
and in conclave they decided how to settle their disputes and to establish
the peace on a firm basis. (27) Khusro also came to the river Tigris, which
is about two days' journey from the city of Nisibis, so that when each
side had decided that the question of the peace was well settled, he could
be escorted to Byzantium. (28) There were many opinions voiced by both
sides as to their differences, among which was Seoses' claim that the land
of Colchis, which is now called Lazica, formerly subject to Persia, had
been seized unjustly by Rome and was now held without any justifica-
54 tion.[71] (29) When the Romans heard this, they were angry that even
Lazica was to be disputed by the Persians. And when they actually said
that Khusro's adoption must be in the barbarian manner, the Persians
could not tolerate it. (30) So each side separated and went home, and
Khusro returned to his father having achieved nothing, greatly grieved at
the way things had turned out, and swearing to have revenge on the
Romans for their insult to him.

(31) Later, however, Mebodes denounced Seoses to Kavadh, saying that
he had deliberately brought up the issue of Lazica, which had not been
part of his master's instructions, in an attempt to sabotage the peace, after
agreeing beforehand with Hypatius, who was by no means well disposed
to his own emperor and did not wish the peace and Khusro's adoption to
come into effect.[72] Seoses' enemies brought him to trial and made many
other accusations against him. (32) So the whole council of the Persians
assembled and tried him, more in malice than by legal process, for they
were very much opposed to his unusual office, and understandably irri-
tated by the man's character. (33) Seoses was not open to bribery and was
a most scrupulous guardian of justice, but he was plagued by the disease
of arrogance to an extent unlike other men. This seems to be endemic

---

[69] Rufinus was a long-serving Roman diplomat, cf. *PLRE* 2, Rufinus 13.

[70] On Seoses and his post, see nn. 28, 30. The Greek Mebodes probably corresponds to the Persian
Māhbōdh, a member of the noble Sūrēn family, likely to have been a general.

[71] Probably in 522 the Lazic ruler Tzath had defected to the Romans from the Persians. See Mal. 17.9
with *RPW*, 130–2, *REF*, 79–80. The negotiations described here took place in 525/6.

[72] The date of Seoses' downfall is uncertain, perhaps in the late 520s. Eastern traditions also report
bitter rivalries at the Sasanian court.

among Persian officials, but even they thought that in Seoses the disease had flourished to a remarkable degree. (34) His accusers made the charges that I have mentioned, and they claimed besides that the man would not live according to established custom or uphold the Persian way of life.[73] (35) They said that he worshipped new gods, and that when his wife died recently he had buried her, although by Persian law it was forbidden ever to cover the bodies of the dead with earth. (36) So the judges condemned him to death; and Kavadh, although seeming to be grieving for Seoses, his friend, was unwilling to rescue him. (37) Not, however, that he let it be known that he was angry with him; he explained that he was unwilling to break the Persian law, even though he owed the man his life, since it was thanks to Seoses most of all that he was alive and was king. (38) So Seoses was condemned and vanished from the world of men. The office began with him and finished with him, for there was no other *adrastadaran salanes*. Rufinus denounced Hypatius to the emperor, (39) and so the emperor deprived him of his command, but after torturing some of his attendants very severely he found that there was nothing whatever to substantiate the accusation and did Hypatius no further harm.[74]

Chapter 12

(1) Although Kavadh was anxious to invade Roman territory, he could not do so forthwith, since he was prevented in the following way. (2) The Iberians who live in Asia have established themselves at the very Caspian Gates, which are to their north. On their left hand is Lazica, stretching towards the west, and on their right towards the east are the Persian peoples.[75] (3) They are a Christian people and keep the customs of this religion more scrupulously than any other men known to us, even though they have long been subject to the king of Persia.[76] (4) At this time Kavadh determined to force them into the observance of his own religion. He ordered their king Gurgenes to comply with Persian

56

---

[73] There are some parallels between these accusations, as reported by Procopius, and those brought against Socrates at Athens. His alleged religious unorthodoxy might reflect his support for the Mazdakites.

[74] There was no lasting damage to his career: he was reappointed *magister militum per Orientem* already in 527.

[75] Lazica, also referred to by Procopius as Colchis, lies on the eastern coast of the Black Sea in today's western Georgia.

[76] The Iberians had been converted already in the fourth century. The kingdom was generally under Persian control. See *ODLA*, Iberia.

customs, including throwing all their dead to the birds and dogs instead of burying them in the ground.[77] (5) So Gurgenes wished to go over to the Emperor Justin and asked to receive pledges that the Romans would never abandon the Iberians to the Persians. (6) Justin gave these very willingly, and he sent Probus, the nephew of the Emperor Anastasius, a patrician, with a large amount of money to Bosporus to recruit a Hunnic army and send it to aid the Iberians.[78] (7) Bosporus is a city by the sea, on the left as you sail into the so-called Euxine Sea, twenty days' journey from the city of Cherson, which is the last in Roman territory.[79] The land between the two belongs to the Huns. (8) The people of Bosporus were formerly autonomous, but recently decided to go over to the Emperor Justin. (9) But when Probus returned from there with no success, the emperor sent the general Peter with some Huns to Lazica to help Gurgenes with all his might.[80] (10) But in the meantime Kavadh had sent a very considerable army against Gurgenes and the Iberians under the generalship of a Persian called Boes, a *varizes* in rank.[81] (11) It was evident that Gurgenes was too weak to stand up to the Persian attack, for the Roman aid was not sufficient, and he fled to Lazica with all the leading Iberians, taking with him his wife and children as well as his brothers, of whom Peranius was the eldest.[82] (12) But when they arrived at the borders of Lazica they waited there and, protecting themselves by the roughness of the country, they made a stand against the enemy. (13) And when the Persians met them they did nothing worthy of note, since things went against them because of the rough terrain.

(14) Later, however, the Iberians came to Byzantium and Peter was sent for by the Emperor. The emperor told him in future to help the Lazi to defend their country even against their will, sending an army with Irenaeus at its head.[83] (15) There are two fortresses in Lazica immediately as one enters from the borders of Iberia, the guarding of which had been

---

[77] Hdt. 1.140 also reports these Zoroastrian burial practices. Procopius' Gurgenes is sometimes identified with the Iberian king Vakhtang Gorgasal, whose exploits are recounted in Georgian literature, but this is now generally doubted.

[78] On Probus see *PLRE* 2, Probus 8. His mission is also attested by Ps.-Zach. 12.7n. Bosporus was earlier known as Panticipaeum; it is today's Kertch. Justinian took over the city soon after 528 following a coup against a pro-Roman Hunnic king, cf. Mal. 18.14.

[79] Cherson is today's Sevastopol; the Euxine Sea is the Black Sea.

[80] On Peter see 2.15.7–9 and *PLRE* 2, Petrus 27.

[81] The name may represent the Persian Bōy; whether *varizes* is a name or a title is uncertain.

[82] The Greek is ambiguous; Peranius was probably Gurgenes' eldest son, however, rather than his eldest brother. See *PLRE* 3, Peranius.

[83] Mal. 18.4 also reports the involvement of Irenaeus in fighting in the Caucasus (dated to 528), cf. *PLRE* 2, Irenaeus 7.

long in the hands of the local people, even though they were oppressed by great hardships, for there is no wheat there or wine or any other good thing.[84] (16) Nor yet is it possible to import anything from elsewhere because of the narrowness of the pass, unless it is carried by men. (17) But the Lazi could live off a kind of millet which grows there, to which they are accustomed. (18) The emperor removed these guards and ordered Roman soldiers to be stationed there to guard the fortresses. (19) At the beginning the Lazi would bring them supplies with difficulty, but later they refused this service, the Romans abandoned these fortresses, and the Persians got control of them without any effort. This happened in Lazica.

(20) The Romans, under the command of Sittas and Belisarius, invaded Persarmenia, which was subject to Persia, plundered a large area and returned, having enslaved a large number of Armenians.[85] (21) These two men were young and sporting their first beards. Both were in the personal bodyguard of the general Justinian, who later held the imperial power together with his uncle Justin. In another invasion of Armenia by the Romans, Narses and Aratius unexpectedly met them and engaged them. (22) Not long afterwards they deserted to the Romans and campaigned with Belisarius in Italy, but at that time they got the best of it in their engagement with Sittas' and Belisarius' troops.[86] (23) Another Roman force under the command of Libelarius from Thrace invaded the land around the city of Nisibis. These troops fled in a straight retreat, even though no one was pursuing them.[87] (24) For this reason the emperor dismissed Libelarius from his command and made Belisarius the commander of the troops in Dara. At that time Procopius, who composed this history, was chosen as his adviser.

59

Chapter 13

(1) Not long afterwards Justin died after declaring Justinian, his nephew, Augustus with him. After this the throne fell to Justinian alone.[88] (2) This

---

[84] The fortresses are later (2.29.18) named by Procopius as Sarapanis and Scanda. Procopius exaggerates the barrenness of Lazica, cf. 2.15.5.

[85] This raid probably took place in 526. Both Sittas and Belisarius were *bucellarii* (bodyguards) of Justinian.

[86] See 1.15.31 with *PLRE* 3, Aratius, Narses 2.

[87] Ps.-Zach. 9.1b probably describes the same debacle in summer 527, though he names the commander as Timostratus; Libelarius is mentioned by Ps.-Zach. at 8.5a–b. Belisarius succeeded Libelarius as *dux* of Mesopotamia.

[88] The joint reign of Justin I and Justinian lasted from 1 March to 1 August 527, when Justin died.

Justinian ordered Belisarius to build a fort in a place called Minduos, which is on the very borders of Persia, on the left as one goes towards Nisibis (fig. 7).[89] (3) He carried out the emperor's wishes with great zeal, and the fort was already rising high with the vast number of workmen. (4) But the Persians forbade them to build any more, threatening that they would soon stop them with actions as well as words. (5) When the Emperor heard this (for Belisarius could not ward off the Persians from there with his available army), he ordered another force to go there, under Cutzes and Buzes, who were then in command of the soldiers in Lebanon.[90] These two were brothers from Thrace, both young, and both reckless in coming to grips with the enemy. (6) So the two armies mustered and came *en masse* to the building site, the Persians to put a stop to it with all their might, the Romans to defend the builders. (7) In a fierce battle the Romans were worsted, and there was a large slaughter. The enemy also captured some alive, (8) among whom was Cutzes. All of these the Persians took to their own country and imprisoned them indefinitely in a cave. The structure of the fort, which no one was any longer defending, they razed to the ground.

(9) Later the Emperor Justinian made Belisarius *magister militum per Orientem* and ordered him to campaign against the Persians.[91] And Belisarius, mustering a very considerable army, went to Dara (fig. 8). (10) Hermogenes came to him from the emperor to aid him in setting the army in order. This man, holding the office of *magister*, had previously been Vitalian's *assessor* when he opposed the Emperor Anastasius.[92] (11) The emperor also sent Rufinus as ambassador, ordering him to remain in the city of Hierapolis by the river Euphrates until he gave the word, for both sides were already giving much discussion to peace. (12) But suddenly someone told Belisarius and Hermogenes that the Persians were expected to invade Roman territory, eager to capture the city of Dara. (13) When they heard this, they made the following preparations for battle. Not far from the gate that lies opposite the city of Nisibis, only a stone's throw away, they dug a deep trench with many paths across it (fig. 11). This trench was not dug straight, but in the following way: (14) in the middle there was a short, straight piece, and there were two crosspieces, one at either end; at the ends of the crosspieces they made straight

---

[89] Location uncertain, perhaps modern Kasriahmethayro, 6.3 km south-east of Dara (see fig. 10). Ps.-Zach. 9.2b and Mal. 18.26 also seem to describe this campaign.

[90] On the two commanders see *PLRE* 3, Buzes, Cutzes. They were *duces* of Phoenice Libanensis.

[91] Belisarius' promotion occurred in April 529, the battle of Dara in 530.

[92] Hermogenes was *magister officiorum*, cf. *PLRE* 3, Hermogenes 1.

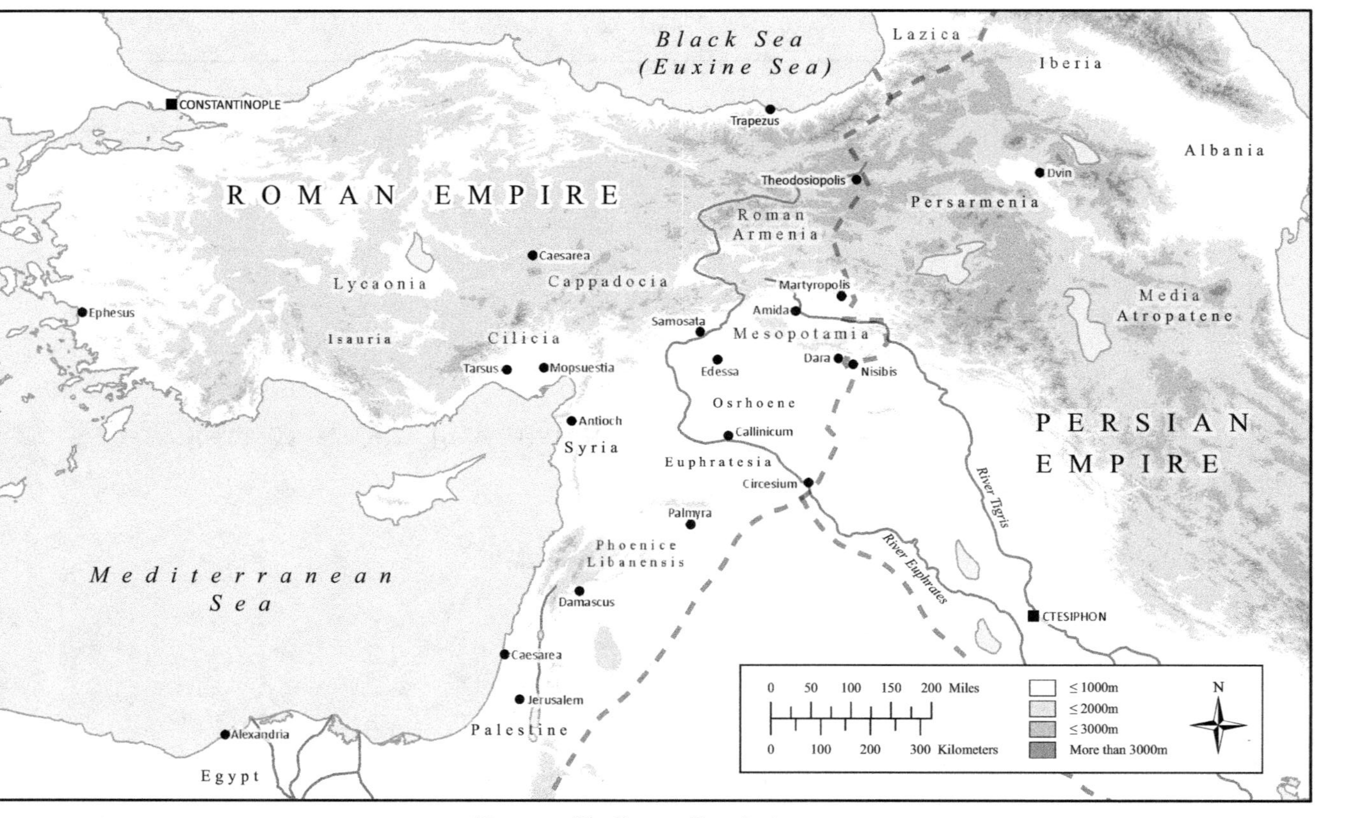

Figure 7   The Eastern Frontier in §27

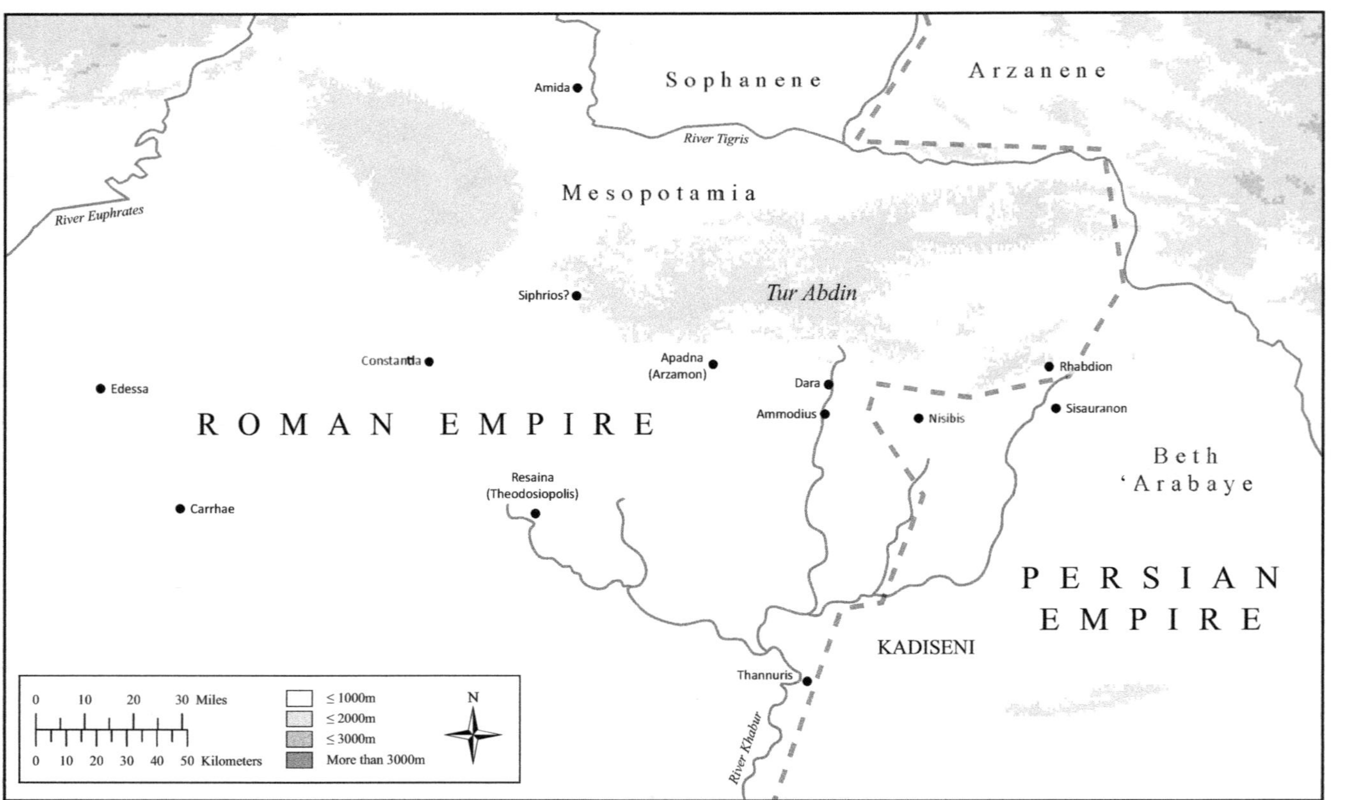

Figure 8   The Frontier Around Dara

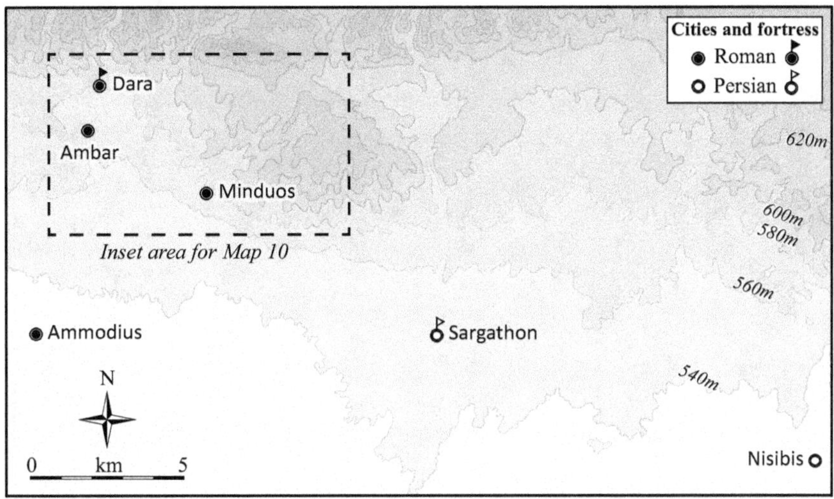

Figure 9   The Frontier Zone Between Dara and Nisibis

ones again over a very long distance.[93] (15) The Persians soon arrived with a large army, and all pitched camp in a place called Ammodius, twenty stades away from the city of Dara (fig. 9). (16) Among the commanders were Pityaxes and Baresmanas, who had only one eye.[94] The commander in chief was a Persian called Peroz, a *mirranes* in rank (this is the Persian name for the office).[95] (17) He immediately sent word to Belisarius telling him to make ready the bath, for he wanted to bathe there on the next day. (18) So the Romans made ready for the battle with great zeal, preparing to fight on the following day.

(19) At sunrise they saw the enemy advancing upon them and took up the following position (fig. 11). The furthermost part of the left straight trench that joined the cross-trench as far as the hill which rises there was held by Buzes with a large number of cavalry and by Pharas, the Herul,[96] with three hundred of his people. (20) On their right, outside the trench, at the angle formed by the cross-trench and the further straight one, were

---

[93] Whether the central trench projected forward from the two flanks is debated: some scholars suppose it lay to the rear. The former is more likely.

[94] Neither general is otherwise known. The names could represent the Persian titles *marzban* (a military official, cf. *ODLA*, marzban) and *petiaxes* (*bdeashkh*), a frontier commander, cf. *ODLA*, Pitiakhsh.

[95] Presumably the same as Malalas' Meran (18.50), said to be the Persian general at Dara. It may be that the reference is to a member of the Mihran house.

[96] The Heruls were a people settled by this point in the Balkans and frequently recruited by the Romans for campaigns, cf. also 2.25.27. On Pharas see *PLRE* 3, Pharas.

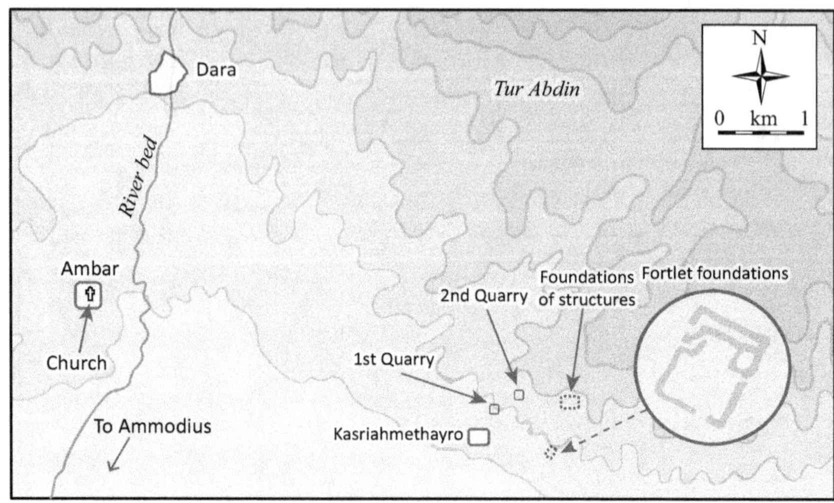

Figure 10　The Immediate Environs of Dara

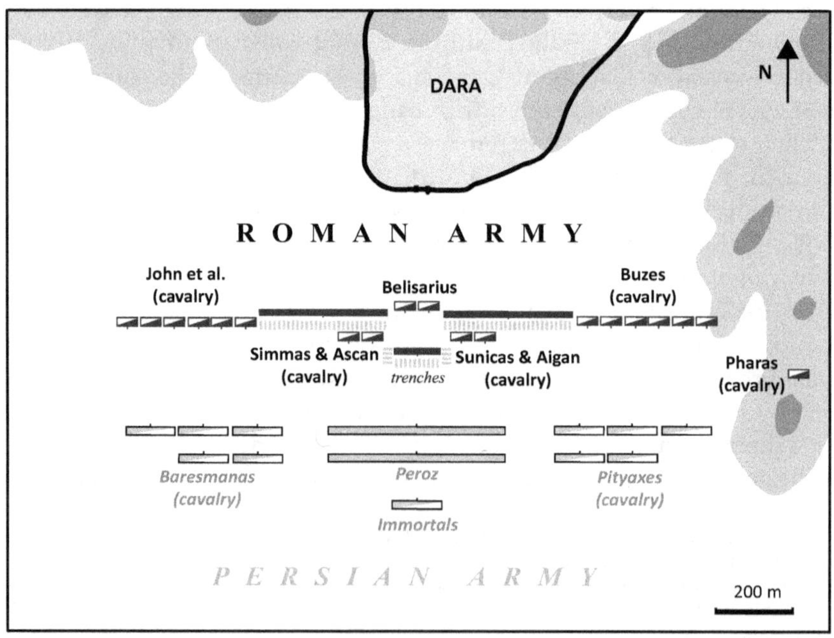

Figure 11　The Dispositions for Battle at Dara

Sunicas and Aigan, both Massagetae by birth,[97] with six hundred cavalry, so that if the troops under Buzes and Pharas were turned, they could advance quickly in a flank action, come up behind the enemy and easily assist the Romans in that position. On the other side there was the same arrangement. (21) A large body of cavalry held the furthermost part of the straight trench, under John, the son of Nicetas, and Cyril and Marcellus. With them also were Germanus and Dorotheus. At the angle on the right six hundred cavalry were stationed, under the command of Simmas and Ascan, both Massagetae, so that, as I have explained, if John's forces were turned, they could leave their position and come up behind the Persians. (22) All along the trench the regular cavalry and the infantry were posted. Behind these Belisarius and Hermogenes and their troops were stationed. (23) In this way the Romans were arranged for battle, some 25,000 in number. The Persian army amounted to 40,000 cavalry and infantry, standing close together forming a massed front, so that the front of the phalanx would be extremely deep. (24) For a long time neither side began the battle; instead the Persians seemed to be marvelling at the discipline of the Romans and at a loss as to what to do under the circumstances.

(25) As the day drew towards evening a detachment of horsemen who were holding the right wing separated themselves from the rest of their company and attacked Buzes and Pharas. (26) The Romans retreated a short distance. The Persians did not pursue them but remained where they were, anxious, I think, not to be surrounded by the enemy. Next, however, the Romans who had been fleeing suddenly charged against them, (27) and not being able to withstand the advance, the Persians retreated to the phalanx.[98] Buzes and Pharas with their forces took up their old position again. (28) In this engagement seven Persians fell, the Romans taking control of the bodies, and thenceforth both sides kept their positions. (29) But one young Persian, riding his horse very near to the Roman army, challenged them all to see if anyone would fight him. (30) No one dared to run the risk, but there was a certain Andreas among Buzes' entourage, not a soldier nor one who had ever engaged in warfare, but a trainer in charge of a wrestling school in Byzantium. (31) He was with the army as Buzes' bath attendant and was a Byzantine by birth. He alone had the courage, without being ordered by Buzes or anyone else,

---

[97] The two commanders may have been *duces*. See *PLRE* 3, Aigan, Sunicas. By 'Massagetae' Procopius means Huns: he deliberately uses a Herodotean term.

[98] The Romans thus, by these Scythian tactics, threw back the probing attack by the Persian right wing.

voluntarily to take on this man in single combat. He got in first while the barbarian was still wondering where to aim, and hit him in the right breast with his spear. (32) The Persian could not withstand the blow from this very strong man, and he fell from his horse onto the ground, whereupon Andreas slaughtered him with a short knife as he lay flat on his back like a sacrificial victim, and a great shout broke out from the circuit wall and from the Roman troops. (33) The Persians were enraged by this and despatched another horseman to take up the task, a brave man of splendid physique, and no youth, but one who actually showed some grey hair. (34) This man rode up to the enemy army, and brandishing the whip which he used to strike his horse, challenged to battle any Roman who was willing. (35) When no one went out to meet him, Andreas came into the open, unnoticed by anyone, even though he had been forbidden by Hermogenes. (36) Both men charged furiously with their spears, and the spears, hurled against their breastplates, were deflected with great force, while the horses, cannoning headlong into each other, themselves fell and threw their riders. (37) The two men, falling next to each other, both struggled hard to get up, but the Persian could not do this because of the hindrance of his size, and Andreas was the first to rise (for his wrestling-school practice enabled him to do so). He struck the other as he was getting up on his knee and killed him as he fell to the ground. (38) Then a shout perhaps even greater than before rose up from the circuit wall and the Roman army, and the Persians broke up their phalanx and retreated to Ammodius, while the Romans came inside the circuit wall singing the paean of victory, for it was already growing dark.[99] (39) And so both sides encamped for the night.

Chapter 14

(1) On the next day 10,000 reinforcements arrived for the Persians, sent for from the city of Nisibis, and Belisarius and Hermogenes wrote this letter to the *mirranes*: 'It is agreed by all men who have even a small share of rationality that peace is the chief good. (2) If then someone were to break it, that person would bear the prime responsibility for the evils that would befall not only his neighbours, but also his own people. The best general, therefore, is he who is best able to make peace out of war. (3) You decided, when matters were firmly settled for the Romans and the

---

[99] The practice of singing the paean was customary after a victory already in the fifth century B.C., cf. e.g. Hdt. 5.1.3, Thuc. 1.50.5, and is attested also for Roman forces.

Persians, to start a war against us for no reason, even though each of our sovereigns is discussing peace and our envoys are already present in the neighbourhood, who will very soon settle our differences by negotiation, unless the results of your invasion are so serious as to dispel this hope of ours. (4) Instead, take away your army to Persian territory as fast as possible, and do not oppose these great blessings, in case you should be responsible for the disasters that, in all likelihood, will befall the Persians.' (5) When the *mirranes* had received and read this letter, he made this reply: 'I would have been influenced by your letter and complied with its requests, had it not been sent by Romans, who are very ready to make promises, but find the fulfilment of their promises by action very difficult and indeed more than can be hoped for, especially when you confirm the agreements by oaths. (6) We therefore reject your deceit and have been forced to come in arms against you. Rest assured, my dear Romans, that there is nothing for you in the future but to fight the Persians. Here we shall either die or grow old, until you show yourselves just to us in your deeds.' This was the *mirranes*' reply. (7) In return Belisarius and his entourage wrote the following: 'Most noble *mirranes*, it is not necessary in all cases to indulge one's arrogance and to heap upon one's neighbours reproaches that they do not deserve. (8) For when we said that Rufinus had come on an embassy and was not far away, we were speaking the truth, as you yourself will soon know. (9) Although you long for warfare, we shall take up our position with the help of God, who, we know, will help us in the danger, moved by the Roman love of peace, and wreaking vengeance upon Persian arrogance and against you who have decided to resist us when we invite you to peace. (10) We shall take up our positions against you, fixing the letters written by both sides on the tops of our standards for the conflict.' (11) This was the content of the letter. And the *mirranes* replied also: 'We too go into battle with our gods on our side, and with their help we shall come against you, and I am confident that tomorrow they will bring the Persians into Dara. (12) Let bath and luncheon be ready for me inside the circuit wall.' When Belisarius and his generals had read this, they prepared themselves for the battle.

(13) On the following day around sunrise the *mirranes* called all the Persians together and made the following speech: 'I am well aware that Persians are courageous in danger not because of their generals' speeches, but because of their own bravery and respect for each other. (14) But when I see you wondering why the Romans, who were not previously accustomed to go into battle without confusion and disorder, recently

withstood a Persian attack with a discipline by no means usual with them, I am resolved to encourage you, so that you may not go wrong under the influence of a false belief. (15) Do not think that the Romans have suddenly become better at warfare, nor that they have acquired more bravery or experience. On the contrary, they have become even more cowardly than before – they are so terrified of the Persians that they dare not form a phalanx without a trench. (16) Not even with this did they begin a battle; when we did not join battle with them, they were overjoyed and went back to the walls, convinced that everything had gone better for them than they had hoped. (17) So they were not thrown into confusion because they have not yet come into the danger of war. If the battle is at close quarters, terror and inexperience will seize them and throw them in all probability into their usual disorder. (18) Such is the condition of the enemy. You, Persians, think of the judgement of the king of kings. (19) For if you do not show yourselves in the current situation to be men worthy of Persian valour, a shameful punishment will encompass you.' (20) With this exhortation the *mirranes* led his army against the enemy.

Belisarius and Hermogenes called all the Romans together in front of the circuit wall and delivered this exhortation: (21) 'You know that the Persians are not wholly invincible, nor yet too strong to die, for you can judge by the previous battle. But no one will deny that though you surpass them in valour and bodily strength, you fall short only in that your discipline towards your officers is inferior. (22) This you can set right without any difficulty. For whereas reversals of fortune are not the sort of thing to be put right by determination, intelligence can easily be the physician for a man's own ills. (23) So therefore, if you are willing to listen to your orders, you will immediately gain for yourselves the superiority in war. For as they come against us, they trust only in our confusion. (24) But if they are now cheated of this expectation, they will retreat just as in the previous engagement. The numbers of the enemy, by which they most terrify you, you should despise. (25) All their infantry is simply a rabble of pitiable peasants, who come to battle for no other purpose than to dig through walls and strip the dead, and perform other services for the soldiers.[100] (26) So they have no weapons with which to trouble the enemy, and they hold before them shields big enough only to defend themselves against enemy missiles. (27) If you are brave in this danger,

---

[100] The criticism of the Persian infantry is borne out by their performance at the battle, see 14.52, and is echoed by other sources.

you will not only conquer the Persians at this moment, but also punish them for their folly, so that never again will they campaign against Roman territory.'

(28) With this exhortation, Belisarius and Hermogenes quickly arranged their soldiers in the former position, since they had seen the Persians advancing towards them. (29) The barbarians, coming up before them, took up their position in line. But the *mirranes* did not station all the Persians against the Romans, but only half, allowing the others to remain behind. (30) These were to relieve the fighters and be fresh when they attacked the enemy, so that they could all fight in continuous succession. (31) He ordered only the corps of the so-called Immortals to remain where they were until he gave the signal.[101] (32) He stationed himself in the middle of the front line, and put Pityaxes in charge of those on the right, and Baresmanas in charge of those on the left wing. Thus both sides were drawn up. Pharas stood beside Belisarius and Hermogenes and said: (33) 'I do not think that if I stay here with the Heruls I can do much harm to the enemy, but if we hide on this slope and then, when the Persians are engaged in the battle, climb up across this ridge and suddenly advance on their rear, shooting at them from behind, we shall in all probability strike the fatal blow.' These were his words, and since Belisarius and the generals approved, he acted accordingly.

(34) Neither side began the battle until midday, but as soon as noon had passed, the barbarians started the engagement. They had put off the moment of the encounter until this time of day because it was their custom to eat only in the evening, whereas the Romans ate before noon, and so they thought the Romans would never hold out so well if they attacked them while they were hungry. (35) First of all each side shot arrows at the other, and the missiles, by their sheer number, produced quite a mist over a wide area. Many fell on both sides, but the barbarians' missiles fell far more densely, (36) for they fought in succession and were always fresh, giving the enemy no hint of what they were doing. Yet even so the Romans did not get the worst of it, for a favourable wind blew from their side against the barbarians and did not allow their missiles to be very effective. (37) When each side had used up all its arrows, they used their spears against each other, and the battle started at closer quarters (fig. 12). The Roman left wing was in the most serious trouble.

---

[101] The Immortals constituted a 10,000-strong unit of elite soldiers, whose strength was always maintained at this number; they existed in the Achaemenid empire of Herodotus' day, cf. e.g. Hdt. 7.83.

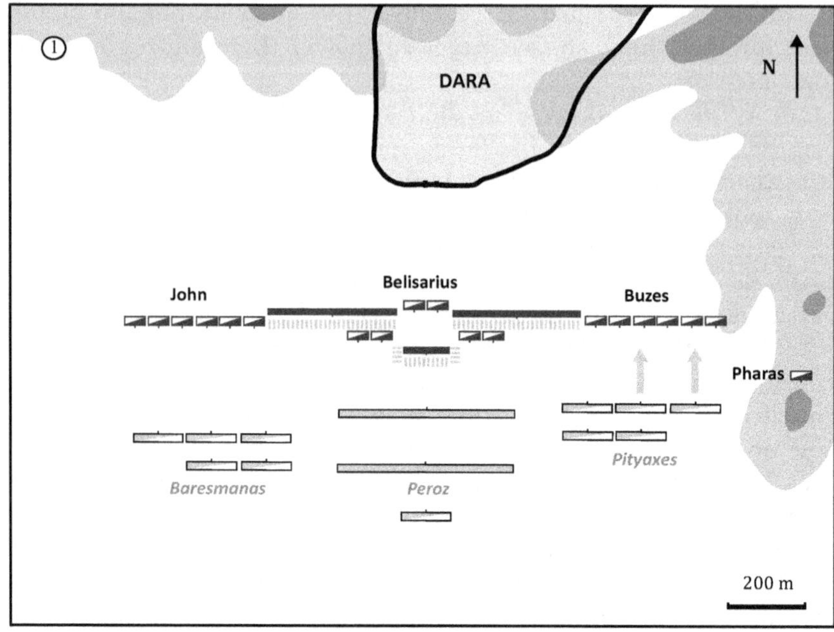

Figure 12   The Battle of Dara (Phase 1)

(38) The Kadiseni,[102] who were fighting there under Pityaxes, coming up in large numbers, suddenly turned the enemy and, following closely on them as they fled, killed many (fig. 13). (39) The troops under Sunicas and Aigan saw this and came against them at a run. But first the three hundred Heruls with Pharas came down upon the enemy's rear from the high ground and gave a wonderful display of valour against the Kadiseni and others. (40) And when the Kadiseni saw Sunicas' troops now coming against them from the flank, they turned to flight. (41) The rout became obvious, for the Romans there joined up with each other and slaughtered many barbarians. (42) On the right wing no fewer than 3000 perished in this reversal, the rest just managing to find safety back in the phalanx. (43) The Romans did not pursue them further, and each side took up its position opposite the other in battle order. These things turned out then in this way.

(44) But the *mirranes* secretly sent troops to the left, including all the so-called Immortals. When Belisarius and Hermogenes observed them,

<hr>

[102] The Kadiseni were a highland people from the Jebel Sinjar, south of Nisibis, and are referred to also by Ps.-Josh. 22 and Ps.-Zach. 9.2a.

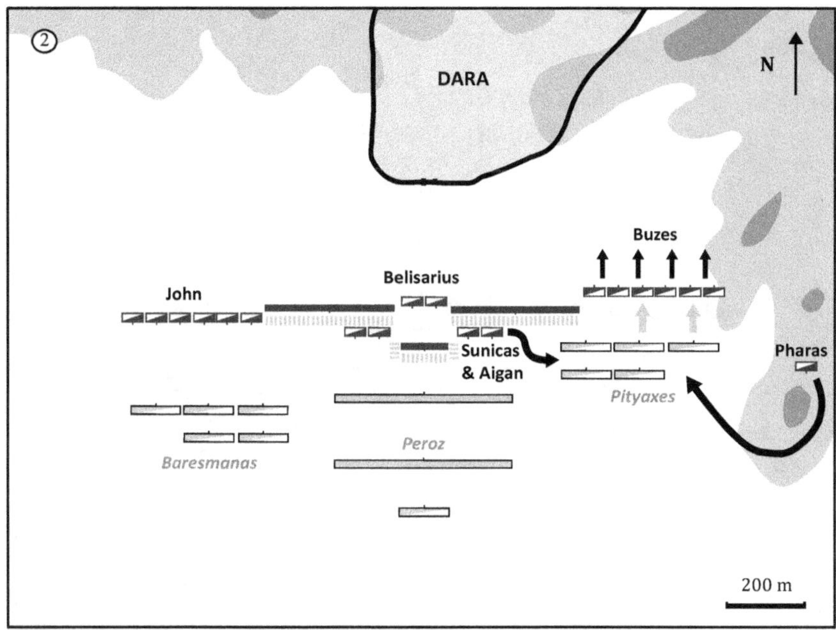

Figure 13   The Battle of Dara (Phase 2)

they gave the command for Sunicas' and Aigan's men, six hundred in number, to proceed to the right-hand angle, where Simmas' and Ascan's men were positioned, and behind them they posted many of Belisarius' men. (45) So the Persians who were holding the left wing under the leadership of Baresmanas advanced at a run with the Immortals against the Romans drawn up opposite them. The Romans could not withstand their attack and turned to flight (fig. 14). (46) Then the Romans at the angle and those who were behind them charged against the pursuers with all their might, (47) and since they met the barbarians from the flank, they divided their army in two, with the majority on the right, but also cutting some off on the left (fig. 15). Among these there happened to be Baresmanas' standard-bearer, and Sunicas made for him and hit him with his spear. (48) Now the Persians who were at the front of the pursuit, realising what danger they were in, wheeled around, abandoned the pursuit and set about the Romans, exposing themselves as a result to enemy fire from both sides – (49) for those who were in flight realised what was happening and turned back again (fig. 16). The corps of the Immortals and the rest of the Persians saw that the standard was at an angle and heading towards the ground. They made

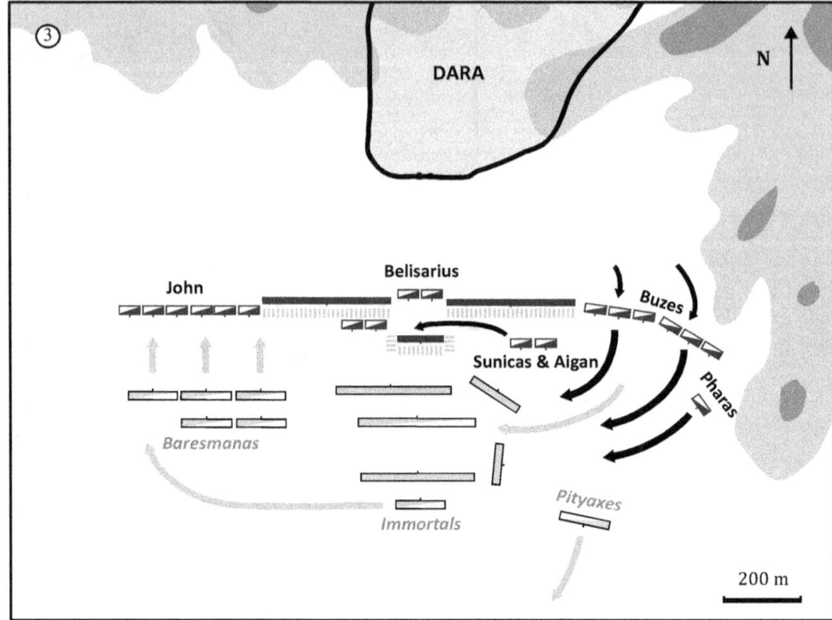

Figure 14   The Battle of Dara (Phase 3)

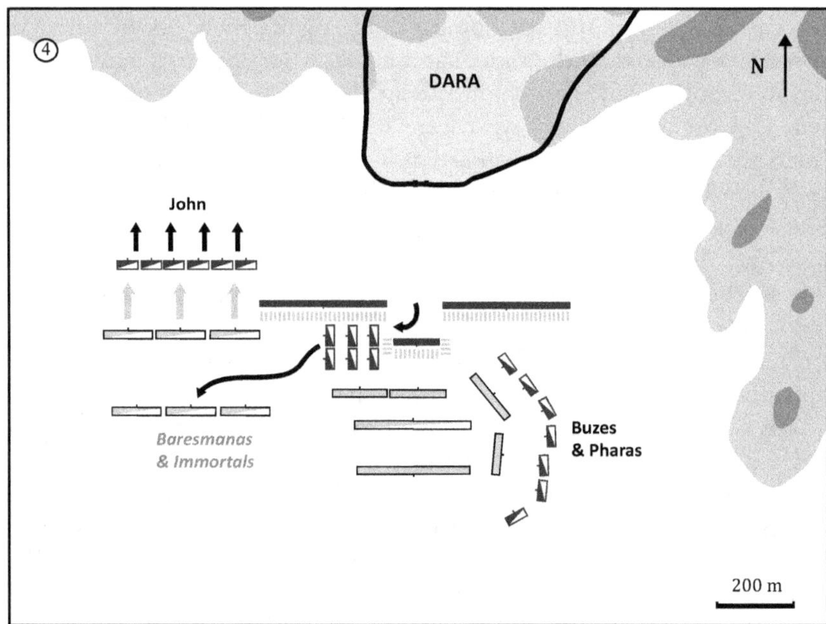

Figure 15   The Battle of Dara (Phase 4)

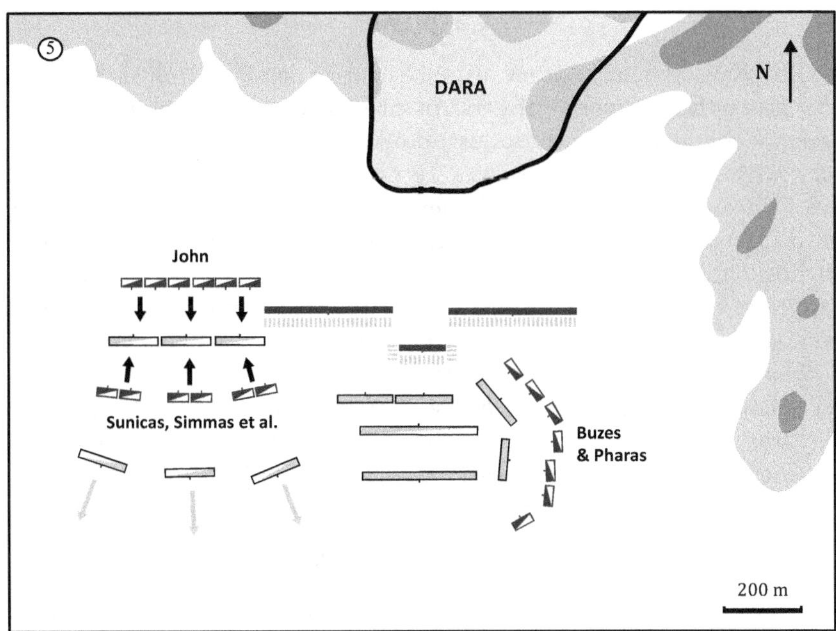

Figure 16   The Battle of Dara (Phase 5)

for the Romans near it with Baresmanas, and the Romans came to meet them. (50) First Sunicas killed Baresmanas, knocking him from his horse onto the ground. At this the barbarians were seized by great fear and had no further thought of valour, but turned to flight in great disorder. (51) The Romans encircled them and killed about 5000. Thus the whole of each army was on the move, the Persians in retreat, the Romans in pursuit.

(52) In this engagement such of the Persian army as were on foot threw down their shields and so were killed by the enemy as they were caught in their confusion. But the Romans' pursuit was short, (53) for Belisarius and Hermogenes would not allow them to go any further. They were afraid that something might happen to make the Persians turn and rout them as they were in their reckless pursuit, and it seemed sufficient to them to keep their victory unspoiled. (54) For on that day the Persians had after many years been defeated in battle by the Romans. So the two sides separated. (55) After this the Persians did not wish to fight the Romans openly, but there were surprise attacks on both sides, in which the Romans did not come off worst. This then was the fate of the armies in Mesopotamia.

74

Chapter 15

(1) But Kavadh sent another army against Roman-controlled Armenia. This army was composed of Persarmenians and Sunitae, who are neighbours of the Alans.[103] Three thousand of the Huns, who are called Sabirs, were with them also, a most warlike people.[104] (2) The general in chief was Mihr-Mihroe, a Persian.[105] When they were three days' journey away from Theodosiopolis, they pitched camp and waited in Persarmenian territory, making their preparations for the invasion. (3) Now Dorotheus happened to be *magister militum per Armeniam*, an intelligent man, with experience of many campaigns, while Sittas held the office of *magister militum praesentalis* and was in command of the whole army in Armenia. (4) When they heard that an enemy army was mustering in Persarmenia, they immediately sent out two of their bodyguards to spy out the size of the enemy forces and report back to them. (5) Both men got inside the enemy camp and found out all the information they desired before they left. (6) As they were on their way to some place thereabouts, they met unexpectedly with the enemy Huns. One of them, Dagaris by name, was caught and taken prisoner, but the other managed to escape and told the whole story to the generals. (7) They made ready the entire army and launched a surprise attack on the enemy camp. (8) The barbarians were overcome with surprise and had no thought of valour, each man fleeing wherever he could. The Romans killed many and plundered the camp, and then returned immediately.

(9) Mihr-Mihroe gathered together his entire force and not long afterwards invaded Roman territory, catching up with his enemies near the city of Satala (fig. 17). There they encamped and remained in a place called Octava, which is fifty-six stades from the city. (10) Sittas therefore led out a thousand men and hid them behind one of the many hills that encircle the city of Satala, which lies in a plain. (11) He told Dorotheus to stay within the circuit wall with the rest of the army, since they did not think themselves capable of meeting the enemy, of whom there were no fewer than 30,000, on level ground, for their own numbers were scarcely half that. (12) On the following day the barbarians came near the wall

---

[103] The Sunitae are referred to in the Armenian sources as Siwnikʻ, whose territories lie east of Dvin, cf. Ps.-Zach. 12.7k(iv), where they are referred to as Sisakan. The Alans occupied the region to the north of the Caspian Gates.

[104] The Sabirs lived north of the Caucasus from where they issued forth intermittently, raiding Roman territory. They were often hired by both Romans and Persians to supplement their forces.

[105] Mihr-Mihroe served with distinction in the Caucasus up to the 550s, cf. *PLRE* 3, Mermeroes, *ODLA*, Mihr-Mihroe.

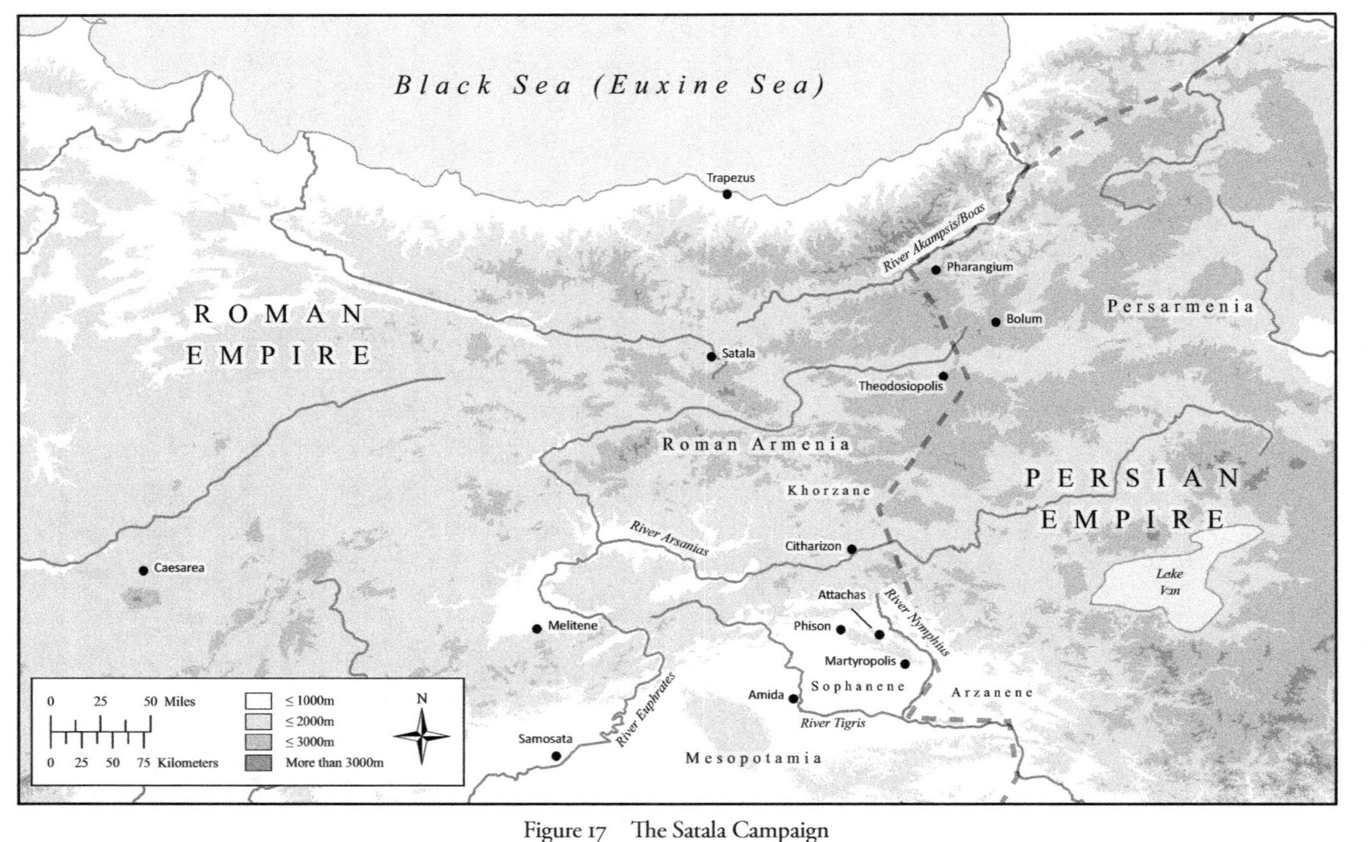

Figure 17   The Satala Campaign

and were keen to encircle it. But they suddenly caught sight of Sittas'
men coming down upon them from the high ground, and unable to estimate their number (it was summer and there was a great deal of dust),
they thought that they were far more numerous, and at once abandoned
their encircling and made every effort to gather themselves together in a
compact space. (13) The Romans forestalled them, divided their own
force into two sections, and attacked them as they retreated from the
walls. When the main Roman army saw this they were encouraged, and
they poured out from the walls and moved against the enemy with all
speed. (14) Thus they had the enemy between their own forces and put
them to flight. But, as I have said already, the enemy had the advantage
in numbers and could still hold out, and there was a fierce battle at close
quarters. (15) Each side kept making sallies against the other and then
retreating, since they were all cavalry. Then Florentius, a Thracian, the
commander of a cavalry unit, dashed into the midst of the enemy,
snatched their general's standard, bent it right down and began to withdraw. (16) He was caught and butchered there, but he was the one who
was chiefly responsible for the Roman victory. When the barbarians
could not see the standard, they fell into panic and confusion and
retreated; after reaching their camp, they remained there quietly, having
lost many men in the battle. (17) On the following day they all retreated
homewards, no one pursuing them; to the Roman army it seemed a great
and memorable feat that so great a number of barbarians should not only
have suffered in their own territory what I have related before this, but
also should have returned after invading enemy territory without
achieving anything, defeated like this by a smaller force.

(18) Then the Romans obtained districts of the Persians in Persarmenia,
acquiring the fortress of Bolum and that called Pharangium, from which
the Persians mine gold and bring it to the king.[106] (19) It happened also that
a short time before this they had reduced the Tzani, who had long been
settled in Roman territory as an independent people. How this happened
will now be related. (20) When one goes from Armenian territory into
Persarmenia, the Taurus is on the right, stretching to Iberia and the peoples
thereabouts, as I have earlier explained,[107] but on the left the road descends
steadily over a long distance and is overhung by sheer mountains covered
all the year round with cloud and snow, (21) from which the river Phasis

---

[106] Pharangium corresponds to the modern İspir in eastern Turkey, Bolum to Armenian Bołberd;
both lie to the east of Theodosiopolis.
[107] See 1.10.1–2.

rises and flows into the land of Colchis.[108] Here from the beginning lived barbarians, the Tzani, who were subject to no one, and were called in earlier times Sani.[109] They used to rob the Romans living around about and lived a very hard life, forever living off stolen goods, for the land bore them nothing that was good to eat. (22) So every year the Roman emperor used to send them a fixed amount of gold, on condition that they should not plunder the land thereabouts. (23) They swore their ancestral oaths to this, but thought nothing of their word, and used to make sudden attacks over a wide area and harass not only the Armenians, but also the Romans who lived next to them as far as the sea, making short invasions and returning home immediately. (24) If by any chance they met a Roman army they would be defeated in battle, but they were not susceptible to complete capture because of the strength of their villages. Now Sittas had defeated them in battle before this war and had managed to win them over completely after much persuasion and practical encouragement.[110] (25) They adopted a more civilised way of life and enrolled in the Roman ranks, henceforth setting out against the enemy with the rest of the Roman army. They also changed their faith in the direction of true piety, all of them becoming Christian. This then was how things were with the Tzani.

(26) As one crosses over their borders there is a deep and very precipitous valley stretching as far as the Caucasus mountains. Here there are very populous regions, and vines and other crops grow there in plenty. (27) For the space of about three days' journey this valley is subject to the Romans, but from that point the territories of the Persarmenians take over; here lies the gold mine that was worked by a local inhabitant called Symeon, by the gift of Kavadh. (28) When this man Symeon saw that both sides were ripe for war, he decided to stop supplying money to Kavadh. (29) So he gave himself and Pharangium up to the Romans, but refused to give to either side the gold from the mine. (30) The Romans did nothing about it, thinking it sufficient for them that their enemy had lost the revenue, and the Persians could not exact it from the inhabitants against the will of the Romans, since the difficulty of the terrain was against them.

---

[108] Procopius confuses two rivers. The river in question here is rather the Boas, also known as the Akampsis. Although at 2.29.16 he still wrongly identifies the Boas/Akampsis and the Phasis (a river that flows westwards down from the Caucasus into the Black Sea), at 8.2.6–9 he correctly distinguishes them.

[109] The Tzani inhabited the highland regions south of the Black Sea and east of Trapezus.

[110] The date of this subjugation is unclear. Some place it in the early 520s, although Sittas would have been very young then (cf. 1.12.21); more likely it took place in 528 or 529. Procopius describes how they were civilised also at *Aed.* 3.6.1–13; Justinian boasts of their submission in the preface of his first *Novel*, cf. Agath. 5.2.4.

(31) About the same time Narses and Aratius, who at the beginning of this war came into conflict with Belisarius and Sittas in Persarmenia, as I have related above, deserted to the Romans with their mother; Narses, the emperor's treasurer, received them (for he too was a Persarmenian by birth) and bestowed large sums of money upon them. (32) When Isaac, their youngest brother, heard of this, he entered secret negotiations with the Romans and surrendered the fortress of Bolum to them, which is very near to the borders of Theodosiopolis.[111] He gave instructions that soldiers should hide themselves somewhere nearby, and he let them into the fortress at night, secretly opening one gate for them. In this way he too came to Byzantium.

Chapter 16

80 (1) Such was the state of Roman affairs. But the Persians, despite their defeat in battle at Dara at the hands of Belisarius, did not decide to withdraw from there until Rufinus, having come into Kavadh's presence, spoke as follows. 'Your brother, O King, sent me with a just reproach, namely that the Persians came against his land under arms for no reason. (2) Yet it would be appropriate for a great king, who has attained such a pinnacle of understanding, to obtain peace in place of war, rather than to inflict unnecessary confusion on both himself and his neighbours when affairs were firmly settled. (3) In connection with this I have come here in person with good hope, in order that in the future the bounties of peace will accrue to both sides.' (4) So spoke Rufinus. Kavadh responded thus: 'O son of Silvanus, in no way try to contest the responsibility, since you above all are aware that you, the Romans, were the most responsible for all the confusion. For we have held the Caspian Gates for the benefit of the Persians and Romans after expelling the barbarians there: the Roman Emperor Anastasius, as indeed you yourself know, when it was possible for him to buy them for money, did not want to, in order that he might not be obliged to spend large sums on behalf of both powers to keep an army there for all time. (5) Since then we have stationed a large army **81** there and have supported it up to the present. Thus we have allowed you to inhabit unmolested the part of your territory that adjoins the

---

[111] On Narses and Aratius see 1.12.21. The other Narses here, the treasurer, is the famous eunuch who went on to defeat the Ostrogoths in the 550s, on whom see *PLRE* 3, Narses 1. The post here described may be that of *cubicularius* or chamberlain. For Isaac see *PLRE* 3, Isaaces 1. Some suppose that all three brothers were members of the Kamsarakan family.

barbarians there and to hold your possessions in complete tranquillity.[112] (6) Yet, as though this were not enough for you, you have built a large city at Dara, a bulwark directed against the Persians, although this was expressly forbidden in the treaty that Anatolius made with the Persians.[113] Henceforth the Persian state has inevitably been burdened with the effort and expenditure of two armies, one in order that the Massagetae would not be able to plunder the lands of both powers with impunity, the other in order to repel your potential incursions. (7) When we recently reproached you about these issues, we asked that one of two alternatives should happen: either an army should be despatched to the Caspian Gates by both sides or the city of Dara should be razed. Not only did you not accept the import of what was said, but you also decided to further your plotting against the Persians by a still greater injury, if I have any recollection of the building work at Minduos.[114] Even now the Romans may choose peace or they may take up their weapons, depending on whether they do justice to us or they come against us. (8) For the Persians will not put down their weapons until the Romans either join them in guarding the Gates fairly and justly or they raze the city of Dara.'

(9) Having made his statement, Kavadh dismissed the envoy after hinting that he would be willing to accept money from the Romans and thus to remove the causes of the war. (10) This was what Rufinus announced to the emperor when he came to Byzantium. Not long afterwards Hermogenes also reached the city and the winter came to an end; and the fourth year of the reign of the Emperor Justinian drew to a close.[115]

82

Chapter 17

(1) At the start of spring a Persian army led by Azarethes invaded Roman territory.[116] There were 15,000 of them, all cavalry. Among them was al-Mundhir the son of Sakkike, who led a vast throng of Saracens.[117] (2) This invasion by the Persians did not unfold in the normal fashion, since they did not invade Mesopotamia as they had previously, but instead the

---

[112] The Persians had long laid claim to subsidies from the Romans for the defence of the Caspian Gates. Kavadh was thus continuing to pursue this policy. Mal. 18.53 also reflects the exchange between Justinian and Kavadh.

[113] Cf. 1.10.13–15, 2.15.

[114] Described at 1.13.1–8.

[115] Procopius marks in Thucydidean fashion (cf. e.g. 3.25.2) the end of the campaigns of 530.

[116] Azarethes may represent the Persian title *hazārbed*, designating a senior court official. Mal. 18.59 renders it as Exarath.

[117] The epithet, 'son of Sakkike', is found in other sources. Sakkike may be his mother or grandmother; Arab sources know of a paternal grandmother, Shaqīqa. See *AEBI*, 225–6.

former Commagene, now called Euphratesia, from where the Persians had never previously campaigned against the Romans, at least as far as we know.[118] (3) But I shall now proceed to explain why the country is called Mesopotamia and why the Persians held off invading through it.

(4) There is among the Armenians a not particularly steep mountain, forty-two stades from Theodosiopolis, lying to the north. Two springs emerge from there, which immediately form two rivers, the one on the right the Euphrates, the other one the Tigris. (5) One of the two, the Tigris, descends directly to the city of Amida with no deviations and without the addition of any further water-sources, save small ones. (6) From there, proceeding northwards, it moves into the land of the Assyrians.[119] The Euphrates, on the other hand, is borne along at the start for a short distance, but then immediately disappears in its course. It does not go underground, however, but rather something amazing happens: (7) a tremendously deep marsh covers the water over a large area, as much as fifty stades in length and twenty in breadth. A large quantity of reeds grows in this mud. (8) So hard is the earth here that it seems to those who come across it just to be solid ground. (9) Indeed, numerous wagons cross here every day, but they are completely incapable of shifting or disturbing the marsh. (10) Every year the inhabitants burn the reeds, in order that the roads not be blocked by them; on one occasion an extraordinary wind struck the region and the fire happened to penetrate to the tips of the roots, and in a small area the water appeared. (11) Within a short time the earth had recovered, restoring to the place its previous form. From there the river proceeds to the land known as Kelesene,[120] where there is the temple of Artemis among the Taurians, from where they say that Iphigenia, the daughter of Agamemnon, escaped with Orestes and Pylades, clutching the statue of Artemis.[121] (12) The other temple, which up to my own times has existed in the city of Comana, is not the one 'among the Taurians'. I shall now reveal how it came into existence (fig. 18).

---

[118] In fact, the Persians had used this route in their third-century invasions.

[119] Rather, it flows eastwards, entering Persian territory, then south-eastwards towards the Persian Gulf. 'Assyria' here probably refers to Lower Mesopotamia, the Sasanian province of Asorestan, cf. *ODLA*, Asorestan.

[120] Kelesene lies south of Satala astride the Euphrates; it is also known as Akilisene and (in the Armenian sources) Ekełeac'.

[121] Procopius refers to the myth (notably treated by Euripides in his play, *Iphigenia in Tauris*) involving Iphigenia, the daughter of King Agamemnon, who was due to be sacrificed in order to allow the Greek ships to set sail for Troy. She was rescued by the goddess Artemis just before the sacrifice and transported to the Taurians, generally supposed to be inhabitants of the Crimea. But Procopius here associates the legend rather with the region of the Taurus mountains. He returns to the legend at *Wars* 8.5.23–4, 22.27–8.

Figure 18   Places Linked to Orestes and Iphigenia

(13) When Orestes escaped in his flight from the Taurians with his
sister, it happened that his body was afflicted with a disease.[122] When he
asked the oracle about the disease, they say that (it responded that) the
problem would not cease until he had built a temple to Artemis in a location similar to the one that existed among the Taurians; there he was to
cut off his hair and to endow the city with the same name.[123] (14)
Therefore Orestes, as he wandered around the region here, found himself
in Pontus and observed a mountain that rose steeply and hung there, as
though suspended, below which the river Iris flowed among the foothills
of the mountain. (15) Consequently Orestes at this point supposed that
this was the place that the oracle had indicated to him, and there he built
a noteworthy city and the temple of Artemis; he cut off his hair and
endowed the city with his name, which has been known as Comana up
to my own time.[124] (16) Nonetheless, despite having accomplished these
things, the disease persisted and even grew worse. The man realised that
he had not executed the instructions of the oracle satisfactorily; again he
wandered everywhere in his search and found a certain place among the
Cappadocians that very closely resembled the one among the Taurians.
(17) I myself have often looked at the place and marvelled greatly, since it
seemed to me that I was among the Taurians. For this mountain is truly
like that other one, since the Taurus is present also here, while the river
Sarus resembles the Euphrates here. (18) Orestes therefore built an
impressive city and two temples here, the one for Artemis, the other for
his sister Iphigenia, both of which the Christians have taken over for
themselves, albeit with no change whatever to the structures.[125] (19) Even
now it is known as Golden Comana, taking its name from the hair of
Orestes that they say he cut off here, thereby escaping his illness. (20)
Some claim that the illness that he escaped was none other than that
madness that possessed him as a result of his slaying of his own mother.
But I shall return to my previous narrative.

(21) The river Euphrates flows to the right emerging from Armenia in
the Taurus and the territory of Kelesene, encompassing a large area;
among the rivers flowing into it is the mighty Arsinus,[126] which is carried

---

[122] The illness is generally portrayed as madness, cf. 17.20, provoked by his slaying of his own mother,
Clytemnestra. The god Apollo directed him to steal the statue in order to be cured, according to
the legend.
[123] The Greek word for hair is *komē*, here thus linked to the city's name of Comana (Komana).
[124] This is Comana Pontica, modern Yeşilırmak.
[125] This is Cappadocian (or Golden) Comana, modern Şar.
[126] The Arsinus is more often referred to as the Arsanias, the modern Murat (Su). The perspective of
Procopius' reference to the 'right' is not clear: the Euphrates heads west and south after merging
with the Arsanias, then bends to the east.

forth from the lands of the so-called Persarmenians. As one would expect, the Euphrates has grown into a large river as it reaches those formerly known as the White Syrians, now called the Lesser Armenians, whose capital city, Melitene, is very noteworthy.[127] (22) From there it flows past Samosata, Hierapolis and all the towns there as far as the land of the Assyrians, where the two rivers join together and, now one, are designated by the name of the Tigris. (23) Now the land that is beyond Samosata on the outside of the Euphrates was long ago called **86** Commagene, but now takes its name from the river.[128] The inner side of the river, which is in the middle of it and the Tigris, is named, as is reasonable, Mesopotamia.[129] A part of it, however, is called not only by this name, but also by certain others. (24) As far as the city of Amida the country is called by some Armenia; Edessa and the places that surround it have taken the name Osrhoene after Osrhoes, a man who was king there in earlier times when the people here were allies of the Persians.[130] (25) Once, therefore, the Persians had taken the city of Nisibis and certain other districts of Mesopotamia from the Romans,[131] whenever they intended to launch a campaign against the Romans, they took no heed of the land beyond the river Euphrates because it is generally waterless and uninhabited. They assembled here (in Mesopotamia) with no difficulty, since it was in their own country and extremely close to the inhabited territory of their enemies, and from here they always undertook their invasions.

(26) When the *mirranes*, vanquished in battle and having lost most of his men, arrived with the remainder of his army on Persian soil, he received a bitter punishment from King Kavadh.[132] (27) For he removed from him the ornament with which he was accustomed to tie the hair on his head, which was made from gold and pearls. This is a great privilege among the Persians, below only the honour of the king. (28) For there it is illegal to wear a gold ring or belt or brooch or any **87** other item whatsoever, unless the individual has been deemed worthy by the king.

---

[127] Melitene had been a legionary base already in the first century A.D. See *ODLA*, Melitene.

[128] It was called Euphratesia or Euphratensis.

[129] 'Mesopotamia' combines the Greek words for river (*potamos*) and middle (*mesos*).

[130] Western (Roman) Mesopotamia constituted a province by the name of Osrhoene. See *ODLA*, Mesopotamia, Roman, and Osrhoene.

[131] In 363, following the Emperor Julian's disastrous invasion of Persia and the accession of the Emperor Jovian (363–4). See *RPLA*, 131–4.

[132] Procopius returns briefly to the aftermath of the Persian defeat of Dara in 530.

(29) From that point Kavadh deliberated as to the means by which he himself should campaign against the Romans. For since the *mirranes* had failed in the way that has been described, he had no confidence in anyone else. (30) While he remained generally at a loss, al-Mundhir, the king of the Saracens, came to him, saying, 'Not all things, O Master, have to be entrusted to fortune, nor should one think that all wars must be successful. For this is neither probable nor in any case appropriate for mankind; rather, this notion is more of an obstacle to those that espouse it. (31) Whenever those who hope for every good thing for themselves fail – if it turns out thus – the hope that should not have guided them (in the first place) pains them more than is appropriate. (32) For this reason, then, given that men cannot always have confidence in fortune, they do not engage in the dangers of war directly, even if they pride themselves on outclassing their enemies in every respect, but instead strive to get around their opponents by deception and by various contrivances. (33) For those for whom the odds are even, victory is not assured. Do not now therefore, O King of Kings, be aggrieved at the failure of the *mirranes*, nor seek to put fortune to the test again. (34) For the cities of Mesopotamia and the region known as Osrhoene, since they are the closest to our borders, are the most fortified of all and filled with such a multitude of soldiers as they have never yet contained; consequently, if we go there, the issue of the contest will not be secure. In the region outside the Euphrates, however, and neighbouring Syria, there is no fortified city or army worthy of mention. (35) This I have often heard from Saracens sent to investigate these districts. (36) There, they say, lies the city of Antioch, the first of all the cities among the Romans of the East in wealth, in size and in population. Moreover, it is unguarded and devoid of soldiers. (37) Its people are concerned for nothing save festivals, luxury and incessant rivalries with one another in the theatres. (38) Consequently, if we go against them unexpectedly, it is by no means unlikely that we shall capture the city through a lightning raid and then return to Persian territory without having met an enemy army, since the soldiers in Mesopotamia will not yet have heard what has happened. (39) Do not think about a shortage of water or any other provisions, for I myself shall guide the army where it seems best to me.'

(40) Kavadh, having heard this speech, could neither resist nor distrust him. For al-Mundhir was highly intelligent and endowed with great experience in war; he was also extremely faithful to the Persians and exceptionally active. Indeed, he humbled the Roman state for fifty

years.[133] (41) For starting from the borders of Egypt, reaching as far as Mesopotamia, he plundered the settlements there, despoiling them each in turn, burning the houses he came across and constantly enslaving tens of thousands of people; most of them he killed for no reason, the remainder he ransomed for large sums. Yet no one at all joined battle with him, (42) for he never made an inroad without forethought. Rather, he did so suddenly and with maximum benefit to himself, so that already he was leaving with all his booty when the generals and soldiers began to learn of the events and to muster against him. (43) But if anyone by some chance was ever able to intercept him, this barbarian fell upon his pursuers while they were still unprepared and not yet drawn up for battle. He routed and annihilated them with no effort, and even once captured all the pursuing soldiers with their commanders.[134] (44) (The commanders) were Timostratus, the brother of Rufinus, and John, the son of Luke, whom indeed he subsequently ransomed, obtaining from them a treasure neither paltry nor trifling.[135] (45) To put it in general terms, this man became the most dangerous and cunning adversary of all to the Romans. The reason for this was that al-Mundhir ruled alone over the Persian Saracens, holding the rank of king; he was always able to make an incursion with his entire army wherever he wanted in the Roman empire. (46) No commander of Roman soldiers, whom they call *duces*, nor chief of the Saracens with whom the Romans had a treaty, who are called phylarchs, was sufficiently strong to oppose al-Mundhir with their followers, for in each province were deployed forces that did not match the enemy's strength.[136] (47) Therefore the Emperor Justinian put al-Harith, the son of Jabala, who ruled over the Saracens in Arabia, in charge of as many tribes as possible; he conferred on him the rank of king, something that had never occurred before among the Romans.[137] (48) Yet al-Mundhir damaged Roman affairs no less, perhaps actually more, while al-Harith during every incursion and combat proved either extremely unlucky or turned traitor as quickly as possible. For so far we

90

[133] Haury's text gives the figure of fifty, though he indicates that he would have preferred to change it to forty; but al-Mundhir's reign did indeed last for some fifty years (c. 505–54). Probably Procopius was rounding up the figure when writing in the late 540s.

[134] See *AEBI*, 225–9, on al-Mundhir's raids, notably in the late 520s.

[135] They were released in 524; the date of their capture is uncertain. See *AEBI*, 230, cf. *PLRE* 2, Timostratus, Ioannes 70.

[136] Mal. 18.16 describes the laborious process of trying to avenge an incursion by al-Mundhir. See *RPW*, 151–3, *AEBI*, 232–3.

[137] Al-Harith, the Jafnid leader, was promoted probably in 529, so as to exercise authority over all the other phylarchs. See *REF*, 88, *AEBI*, 234–5.

know nothing clearly about him.[138] Thus it happened that al-Mundhir
plundered the entire East – with no one to oppose him – for a very long
time, since he turned out to be remarkably long-lived.

Chapter 18

(1) Therefore at this point, delighted with the man's advice, Kavadh
selected 15,000 men and put in command of them a Persian called
Azarethes, a man particularly good at warfare, and commanded
al-Mundhir to lead the way for them. (2) They crossed the river
Euphrates in Assyria, and after advancing through uninhabited country
they made a sudden and unexpected invasion of the region called
Commagene. (3) This was the first Persian invasion from there into
Roman territory, so far as I can discover by hearsay or by any other
means, and it took all the Romans by surprise. (4) When Belisarius heard
about it, he was at first at a complete loss, but then decided to come to
help with all speed. Putting an adequate garrison in each town, so that
Kavadh and the other enemy army might not find Mesopotamia altogether undefended if they came there, he went himself to face them with
the rest of the army. They crossed the river Euphrates and eagerly pressed
forward. (5) The Roman army comprised about 20,000 infantry and
cavalry, and of these no fewer than 2000 were Isaurians. (6) All the
cavalry commanders were those who had previously withstood the
Persians and the *mirranes* in the battle at Dara, but the infantry
commander was one of the Emperor Justinian's bodyguards, Peter by
name. (7) Longinus and Stephanacius were in command of the Isaurians.
There al-Harith joined them with the Saracen army. (8) When they
reached the city of Chalcis, they pitched camp and waited, for they had
heard that the enemy were at a place called Gabbulon, 110 stades from
Chalcis.[139] (9) When al-Mundhir and Azarethes learnt of this, they were
overcome with fear and refused to go any further; instead they decided to
go home at once. So they retreated, with the river Euphrates on their left,
and the Roman army followed behind them. (10) And in the place where
the barbarians encamped each night, the Romans would always stay on
the following night. (11) Belisarius deliberately refused to allow the army
to go further, since he did not want to meet the enemy in an engagement, thinking it sufficient that the Persians and al-Mundhir should have

[138] But cf. 2.28.12–14, where Procopius appears to revise his views.
[139] According to Mal. 18.60, the Persians actually penetrated further north and fell victim to some
counter-attacks by Sunicas.

invaded Roman territory and then retreated from it like this and were on their way home without achieving anything. (12) Consequently everyone secretly abused him, both officers and men, but no one reproached him to his face.

(13) Finally the Persians encamped on the bank of the Euphrates, opposite the city of Callinicum (fig. 19).[140] From there they intended to march through territory inhabited by no man, and thus to leave Roman territory. (14) They were no longer inclined to proceed as they had previously, keeping close to the river bank. The Romans, after spending the night in the city of Sura, came upon their enemy as they were already packing up for their departure. (15) On the following day fell the festival of Easter, which Christians observe more solemnly than any other. On the day before this festival it is their custom not only to abstain from food and drink for the whole day but also to prolong their fast long into the night.[141] (16) So Belisarius then, seeing all the men longing to attack the enemy, and wanting to change their minds (for Hermogenes, who had just returned from the emperor on an embassy, was of the same opinion as him),[142] called together all those present and addressed them:

(17) 'Where are you going, Romans? What has made you want to take upon yourselves an unnecessary danger? It is usually thought that the only victory that is not counterfeit is to suffer no disaster at the hands of the enemy – and fortune and the fear that we inspire in the enemy have granted us that. (18) It is surely better to enjoy our present benefits than to look for them when the opportunity is past. The Persians were spurred on by great hopes in their expedition against the Romans, but now they have lost everything and have been put to flight. (19) So if we force them against their will to change their plan of retreat and come to grips with us, we shall gain nothing if we are victorious – (20) for why should one rout someone already in flight? – while perhaps if we fail we shall lose the victory that we have won; nor shall we be deprived of it by the enemy, but will be relinquishing it ourselves. And we shall abandon the emperor's land to lie open to the enemy hereafter without defenders. (21) This too you should consider: God always helps men in danger when it is forced upon them, not when it is self-chosen. (22) Furthermore, you will find that men who have nowhere to turn will

---

[140] Callinicum, ar-Raqqa today, lies on the north bank of the Euphrates.

[141] Easter Day fell on (Sunday) 20 April in 531. Fasting was common on Good Friday, through to the Saturday (the day on which the battle was fought).

[142] I accept a slight emendation of the text here, which alters the sense from Haury's; some other translations suppose that Hermogenes agreed with the men in wanting to engage the enemy.

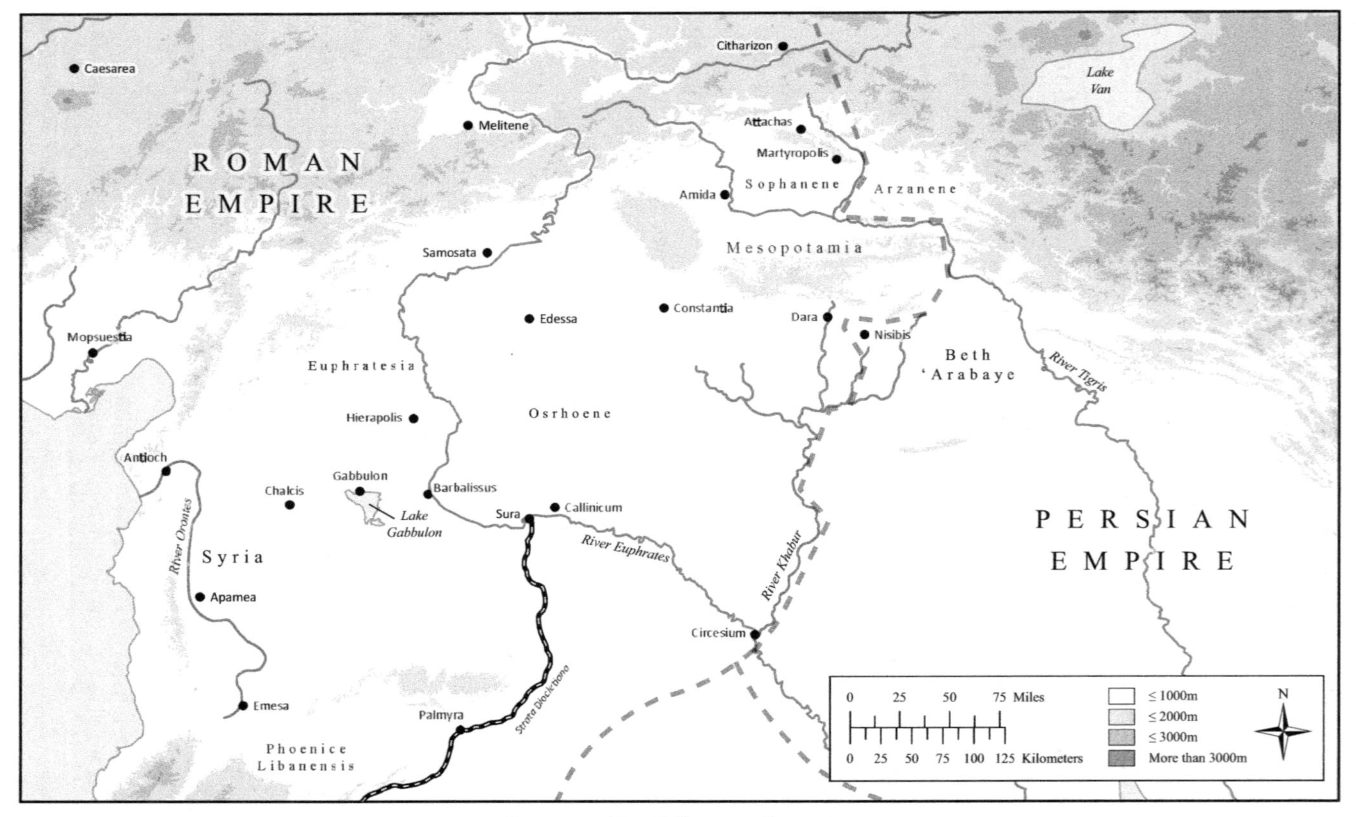

Figure 19   The Callinicum Campaign

fight bravely even against their will, while we have many things against us in the encounter, (23) for many have come on foot, and we are all fasting. I refrain from mentioning that some have not arrived even now.' These were Belisarius' words.

(24) But the army insulted him, and not silently or in secret. They actually came up to him and shouted to his face that he was a coward who wanted to damp down their enthusiasm; even some of the officers displayed their boldness in this way and joined in this poor behaviour. (25) Belisarius was taken aback by their shamelessness and reversed his advice, now giving the impression that he was urging them on against the enemy and drawing them up in battle formation. He said that he had not known their eagerness to fight before, but that now he was full of confidence and would advance against the enemy in better hopes. (26) He formed up a front-facing phalanx and made the following dispositions (fig. 20). On the left wing near the river he stationed all the infantry, on the right, where the ground was steep, al-Harith and all the Saracens with

95

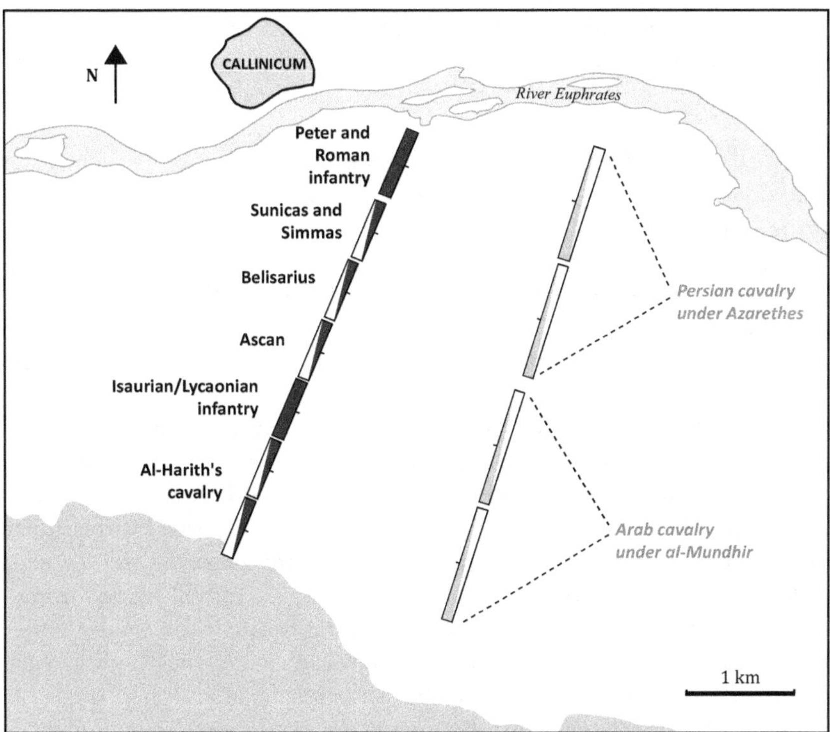

Figure 20   The Battle of Callinicum

him, and he positioned himself with the cavalry in the middle. These were the Roman positions. (27) When Azarethes saw the enemy massing in battle formation, he made this speech of encouragement:

'Though you are Persians, no one would deny that if someone gave you the choice, you would exchange your valour for your lives. (28) But I say that this choice is not open to you, even if you wish it, for this reason. For those who can escape their dangerous position and go on living in dishonour, it is not unnatural, if they wish it, that they should choose pleasure instead of the highest good, but for those who must die, either gloriously before the enemy, or else shamefully brought for punishment by their ruler, it would be utter folly not to choose the more glorious course instead of the shameful one. (29) Since this is so, I believe that all of you should go into this battle thinking not only of the enemy but also of your master.'

96 (30) With this exhortation Azarethes positioned his phalanx opposite the enemy, the Persians holding the right, and the Saracens the left. At once the two sides joined battle. (31) The fighting was very hard. Arrows flew thickly from both sides over a wide area and caused great slaughter on each side, and some men came into the space between the armies and performed feats of valour, but the Persians died in greater numbers from the arrows. (32) Their arrows were undoubtedly greater in number, since nearly all the Persians are archers and are taught to shoot much faster than any other men, (33) but they were shot from feeble bows, not tautly strung, and when they hit a Roman's corselet or helmet or shield, they snapped and could not harm the man who was hit. (34) The Roman arrows are always fired at a slower rate, since they are shot from very taut bows that are drawn hard (and, one could add, by stronger men), and can easily injure those whom they hit, far more than the Persians', for no armour can withstand their force.

(35) By now two parts of the day had passed, and the battle was still undecided. But then, by a concerted plan, the best of the Persian army attacked the enemy right wing, where al-Harith and the Saracens were **97** drawn up. (36) They broke ranks and split into two parts, by this move bringing upon themselves the suspicion of having betrayed the Romans to the Persians. They could not hold off the attack and all turned immediately to flight. (37) So the Persians, breaking through the enemy ranks, at once found themselves behind the Roman cavalry. The Romans were now weary from their journey and from the battle, and all had spent the day so far fasting; harried by the enemy on both sides, they could not hold out. Most fled headlong and reached the islands in the river, which

were not far away, but some stayed there and performed remarkable and memorable feats against the enemy. (38) Among these was Ascan, who, after killing many notable Persians, was gradually cut to pieces and finally fell, leaving many stories about him to circulate among the enemy. With him died eight hundred other men in this battle, fighting bravely, and nearly all the Isaurians with their officers, not having dared even to raise their arms against the enemy. (39) They were quite inexperienced in this sort of thing, for they had come from farming straight into the dangers of war, of which they had previously known nothing. (40) Yet they most of all in their ignorance of war had just now been eager for battle and taunted Belisarius with cowardice. They were not all Isaurians, however; the majority were Lycaonians.[143]

(41) Belisarius remained there with a few men, as long as he saw Ascan and his men holding out, and fought the enemy himself with his companions. (42) But when some of them fell and others turned to flight wherever they could, he too fled with his followers and came to the phalanx of infantry who were still fighting under Peter – only a few in number, for most of them too had fled. (43) There he himself gave up his horse and told all his followers to do the same, and to fight the attackers with the rest as foot soldiers. (44) The Persians who were in pursuit did not carry on the chase for very long, but came back and set about Belisarius and the infantry with the rest of the army. Belisarius and his men turned their backs to the river, so that the enemy could not encircle them, and fought off their attackers as best they could. (45) Again there was a fierce battle, albeit not evenly matched, for they were foot soldiers, and very few in number, fighting the whole of the Persian cavalry. Even so, the enemy could neither rout them nor overpower them in any other way. (46) They were massed together shoulder to shoulder in a small space, and protected themselves very closely with their shields; thus they could fire at the Persians more successfully than they could be fired upon by them. (47) Often, after giving up, the Persians would charge them, trying to throw them into confusion and break up their formation, but they had to retire again without success, (48) for their horses were unsettled by the clash of shields and reared and panicked with their riders. So both sides went on until late in the day. (49) But when night had already come on, the Persians retired to their camp and Belisarius, finding a cargo vessel, put in at the island in the river with a few men, while the other Romans reached it by swimming. (50) On the next day the

---

[143] Lycaonia lies just north of Isauria in central Asia Minor.

Romans, once numerous cargo vessels had arrived from the city of Callinicum, were conveyed there; the Persians stripped the corpses and all went home. Yet they found as many of their own corpses as of the enemy's.[144]

(51) When Azarethes reached Persia with his army, even though he had done well in the battle, he found Kavadh very ungrateful for the following reason. (52) The Persians have a custom that when they are about to go on an expedition against an enemy, the king sits on the royal throne, with a number of baskets there in front of him, and the general who is expected to lead the army against the enemy is present; the army passes before the king, man by man, and each throws an arrow into the baskets. After this they are sealed with the king's seal and kept, and when the army returns to Persia each of the soldiers takes one arrow from the baskets. (53) And so, after counting the arrows which are not taken by the men, the officers in charge tell the king the number of soldiers who have not returned, and in this way it is clear how many have perished in the war. (54) This has been the Persian custom since ancient times. When Azarethes came before the king, Kavadh asked him whether he had subdued any Roman possession, since he had gone out against the Romans with al-Mundhir with the purpose of reducing Antioch. Azarethes replied that he had not captured any place but that he had defeated Belisarius and the Romans in battle. (55) Then Kavadh ordered Azareth's army to pass before him, and each man took an arrow from the baskets, as was the custom. (56) But many arrows were left, and the king reproached Azarethes for his victory and from then onwards held him in very low esteem. Such then was the conclusion of this victory for Azarethes.

Chapter 19

(1) The idea then occurred to the Emperor Justinian to enter into an association with the Ethiopians and Homerites to harm the Persians.[145] I shall now proceed to relate where in the world these men live and how the emperor hoped that they would be useful to the Romans. (2) The boundaries of Palestine extend eastwards to the sea called Red (fig. 21). (3) This

[144] Procopius' account strives to exculpate Belisarius for the defeat. Mal. 18.60 offers a less rosy view of the general's performance. See *RPW*, 200–7, for a detailed discussion. Even if Malalas' version reflects an official report, Procopius may yet be closer to the mark. Ps.-Zach. 9.4 also has a brief account of the battle.

[145] The Homerites, also known as Ḥimyarities, inhabited southern Arabia, today's Yemen.

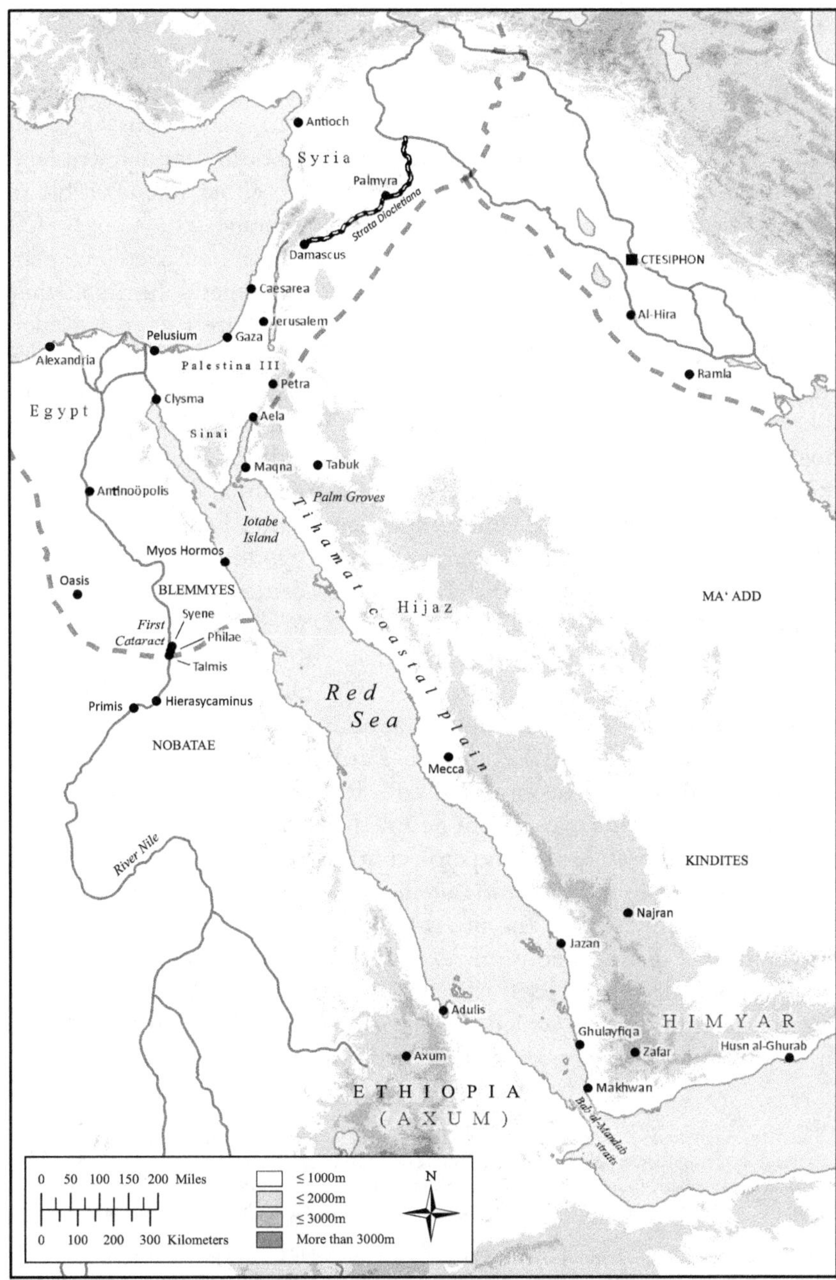

Figure 21   The Arabian Peninsula, Ethiopia and Egypt

sea has its starting-point in India and ends here, in the Roman empire.[146] A city called Aela is situated on the coast of the empire here, where the sea, as I mentioned, comes to an end, forming an extremely narrow strait.[147] As one sails from there into the strait, the mountains of Egypt stretch out southwards on the right; on the other side an uninhabited land extends northwards over a wide area. The land on either side is visible to one sailing into the sea, as far as the island called Iotabe, which lies no less than a thousand stades from Aela.[148] (4) There Jews had lived independently from of old, but during the reign of this Emperor Justinian they had become Roman subjects. (5) From this point a great open sea takes over. Those who sail into it no longer see the land on their right; but when night falls, they always moor on the left bank. (6) For it is impossible to sail in this sea in the dark because it happens to be filled with shoals over a wide area. (7) But there are many harbours there, formed not by the hands of men but by the nature of the terrain, and consequently it is not hard for sailors to find a mooring wherever they happen to be.

Saracens occupy the coastline immediately beyond the frontier as one crosses over from Palestine; (8) they have been settled in the Palm Grove from of old.[149] (9) The Palm Grove lies inland, stretching over a vast area, where absolutely nothing grows other than palm trees. (10) Abu Karib, the ruler of the Saracens there, presented this Palm Grove to the Emperor Justinian as a gift, and the emperor appointed him phylarch over the Saracens in Palestine.[150] (11) And Abu Karib kept the land consistently free from raiding, since he appeared both fearsome and remarkably energetic to the barbarians over whom he ruled and no less so to his enemies. (12) In theory therefore the emperor controls the Palm Grove, but it is absolutely impossible for him to take his share of the lands here. (13) For a land completely desolate and utterly waterless lies in between (the Palm Grove and the Roman empire), extending for a distance of ten days' journey. The Palm Grove itself is of no worth whatever: Abu Karib gave a present merely in name, which the emperor accepted in full knowledge. This then is how things are with the Palm Grove. (14) Next to these men,

---

[146] 'India' is a vague term in ancient sources: in the present context it probably refers to the Horn of Africa, but it could also apply to southern Arabia or, of course, India itself.

[147] Aela, at the northern end of the Gulf of Aqaba, is today's Aqaba in Jordan. See *ODLA*, Aila.

[148] Iotabe is likely to be modern Tiran, 200 km south of Aela, where the Gulf of Aqaba opens into the Red Sea.

[149] The Palm Grove (Phoinikōn) lies in the Ḥijāz of today, probably in the vicinity of Tabūk.

[150] Abu Karib (Abū Karib, Abokharabos) was the brother of the Jafnid ruler al-Harith (al-Ḥārith); he became phylarch of Palestine (perhaps all three Palestinian provinces) in the late 520s and was still alive in 547. His importance is confirmed in documentary sources, cf. *AEBI*, 323–4.

other Saracens occupy the coast, who are called the Maddeni and are subjects of the Homerites.[151] (15) These Homerites live in the land beyond, next to the seashore. They say that many other peoples are settled beyond them, as far as the man-eating Saracens. (16) Beyond them, moreover, lie the Indian races. But let each person tell of these peoples as he wishes.

(17) More or less opposite the Homerites, on the facing mainland, there live the Ethiopians, who are called Auxomites because their royal palace is in the city of Auxomis.[152] (18) The sea between them extends over a distance that, with a moderately favourable wind, takes five days and nights to cross, (19) for in this region they are accustomed to sail also by night, since there are no shoals here. This sea is called by some the Red Sea: the waters beyond it for one sailing up to the coast and the city of Aela have acquired the name 'the Arabian Gulf'. (20) For the territory from here as far as the borders of the city of Gaza was formerly named Arabia, since the king of the Arabs had his royal palace in those earlier times at the city of Petra.[153] (21) The harbour of the Homerites from which they are accustomed to set off to sail to the Ethiopians is called Bulicas.[154] (22) Having sailed across this sea they invariably drop anchor at the harbour of the Adulitae: the city of Adulis is twenty stades distant from the harbour, for it is cut off by such a small distance from the coast, while from the city of Axum it is twelve days' journey.[155]

(23) Now all the ships that exist in India and in this sea are not constructed in the same manner as other ships, for they are not coated with pitch or any other substance; moreover, their planks are not held together by iron nails passing right through them, but they are rather bound together by rope-knots. (24) The grounds for this are not those that many suppose, that there are certain rocks there that draw the iron to themselves: the proof of this is that such a fate has never befallen any Roman ships sailing from Aela into this sea, even though they are equipped with a lot of iron. Rather, the reason is that the Indians and Ethiopians possess neither iron nor any other material suited to such

[151] The Maddeni (Ma'add in the Arabic sources) were a confederation that exercised great influence in the centre of the Arabian peninsula.

[152] The people are more commonly known as Axumites (or Aksumites) and the city as Axum (Aksum); they are situated in today's Ethiopia.

[153] An allusion to the Nabataean kingdom whose capital lay at Petra (in modern Jordan), which was annexed to the Roman empire by Trajan at the start of the second century A.D.

[154] Various identifications have been proposed, the most recent being the modern Jāzān in Saudi Arabia, close to the border with Yemen.

[155] Adulis is the modern Zula in Eritrea, which lies 7 km from the sea.

needs.[156] (25) Moreover, they are not able to buy these things from the Romans, since such a practice is explicitly forbidden by law, (26) for death is the penalty for the person caught doing so.[157] Such is the state of affairs as regards the so-called Red Sea and the land on either side of it.

(27) From the city of Auxumis to the Egyptian frontier of the Roman empire, where the city called Elephantine is situated, lies a journey of thirty days for an active man. (28) Here are established many peoples, among whom are the Blemmyes and Nobatae, tribes that are extremely populous. The Blemmyes inhabit the interior of this territory, while the Nobatae occupy the lands around the river Nile.[158] Previously these were not the limits of the Roman empire, but they extended beyond for a distance of a further seven days' journey. (29) When, however, the Emperor Diocletian arrived there, he realised that the tribute of the villages there was of minimal worth, since it happens that the land there is extremely narrow: for not far from the Nile high rocks rise up and dominate the rest of the terrain.[159] Yet from of old a large contingent of soldiers had been established here, whose expenses greatly burdened the treasury; at the same time, the Nobatae who formerly lived around the city of Oasis constantly plundered all the villages there.[160] So Diocletian persuaded the barbarians to move off from their own homelands and to settle around the river Nile; and he agreed to grant them large cities and much land of a quality remarkably superior to that in which they had lived hitherto. (30) In this way he thought that they would no longer trouble the villages around Oasis and would lay claim to the land granted to them, since it was now their own, and that they would ward off the Blemmyes and the other barbarians, as might be expected. (31) Since these proposals pleased the Nobatae, they undertook forthwith the migration that Diocletian had ordained for them; and they occupied the cities of the Romans and all the land on either side of the Nile from the city of Elephantine southwards. (32) At that time this emperor laid down that every year a specified sum of gold should be given to the Blemmyes on the condition that they should no longer plunder the land of the Romans. (33) But although they have collected this sum up to my day, they nonetheless overrun the villages there. Thus, it appears, there is

---

[156] Such boats are attested, built of teak or coconut wood, in the Indian Ocean.

[157] Confirmed by *C.J.* 4.41.2 (455/7).

[158] Procopius' placing of the tribes is broadly correct for the sixth century: the Nobatae (also known as Nobades) in the Nile valley, the Blemmyes to the east.

[159] Diocletian visited Egypt's southern frontier in 298.

[160] Oasis refers to the Kharga oasis west of the Nile in Upper (southern) Egypt. See *ODLA*, Oasis (Great Oasis).

no way for barbarians to keep faith with the Romans save through fear of soldiers ready in defence. (34) Nonetheless this emperor, after he had found out about an island in the river Nile very close to the city of Elephantine, erected certain common temples and altars there for both the Romans and these barbarians; and he established priests of both sides in this fortress, believing that their friendship would be more secure through their sharing of the sanctuaries. (35) He therefore named the place Philae.[161] Both peoples, the Blemmyes and the Nobatae, believe in the gods in whom the Hellenes believe, and they revere both Isis and Osiris, and not least also Priapus. (36) The Blemmyes, moreover, used to sacrifice people to the sun. These barbarians indeed maintained these temples in Philae up to my day, but the Emperor Justinian decided to destroy them. (37) At any rate Narses, the commander of the soldiers there, a Persarmenian by birth, whose defection to the Romans I mentioned earlier, destroyed the temples upon the orders of the emperor; he kept the priests in prison and sent the statues to Byzantium.[162] I shall now return to my earlier account.

Chapter 20

(1) Around the time of this war Hellesthaeus,[163] the king of the Ethiopians, a Christian with the greatest zeal for this faith, learnt that the Homerites of the mainland opposite – many of whom were Jews, while many others revered the ancient faith, which people now call Hellenic – were plotting against the Christians there on a large scale.[164] He therefore gathered a fleet of ships and an army and set off against them. Having defeated their king in battle and killed many of the Homerites, he appointed another king there, a Christian, a Homerite by birth, Esimiphaeus by name.[165] He instructed him to pay a tribute to the

107

---

[161] The etymology is false but found in numerous other sources. 'Philae' would mean '(female) friends', presumably the Blemmyes and the Romans. See also *ODLA*, Philae.

[162] See 1.15.31 on Narses' defection. He probably shut the temple in 535; soon afterwards a mission was sent to convert the Nobatae. The temple had in any case been waning for a long time before this formal closure.

[163] Hellesthaeus is often referred to as Kālēb; Procopius gives a version of his throne name 'Ella 'Aṣbeḥa, 'he who has brought the dawn'. Procopius fails to date these events precisely: they need not have taken place in 531 exactly.

[164] Harsh persecution by Jewish or Judaising rulers had taken place over the preceding decades, culminating in the execution of numerous Christians at Najrān in Ḥimyar in November 523. The Ḥimyarite ruler Yūsuf (Joseph) As'ar Yath'ar, also referred to as dhū-Nuwās and Masrūq, unsuccessfully opposed the Ethiopian intervention. See *AEBI*, 145–8.

[165] The ruler is called Sumūyafa' Ashwa' in inscriptions. The Ethiopian campaign took place in 525.

Ethiopians every year and returned home. (2) Among the Ethiopian army there were many slaves and people disposed towards mischief who were wholly unwilling to follow the king. After being left behind there, they remained on account of their enthusiasm for the land of the Homerites, which is extremely good.

(3) This force rose up a little later, along with certain other individuals, against King Esimiphaeus, imprisoned him in a fortress there, and appointed another king for the Homerites, Abramus by name.[166] (4) This Abramus was a Christian, but a slave of a Roman in the Ethiopian city of Adulis whose occupation was maritime trade. (5) When Hellesthaeus learnt this, he was eager to obtain vengeance for the injustice to Esimiphaeus on Abramus and those who had risen up with him. He sent against them an army of 3000 men and a commander drawn from his own relatives. (6) This army did not want to return home but preferred to stay there, in a good land. So the soldiers secretly entered negotiations with Abramus unbeknownst to their commander and after they came into battle with their enemies, when they were in the fray, they killed their commander, joined the ranks of the enemy army and remained there. (7) Greatly enraged, Hellesthaeus despatched another army against them, which entered battle with Abramus' force, but was decisively defeated in the engagement and immediately withdrew homewards. After this, the Ethiopian king grew afraid and no longer undertook any campaigns against Abramus. (8) When Hellesthaeus died, Abramus agreed to pay tribute to the one who inherited the Ethiopian throne from him, and thus he secured his rule. These things, however, took place subsequently.[167]

(9) At that time the Emperor Justinian, in the reign of Hellesthaeus in Ethiopia and Esimiphaeus among the Homerites, sent Julian as an ambassador, asking both parties to aid the Romans in their war against Persia because of their shared faith.[168] His idea was that the Ethiopians, by buying raw silk from the Indians and selling it to the Romans, might themselves earn a large sum of money, and at the same time do the Romans this single favour – they would no longer be forced to hand over their own money to their enemies.[169] This is the raw silk from which they make clothing which the Greeks in ancient times used to call Persian, but

---

[166] Also referred to as Abraha. The name may not invoke the biblical patriarch but rather be an Ethiopic one meaning '(God) has illuminated'.

[167] It is uncertain when Hellesthaeus (Kāléb) died, though it was certainly before 547, when a rapprochement between Abraha and Ethiopia (Aksum) is attested.

[168] See the Appendix, p. 213, on this mission and others reported by Nonnosus, cf. *PLRE* 3, Iulianus 8.

[169] Procopius' interest in the silk trade is visible also in *Anecd.* 25.13–26, cf. *Wars* 8.17.1–8. See *ODLA*, silk and silk trade.

which they now call 'silk'. He intended also that the Homerites should make the exiled Qays phylarch of the Maddeni and with a large army of Homerites and Saracen Maddeni invade Persian territory. (10) This Qays was from a family of phylarchs and particularly good at warfare, but he fled to an utterly uninhabited land after killing one of Esimiphaeus' relatives.[170] (11) Both kings sent back the envoy with the promise that they would fulfil the request, but neither did what he had agreed. (12) The Ethiopians could not buy the silk from the Indians because the Persian merchants were always at the harbours where the Indian ships first anchor, since they live in the adjoining districts and buy up all the cargoes.[171] It seemed hard to the Homerites that they should leave their country and go on a lonely and long journey against an enemy that was far more warlike. (13) Likewise later Abramus, when he had strengthened his rule and made it as firm as possible, made many agreements with the Emperor Justinian to invade Persian territory, but only once actually set out on the journey, and then came back immediately. Thus did Ethiopian and Homerite affairs turn out for the Romans.

110

Chapter 21

(1) At this juncture, immediately after the battle at the Euphrates, Hermogenes came on an embassy to Kavadh. But he achieved no agreement about peace, which was the purpose of his visit, since he found Kavadh still bursting with rage against the Romans; so he returned without success. (2) Belisarius was summoned by the emperor and came to Byzantium, relieved of his command in order to campaign against the Vandals.[172] (3) Sittas, on the orders of the Emperor Justinian, came to guard the East. (4) The Persians again invaded Mesopotamia with a large army under the command of Khanaranges and Aspebedes and Mihr-Mihroe.[173] (5) Since no one dared to engage them, they pitched camp and laid siege to Martyropolis, where Buzes and Bessas were stationed with a garrison.[174] (6) This city lies in the district called Sophanene, 240 stades

111

---

[170] See the Appendix, p. 215, on Qays who, later in the 530s, evidently grew much more powerful.

[171] The reference is probably to Sri Lanka, where Roman coins show contact for much of Late Antiquity.

[172] In fact, Belisarius had been sacked after his defeat. Only in 533 did he set out against the Vandals.

[173] The first name is most likely a rendering of the title *kanārang*, cf. 1.5.4. Similarly Aspebedes probably reflects a Persian title and is unlikely to be the same person as that mentioned at 1.9.24 (and 1.11.5). On Mihr-Mihroe, see 1.15.2.

[174] Further details on the final stages of the war are found in Mal. 18.61–70 and Ps.-Zach. 9.4–7, cf. *REF*, 94–6.

to the north of the city of Amida. It is on the river Nymphius, which divides Roman and Persian territory.[175] (7) So the Persians began to besiege the circuit wall. (8) At first the besieged bravely held them off, but they were not expected to hold out for long, for the circuit wall was in most parts easily assailable and could be taken by a Persian siege extremely easily. And the defenders did not have enough provisions, nor war machines, nor anything else of note that they could use for defence. (9) Sittas and the Roman army came to a place called Attachas, 100 stades from Martyropolis, and did not dare to go any further, but pitched camp there and waited. (10) Hermogenes was with them again, having arrived from Byzantium on an embassy. In the meantime the following event occurred.

(11) It has long been customary among both Romans and Persians to maintain spies at public expense; these spies go in secret to the enemy to observe in detail what they are doing and to return and inform their commanders.[176] (12) Many of them naturally display the greatest loyalty to their fellow countrymen, but some do indeed betray secrets to the enemy. (13) At this time, then, a spy sent from the Persians to the Romans came before the Emperor Justinian and gave him information about the doings of the barbarians, including the news that the Massagetae were just on the point of going to Persia so as to damage Roman interests,[177] and that from there they were ready to join with the Persian army and march against the Roman empire. (14) When the emperor heard this, having evidence already of the man's truthfulness to him, he bribed him with a substantial sum of money to go to the Persian army that was besieging the people of Martyropolis and tell the barbarians there that these Massagetae had been bribed by the Roman emperor and were just about to attack them. (15) The spy did this; when he reached the barbarian camp, he told Khanaranges and the others that an army of Huns hostile to them would very soon come to help the Romans. (16) And when they heard this they were terrified and did not know what to do in the circumstances.

(17) In the meantime it happened that Kavadh fell seriously ill. Summoning one of the Persians who was closest to him, Mebodes by name, he consulted with him about Khusro and the kingship, and said that he was afraid that the Persians would want to cast aside his wishes.[178]

---

[175] The Nymphius is today's Batman Su.
[176] On spies in this period see also *Anecd.* 30.12–14 and *ODLA*, spies and spying.
[177] The Massagetae (Huns) here referred to are the Sabirs.
[178] On Mebodes see 1.11.25.

(18) Mebodes asked him to leave the statement of his wishes in writing, and to be confident that the Persians would never dare to overlook it. (19) So Kavadh laid it down openly in his will that the Persians should make Khusro king. Mebodes himself wrote the document, and immediately Kavadh vanished from the world of men.[179] (20) When the customary rites had been performed at the king's burial, Kaoses, taking confidence from the law, tried to assume the honour, but Mebodes prevented him, saying that no one should come to the throne at his own instigation, save by the vote of the Persian nobles. (21) So Kaoses handed the decision in the matter over to the authorities, never suspecting that there would be any opposition to him. (22) But when all the Persian nobles were gathered together for this purpose and were seated, Mebodes read out the document and revealed Kavadh's wishes concerning Khusro, and they all remembered Kavadh's great qualities, and proclaimed Khusro king of Persia on the spot.

(23) In this way Khusro came to the throne. But at Martyropolis Sittas and Hermogenes were afraid for the city, for it was in peril and they could not defend it in any way, and so they sent some men to the enemy who came before the generals and said this:

(24) 'You have failed to notice that you are needlessly standing in the way of the king of Persia and of the blessings of peace for each state. An embassy from the emperor is here at this moment, which is set to go to the king of Persia and resolve our differences and make a truce with him. Leave Roman territory as soon as you can, and allow the envoys to do what will benefit both sides. (25) We are ready also to give as hostages on their behalf men of high rank, so that matters may soon be finalised in practice.'

These were the words of the Roman envoys. (26) And a messenger also happened to have arrived from the palace, who announced to them that Kavadh had died, and that Khusro, the son of Kavadh, had been made king of Persia, and that in this way matters hung in the balance for them. (27) As a result the generals were pleased to accept the overtures from the Romans, since they were also afraid of the Hunnic attack. So the Romans at once handed over as hostages Martin and one of Sittas' bodyguards, Senecius by name. And the Persians raised their siege and made a direct retreat. (28) Not long afterwards the Huns invaded Roman territory, but when they did not find the Persian army there they all returned home after making only a short incursion.[180]

---

[179] Mal. 18.68 dates Kavadh's death to September 531, which fits with what is described here.
[180] The invasion is dated to December 531 by Syriac sources: see *RPW*, 210–11.

Chapter 22

(1) Rufinus, Alexander and Thomas set out at once as ambassadors with Hermogenes and reached the king of Persia at the river Tigris.[181] (2) When Khusro saw them he released the hostages. The ambassadors tried to soothe Khusro with many blandishments that were far from fitting for Roman envoys. (3) Khusro grew more pliant towards them and agreed to make with them a peace with no limit, at the price of one hundred and ten *centenaria*, on condition that the commander of the troops in Mesopotamia should no longer in the future be stationed in Dara, but should be permanently in Constantia, where he used to be. He said that he would not give up the fortresses in Lazica, though he demanded that he himself should receive back from the Romans both Pharangium and the fortress of Bolum. (4) The *centenarium* weighs a hundred pounds, from where it gets its name, for the Romans call a hundred *centum*.[182] (5) This gold, he demanded, should be given to him in return for the Romans not being obliged to pull down the city of Dara or share with the Persians the garrisoning of the Caspian Gates. (6) The ambassadors accepted all the terms except for the fortresses, which they said that they could not give up without the emperor's knowing about it first. (7) So they decided that Rufinus should go to Byzantium on this mission and that the others should remain until he returned; a period of seventy days was allowed for Rufinus to return. (8) And when Rufinus reached Byzantium and told the emperor Khusro's wishes concerning the peace, the emperor commanded them to make the peace on these terms.

(9) In the meantime a false rumour reached Persia, which announced that the Emperor Justinian had become angry and executed Rufinus. Khusro was up in arms at this and in a great passion set out against the Romans with all his army. But in the meantime Rufinus returned and met him not far from the city of Nisibis. (10) Accordingly, they went themselves to the city, and since they were going to ratify the peace treaty, the legates brought the money there. (11) But the Emperor Justinian already regretted having surrendered the fortresses in Lazica, and he wrote a letter to the envoys explicitly refusing to give them up to the Persians. (12) Khusro therefore no longer consented to make the treaty, and then it occurred to Rufinus that he had advised bringing the money

---

[181] Procopius passes over a hiatus in negotiations during which Justinian refused to recognise Khusro as the new Persian king, an approach he swiftly abandoned. See *RPW*, 211.

[182] The sum proposed amounts to just under 3600 kg of gold.

into Persian territory more hastily than was safe. (13) At once he flung himself to the ground and, with his face touching the floor, begged Khusro to send the money with them and not to campaign right away against the Romans, but to put off the war to another time. (14) And Khusro told him to get up, promising that he would grant his requests. So the envoys came to Dara with the money and the Persian army retreated.

(15) Then Rufinus' fellow ambassadors held him in the gravest suspicion; they slandered him to the emperor, basing their impression on the fact that Khusro had been persuaded to agree to everything that he asked.[183] (16) But the emperor did him no harm as a result of this. Not long afterwards Rufinus and Hermogenes were sent again to Khusro; at once they came to an agreement about the treaty, the terms being that each side should restore whatever places they had taken from the other in this war, and that there should no longer be a military post in Dara. And it was decided that the Iberians should choose whether to remain there in Byzantium or to return to their native country. There were many who stayed and many who returned to their own country. (17) So they made the so-called 'Endless Peace' in what was already the sixth year of Justinian's reign.[184] (18) The Romans surrendered Pharangium and the fortress of Bolum to the Persians with the money, and the Persians surrendered the Lazic fortresses to the Romans. The Persians gave up Dagaris to the Romans, receiving an important man in return for him.[185] (19) Later this Dagaris many times defeated Huns who invaded Roman territory, and drove them out, for he was remarkably good at warfare. Both sides thus ratified the mutual treaty in the way described.

Chapter 23

(1) But at once each king suffered a revolt by his subjects. I shall now go on to describe how this took place. Khusro, the son of Kavadh, was unstable in temperament and extraordinarily fond of novelty. (2) Accordingly, he was always full of disturbances and confusion himself,

[183] On Rufinus' links to Khusro and Kavadh, see 1.11.5 and cf. Ps.-Zach. 9.7.

[184] Probably in September 532. Despite the doubts of certain scholars, it is clear that the peace was supposed to last indefinitely; such agreements often expired upon the death of one ruler, but evidently this was intended to be exceptional. A minor clause in the treaty may have allowed Athenian philosophers who had recently sought refuge at the Persian court to return home, on which see Agath. 2.31.4.

[185] Perhaps, it has been suggested, a certain Pīrān-Gušnasp, also known as Mar Grigor, a Persian general who had converted to Christianity and whose life is preserved in a Syriac source.

and he was the cause of the same effect in others. (3) The most active Persians, therefore, dissatisfied with his rule, had in mind to appoint for themselves another king of Kavadh's house. (4) They were very eager for Zames to rule, which was forbidden by law because of his damaged eye, as I have explained, so they thought the matter over and decided that it would be better for them if they made king his son Kavadh, who had the same name as his grandfather, and that Zames, as his son's guardian, should direct Persian affairs as he thought fit.[186] (5) They came to Zames and told him their plan, and with much enthusiastic encouragement urged him on to the undertaking. He liked the idea, and so they decided that they would attack Khusro at a suitable moment. But the plan became known and reached the king, and he put a stop to what was going on. (6) Khusro put to death Zames himself and all of his and Zames' brothers with their whole male descent, and as many of the Persian nobles as had come to lead the plots against him or to partake of them in any way. Among them was Aspebedes, Khusro's mother's brother.[187]

(7) Kavadh the son of Zames he could not himself put to death, however, for he was still being reared under the care of the *kanarang*, Adergudunbades.[188] But he commanded the *kanarang* himself to make away with the child whom he was bringing up. He did not think it right to distrust the man and could not force him in any other way. (8) So the *kanarang*, on hearing Khusro's commands, in grief and weeping at his lot told his wife and Kavadh's nurse what the king commanded. And his wife, weeping, seized her husband's knees and begged him on no account to kill Kavadh. (9) So they discussed the matter and decided to bring the boy up in the safest possible concealment, telling Khusro as quickly as possible that Kavadh had vanished from the world of men. (10) They told the king this and hid Kavadh so well that they allowed no one to see him, except for Varrames, their own son, and one of the servants who seemed absolutely loyal to them. (11) But as time went on and Kavadh grew up, the *kanarang* was afraid that the matter might come to light, so he gave money to Kavadh, telling him to go and save himself wherever he might be able to flee. At this time, then, the *kanarang* by these means escaped the notice of Khusro and everyone else.

---

[186] On Zames see 1.11.35.

[187] Cf. 1.11.5 on Khusro's uncle.

[188] On Adergudunbades see 1.6.18. The episode that follows is highly reminiscent of the saving of the life of Cyrus the Great, whom the Median King Astyages had wanted to be killed, recounted by Hdt. 1.108–12.

(12) But later Khusro invaded the land of Colchis with a large army, as I shall relate presently.[189] (13) With him went Varrames, the son of this *kanarang*, taking with him among his servants the one who had shared with him the secret about Kavadh.[190] There Varrames told the king the whole story about Kavadh, and produced the servant to confirm everything. (14) When Khusro heard this, he was seized with rage and was very angry that he should have suffered such a thing from a subject; being unable to bring the man into his hands, he devised this plan.

(15) When he was about to return home from the land of Colchis, he wrote to this *kanarang*, saying that he had decided to invade Roman territory with his whole army, not, however, in one place, but by dividing into two the Persian army so that he could invade the enemy both inside and outside the river Euphrates. (16) He himself would of course lead one part of the army into enemy territory, and he would allow no other of his subjects the privilege of holding the same honour as the king, except the *kanarang* himself, as a reward for his valour. (17) Therefore he must come to him with all speed on his withdrawal, so that he could explain everything to him, and give him all the instructions that would be of service for the expedition, and he must tell his attendants to come behind him on the road.

(18) When the *kanarang* received this message, he was overjoyed at the honour the king was doing him. He prepared at once to carry out the instructions, quite unaware of his own plight. (19) But as he was on his way he could not stand the hardship (for he was a very old man) and fell off his horse through letting go of the reins, and broke his leg. So he had to stay there and be looked after. The king came to the place and saw the *kanarang*. (20) Khusro told him that he could not join in the expedition with his foot in that state, but that he must go to one of the fortresses in the area and get medical assistance there. (21) In this way Khusro sent the man to his death. Following behind with him went men ordered to kill him in the fortress, a man who, among the Persians, was an undefeated general both in name and in fact, and who had made war against twelve barbarian peoples and subdued them all for King Kavadh. (22) When Adergudunbades had vanished from the world of men, his son Varrames was given the office of *kanarang*. (23) Not long afterwards either Kavadh the son of Zames himself or some other man assuming his name came to Byzantium – yet he was very like King Kavadh to look at. (24) The

121

122

---

[189] This is the invasion of Lazica in 541 described at 2.17.
[190] The name Varrames represents a Greek rendering of Bahrām or Wahrām.

Emperor Justinian, though doubtful about him, received him graciously as the grandson of King Kavadh and held him in high honour.[191] This then was what happened with the Persians who rebelled against Khusro.

(25) Later Khusro also did away with Mebodes for the following reason.[192] The king was dealing with an important matter and he told Zabergan, who was present, to summon Mebodes. But Zabergan happened to be at odds with Mebodes.[193] When he found him, he came upon him drilling soldiers under his command. He told him that the king was summoning him to come as quickly as possible. (26) He replied that he would come at once, as soon as he had finished what he had in hand, but the other, spurred on by his dislike of him, told Khusro that Mebodes said that he was very busy and would not come for the present. (27) So Khusro was seized with anger at this and sent one of his attendants to tell Mebodes to come to the tripod. What this means I shall explain immediately. (28) An iron tripod has always stood in front of the palace. When a Persian hears that the king is angry with him, he is not allowed to flee to a temple or anywhere else, but must sit by this tripod and await the king's decree; and no other man dares to protect him. (29) There Mebodes sat for many days in a pitiful state, until someone seized him and killed him at Khusro's order. This was how his good service to Khusro turned out for him.

Chapter 24

(1) At about the same time[194] a popular uprising suddenly broke out in Byzantium, which turned out, contrary to expectation, to be very serious, and which ended by greatly harming both the people and the senate. This is how it came about. (2) The population in every city has long since been divided into Blues and Greens, but it is only recently that for the sake of these names and the seats which they take when watching the games, they spend their money and subject themselves to physical violence of the most bitter kind, and will even die a death of

---

[191] He later took part in the war against the Goths in Italy, *Wars* 8.26.13, cf. *PLRE* 3, Cavades.

[192] Later probably means after the fall of Adergudunbades, during the 530s.

[193] Zabergan may have been involved in negotiating the Eternal Peace and later accompanied Khusro in his invasion of Roman territory in 540. Proc. *Anecd.* 2.32–3 alludes to a visit on his part to Constantinople. His name recalls that of the nobleman Zarvan in Firdausi's *Shāhnāmah*, who brought down his rival Māhbōdh.

[194] Evidently not the same time as the death of Mebodes, just described, but rather in January 532. The Nika riot is reported also by Mal. 18.71, *Chr. Pasch.* 620–9 and Theoph. 181, 184–6; a few other sources, like Marc. *com.* a.532 add a few details. See *ODLA*, Nika Riot.

the utmost dishonour. (3) They fight against those sitting opposite them, not knowing why they put themselves in this danger, yet knowing full well that even if they overcome their enemies in the fight, it remains for them to be dragged off to prison at once, and then to perish after horrible torture. (4) They have a senseless hatred of their neighbours, which is perpetual and never-ending, and it yields neither to marriage connection nor to ties of family nor to bonds of friendship, even if the opposing sides in this matter of colours are brothers or something similar. (5) They care for nothing, human or divine, in comparison with victory in these disputes. If a sacrilege to God is committed by anyone, or if the laws and the state are assailed by friends or enemies, they do not think it their concern, even though they may actually be short of food and in desperate straits because of their attacks on the state, so long as it goes well for their 'party' – for this is the name they give to their fellow partisans. (6) Even women share with them in this pollution, not only following their husbands, but even opposing them if necessary, although they never go to the theatres at all or have any other reason to spur them on.[195] For my part, I can only call this a disease of the soul.[196] This then is the state of affairs in the cities and in every citizen body.

(7) At that time the authorities in charge of the people in Byzantium arrested and led off some of the partisans to their death. But the two sides made common cause and concluded an agreement between them.[197] They seized those being led away and then went straight to the prison and released all those who were imprisoned there for rebellion or for any other offence. (8) The servants attending the city officers were killed for no reason, and any innocent citizens that were there fled to the mainland opposite. The city was fired as if it had fallen into enemy hands. (9) The church of Sophia, the baths of Zeuxippus, and the part of the royal palace from the outer gateways to the so-called House of Ares were burnt down and destroyed,[198] and besides these both the great porticoes that go to the forum named after Constantine, many houses, and a great deal of

---

[195] If by 'theatres' Procopius means the hippodromes, then *NovJ.* 22.15.2 of 535 contradicts him: women were able to attend, albeit with the permission of their husband.

[196] An expression found already in Plato, *Tim.* 87c2.

[197] The riot was sparked when two partisans, one Blue, one Green, survived a bungled execution by hanging and were rescued. The supporters united to demand their release.

[198] The 'outer gateways' translates the Greek Propylaea. The 'House of Ares' might be the guards' quarters next to the Chalke (bronze) gate. But with a slight modification the text might refer rather to the 'Area' or 'Araia': a 'tribunal of the Araia/Area' is attested in front of the Triklinos of Nineteen couches (in the palace complex). See fig. 22.

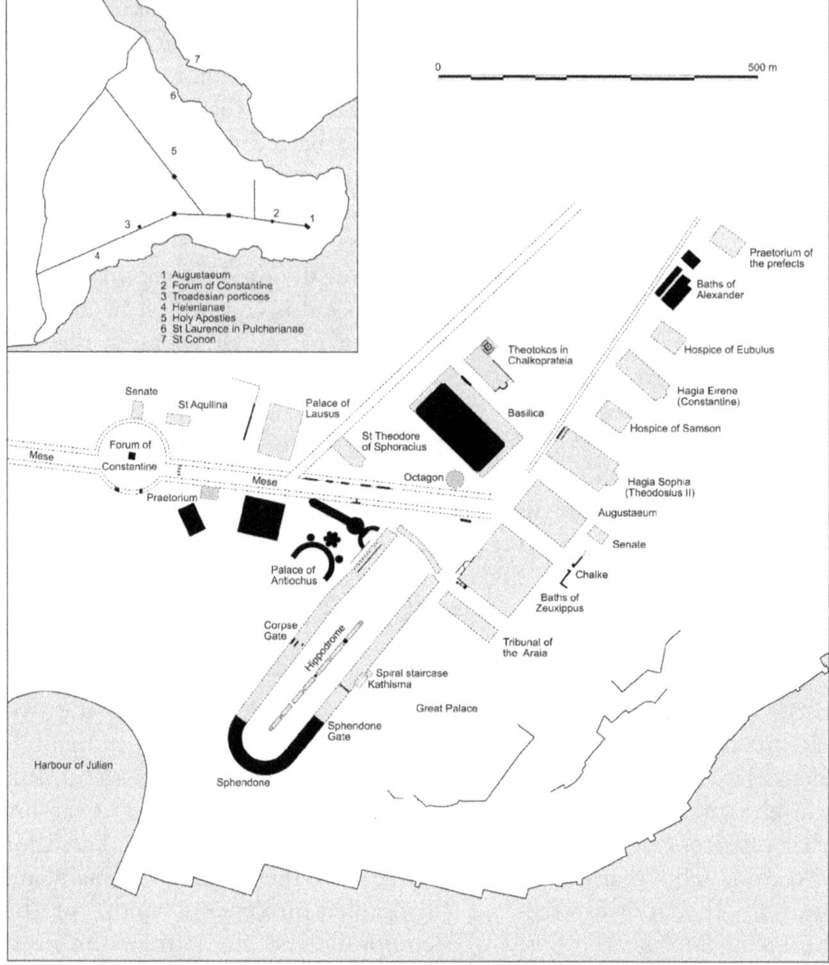

Figure 22 Constantinople at the Time of the Nika Riot

treasure belonging to rich men. (10) The emperor and his consort and some of the senators shut themselves up and waited in the palace. The people passed around among themselves as their watchword 'Nika', and from this the event has taken its name up to the present day.[199]

(11) At that time the praetorian prefect was John, the Cappadocian, and Tribonian, a Pamphylian by birth, was the emperor's adviser (the

[199] The events here described took place on Tuesday–Wednesday 14–15 January. 'Nika', i.e. 'conquer', 'win', was a frequent chant of the circus partisans.

Romans call this man *quaestor*).[200] (12) One of these two, John, had no experience in liberal conversation and education. He learnt nothing from his attendance at school except how to read, and badly at that, yet he was the most capable man of our time, as far as native wit goes. (13) He could always recognise what ought to be done and find a way out of difficulties. But he was the wickedest man on earth and used his native ability to this end; no respect for God or man ever entered his head – instead he sought to destroy many men's lives and raze whole cities for the sake of gain. (14) In a short time he amassed a great deal of money and flung himself into an endless drinking bout. He would plunder the property of subjects of the empire until it was time for lunch, and then he would idle away the rest of the time in drunkenness and in wanton acts of the flesh. (15) He could not restrain himself; he would go on eating until he was sick. He was always ready to steal money, and even readier to waste and squander it. This was what John was like. (16) Tribonian, on the other hand, was both possessed of natural talent and as well educated as any of his contemporaries, but he was extraordinarily greedy for money and was always capable of selling justice for gain; and every day, as a general rule, he spent his time repealing some laws and proposing others, selling either service to applicants according to their need.

   (17) While the people carried on its internal war over the names of the colours, no one paid any attention to the harm that these two men were doing to the state. But when the factions made common cause, as I have mentioned above, and took up the rebellion together, they openly reviled them all over the city and went around looking for them to kill them. So the emperor, wishing to associate himself with the people, immediately deprived both of their offices. (18) He made Phocas, a patrician, praetorian prefect, a man of great intelligence and well able to serve justice. He ordered Basilides to hold the office of *quaestor*, a man known among the patricians for fairness and generally respected.[201] (19) But the rebellion did not abate under them either. On the fifth day of the rebellion, about evening, the Emperor Justinian told Hypatius and Pompey, the nephews of the late Emperor Anastasius, to go home at once, either suspecting that they were plotting some mischief against his person or because fate

---

[200] On John see *PLRE* 3, Ioannes 11 and *ODLA*, John the Cappadocian. On Tribonian, *PLRE* 3, Tribonianus 1, *ODLA*, Tribonian. He was instrumental in Justinian's codification of Roman law.

[201] Phocas is praised also by Joh. Lyd. *De Mag.* 3.72; he was later disgraced himself, accused of paganism. See *PLRE* 2, Phocas 5, *ODLA*, Phocas. On Basilides see *PLRE* 3, Basilides. Procopius omits the replacement of the city prefect Eudaemon by Tryphon.

was actually leading them to this.[202] (20) But they were afraid that – as did actually happen – the people might force them to assume the throne, and they said that they would not be doing right if they abandoned their emperor when he was in such danger. (21) When the Emperor Justinian heard this he was confirmed in his suspicions and commanded them to go at once. So these two men went home and, while it was still night, they stayed there.

(22) On the following day at sunrise the people discovered that both of them had left the palace where they had been staying.[203] The whole mob therefore set off after them at a run, and made to proclaim Hypatius emperor, and were about to bring him to the Forum to take over the power. (23) But Hypatius' wife, Maria, who was an intelligent woman well known for her discretion, clung to her husband and would not let him go. She cried and wailed and told all her friends that the people were leading him to his death. (24) The people were very violent, however, and against her will she had to let her husband go; and the mob brought him against his will to the Forum of Constantine and called on him to adopt the purple. Putting a golden torque on his head (for they had no diadem nor any other of the emperor's customary ornaments), they proclaimed him emperor of Rome. (25) Now the senators were assembling, those of them who had not been left in the imperial palace, and many expressed the opinion that they should go to the palace and fight. (26) But a senator called Origen came forward and said this: 'Our present crisis, Romans, cannot be resolved save by war.[204] Now war and imperial power are generally agreed to be the greatest things in the world. (27) Important actions are not such as to be settled by a momentary crisis, but only by wise counsels and physical effort, displayed by men over a long period. (28) So if we are to attack the enemy, our fate will stand on a razor's edge, and we shall be staking our all in a moment of time, and in what follows we shall either abase ourselves before Fortune or else revile her utterly – (29) for in swift-moving situations, the power of Fortune is generally decisive. But if we take our time in settling the present crisis, we shall not be able to take Justinian in the palace, even if we wish – he will soon enough be glad if someone lets him escape. (30) For when authority is ignored it ebbs away, its strength diminishing day by day. We have other palaces, the Placillianae and that called after Helen, from which this

---

[202] The two men were dismissed from the palace on the evening of Saturday 17 January.
[203] Procopius omits Justinian's failed attempt on the Sunday morning to conciliate the people in the hippodrome.
[204] Origen is not otherwise known.

emperor ought to carry on the war and settle everything else for the best.'[205] (31) These were Origen's words. But the rest were more impetuous, as a crowd usually is, and thought that the present moment was the best time; Hypatius (for he was fated to come to a bad end) was no less keen in urging them to lead the way to the hippodrome. But some say that he came there on purpose, because he was well disposed to the emperor.

(32) The emperor's companions were debating whether it would be better for them to stay or to flee by ship. Many arguments were put forward on both sides.[206] (33) The Empress Theodora said: 'As to whether it is unseemly for a woman to be bold among men, or to be daring when others are full of fear, I do not think that the present crisis allows us to consider the matter one way or another. (34) For those in extreme danger nothing else seems best than to deal with the situation in the best way. (35) For my part, I consider that now of all times flight would be counter to our interests, even if it brings safety. Once a person is born, they cannot escape dying, but for one who has held the imperial power it would be unbearable to become a fugitive. (36) May I never be parted from this purple, and may I never live to see the day when men who meet me will not address me as their mistress. If you wish to be saved, Emperor, that is not difficult. (37) We have great resources of wealth; there is the sea, here are the boats. But take care in case when you have saved yourself you wish that you could exchange your safety for death. I am in agreement with the old saying, "Royalty is a good winding sheet".'[207]

(38) At these words from the empress, they were all inspired with courage and began to debate how they could defend themselves if anyone attacked them. (39) Now the soldiers, including those who were stationed at the emperor's residence, were not well disposed to the emperor and did not want to take part in the fighting openly; they were waiting for the outcome of events. (40) The emperor put all his hope in Belisarius and Mundus. One of the two, Belisarius, had just returned from the Persian war, and among his powerful and remarkable suite he had a large number of spearmen and guards who had been trained in battle and in the perils

---

[205] The palaces of Placillianae (named after Flaccilla, the wife of Theodosius I) and Helenianae (named after Constantine's mother) had imperial associations; the latter was where the Emperor Leo (457–74) had changed his robes when acceding to the throne.

[206] Theoph. 184 confirms that discussions took place about the possibility of flight. But Theodora's speech is likely to be mainly, if not entirely, Procopius' own creation. On the empress in general see *ODLA*, Theodora.

[207] A well-known saying, though applied initially to 'tyranny' rather than 'royalty'.

of war. (41) Mundus, appointed *magister militum per Illyricum*, had been summoned back to Byzantium for some purpose, and by some chance happened to have brought with him Herul barbarians.[208]

(42) So when Hypatius came to the hippodrome, he went straight up to where it is customary for the emperor to sit, and he sat down on the imperial throne, from which the emperor always watches the equestrian and athletic contests.[209] (43) Mundus came from the palace through the gate where there is a spiral staircase, so called because of its spiral descent.[210] (44) Belisarius first went straight up to Hypatius and the imperial throne, and when he came to the nearby room where there have always been soldiers on guard, he shouted to the soldiers to open the gate for him as quickly as possible, so that he could reach the usurper. (45) But the soldiers had decided to help neither side until one of them was clearly on top; they pretended not to hear and evaded the issue. (46) Belisarius therefore turned back to the emperor and assured him that all was lost, (47) for the soldiers garrisoning the palace were in rebellion against him. So the emperor told him to go to the so-called Chalke and the outer gateways there. (48) Belisarius, with great difficulty and not without considerable effort and danger, made his way up to the hippodrome. (49) When he came to the Blue portico, which is on the right of the emperor's throne, he planned to get to Hypatius first, but there was a small door there which was closed and guarded inside by Hypatius' soldiers, and he was afraid that, while he was struggling in the confined space, the crowd might join forces, kill him and his men, and have an easy and effortless path to the emperor. (50) He decided that he must attack the crowd standing in the hippodrome, which was of enormous size and pushing and shoving in great disorder, and he drew his sword from its scabbard and, telling the rest to do the same, he advanced against them at a run, shouting. (51) The crowd was massed together anyhow, in no sort of battle order, and when they saw soldiers under arms with a great reputation for valour and military experience mercilessly brandishing their swords, they turned to flight. (52) In the shouting that naturally ensued, Mundus, who was standing nearby, wished to join the fight (he was a man of great daring and energy), but did not know what to do in the circumstances. When he judged that Belisarius was engaged in combat, he immediately

---

[208] Mundus, also referred to as Mundo, had been appointed to replace Belisarius in the East; he was a Gepid leader. See *PLRE* 2, Mundo, *ODLA*, Mundus (Mundo).

[209] This is the *kathisma*, the imperial box, depicted (e.g.) on the base of the Obelisk of Theodosius in Istanbul in the centre of what was the hippodrome.

[210] The Greek word is *kochlias*, which means 'snail'.

entered the hippodrome by the gate called the Gate of the Corpse. (53) Then Hypatius' supporters were hit on all sides and cut to pieces. When the defeat became obvious, and many of the people had already been killed, Boraides and Justus, cousins of the Emperor Justinian, pulled Hypatius down from the throne, no one daring to raise a hand against them, and took him and handed him over to the emperor, together with Pompey. (54) More than 30,000 of the people died on that day.[211] The emperor ordered the two to be kept under close arrest. (55) At this Pompey wept and moaned in a most pitiful way, for he was not at all the sort of man accustomed to such misfortunes. But Hypatius rebuked him and said that men about to die without justice ought not to lament. (56) He said that in the beginning they had been forced against their will by the people, and that later, when they came to the hippodrome, they had meant no harm to the emperor. But the soldiers killed both of them on the following day and threw their bodies into the sea.[212] (57) The emperor assigned their money to the treasury, together with that of all the senators who had supported them. (58) Later, however, he restored to all of them, including the sons of Hypatius and Pompey, the rank they had previously held and such of their money as he had not given to certain of his friends.[213] This was the end of the revolt in Byzantium.

134

Chapter 25

(1) Tribonian and John, having been thus relieved of their posts, were later both restored to the same offices.[214] (2) Tribonian lived on in office for many years and eventually died of disease, suffering no further harm from anyone.[215] He was crafty and generally agreeable, well able to conceal his disease of avarice by the excellence of his education. (3) But John, who was equally unpleasant and disagreeable to everybody, and would beat anyone he met and plunder men's entire fortunes without any justification, met with a correct and just punishment in his tenth year of office for his wicked way of life. This is how it came about.

(4) Theodora the empress hated him more than anyone. And John, though he had given offence to her by his misdeeds, far from resolving to

---

[211] Sources differ as to the number of casualties: some put the losses as high as 80,000.

[212] The executions took place on Monday 19 January.

[213] Already at the start of 533 Anastasius' nephew Probus and others were recalled from exile. See *PLRE* 2, Probus 8.

[214] In October 532 John is attested back in office; Tribonian was appointed *magister officiorum* in 533 then resumed his former post in 535.

[215] He probably died of the plague in 542.

flatter her and win her over by favours, openly plotted against her, slandering her to the emperor without a blush for her high rank or any thought for the extraordinary love that the emperor bore her.[216] (5) When the empress heard what he was doing she began to contemplate killing the man, but had no means to achieve this, since the Emperor Justinian thought highly of him. (6) But when John heard of the empress' attitude towards him, he was terrified. (7) Whenever he went to his bedroom to sleep he thought every night that a barbarian would spring on him and kill him. He would remain without sleep, continually peering out of the room and scrutinising all its entrances, even though he had gathered around him many thousands of spearmen and guards, something which had never before been granted to any prefect. (8) But when day dawned he forgot all his fears of things human and divine and was again the bane of all Romans, individually and *en masse*. For the most part, he mixed with magicians and on the strength of impious prophecies deduced that the imperial power would be his; he made an exhibition of himself, walking on air, completely carried away by his hopes for the throne. (9) Yet his wickedness and unnatural way of life did not lessen or abate one jot. (10) He was completely without thought of God – if ever he went into a church to pray and to spend the night in vigil there, he did not observe Christian practices, but put on a rough cloak more appropriate for a priest of the old faith, which they now call 'pagan',[217] and recited all night long sacrilegious words which he had learnt by heart, so that the emperor's will might be even more subject to him and that he himself might be immune from harm at the hands of any person.

(11) In the meantime Belisarius, who had subdued Italy, was summoned by the emperor and arrived in Byzantium with his wife Antonina in order to prepare an expedition against Persia.[218] (12) He was naturally greatly honoured and esteemed by all; only John disliked him and plotted against him, for the simple reason that, whereas Belisarius enjoyed outstanding popularity, he drew upon himself universal opprobrium. With the hopes of the Romans upon him, Belisarius set off against the Persians, leaving his wife behind in Byzantium. (13) And Belisarius' wife Antonina, who was better able than anyone to conceive the inconceivable, devised this way of doing a good turn to the empress.

---

[216] Procopius offers a similar account of their poor relations at *Anecd.* 17.38, where he adds that he almost succeeded in provoking a rift between emperor and empress.

[217] Literally 'Hellenic', cf. 1.20.1. Procopius' allegations of paganism are not generally believed.

[218] Belisarius returned from Italy in summer 540 and was despatched to the East in the following year, as described at 2.14.8–13. On Antonina see *PLRE* 3, Antonina 1, *ODLA*, Antonina.

John had a daughter called Euphemia, well known for her sobriety, but very young and therefore all too easily led; her father loved her dearly, for she was his only child. (14) This girl Antonina coaxed for many days and managed to win over completely as a friend, sharing her secrets with her. (15) On one occasion, when only Euphemia was with her in her room, she pretended to lament her present lot, saying that although Belisarius had increased the extent of the Roman empire, had captured two kings and brought back such a quantity of wealth to Byzantium, Justinian was ungrateful to him. She continued to rail about the injustice of the state generally. (16) Euphemia was overjoyed at these words (for she too disliked the present government because of her fear of the empress) and said: 'But my dear friend, you are yourselves responsible, for you will not use the power that is open to you.' (17) But Antonina replied: 'No, my daughter, for we cannot stir up revolution in the army unless some of those here at home support us in the attempt. If only your father were willing, we could easily attempt it and accomplish whatever God wills.' (18) When Euphemia heard this, she promised eagerly that it should be done and at once went and told her father of this. (19) He was delighted with the news (for he imagined that this business was offering him a path to the fulfilment of the prophecies and to the throne) and at once agreed, without any hesitation, telling his daughter to ensure that he could meet Antonina on the following day and give proof of his loyalty. (20) When Antonina heard of John's attitude, she wanted to divert the man as far as possible from suspicion of the truth, and she said that it was not now convenient for her to meet him in case any suspicion should arise and put a stop to the plan, but that she was just about to join Belisarius in the East. (21) So when she had left Byzantium and reached the suburb called Rufinianae, which belonged to Belisarius, John should come there to meet her and see her off, and there they would discuss the whole affair and exchange pledges of loyalty.[219] This message seemed sensible to John, and a day was appointed for the meeting. (22) The empress heard the whole story from Antonina and praised her plan, and by her encouragement increased her enthusiasm for it still further.

(23) When the appointed day came, Antonina said goodbye to the empress and left the city, soon coming to Rufinianae, since she would start her journey to the East on the following day; John, too, came there by night, ready to carry out their agreement (fig. 23). (24) But the

137

138

---

[219] Rufinianae is on the Asiatic shore of the Bosporus, just to the south-east of Chalcedon. See *ODLA*, Rufinianae. Proc. *Anecd.* 2.16 adds that Antonina also bound herself by oaths.

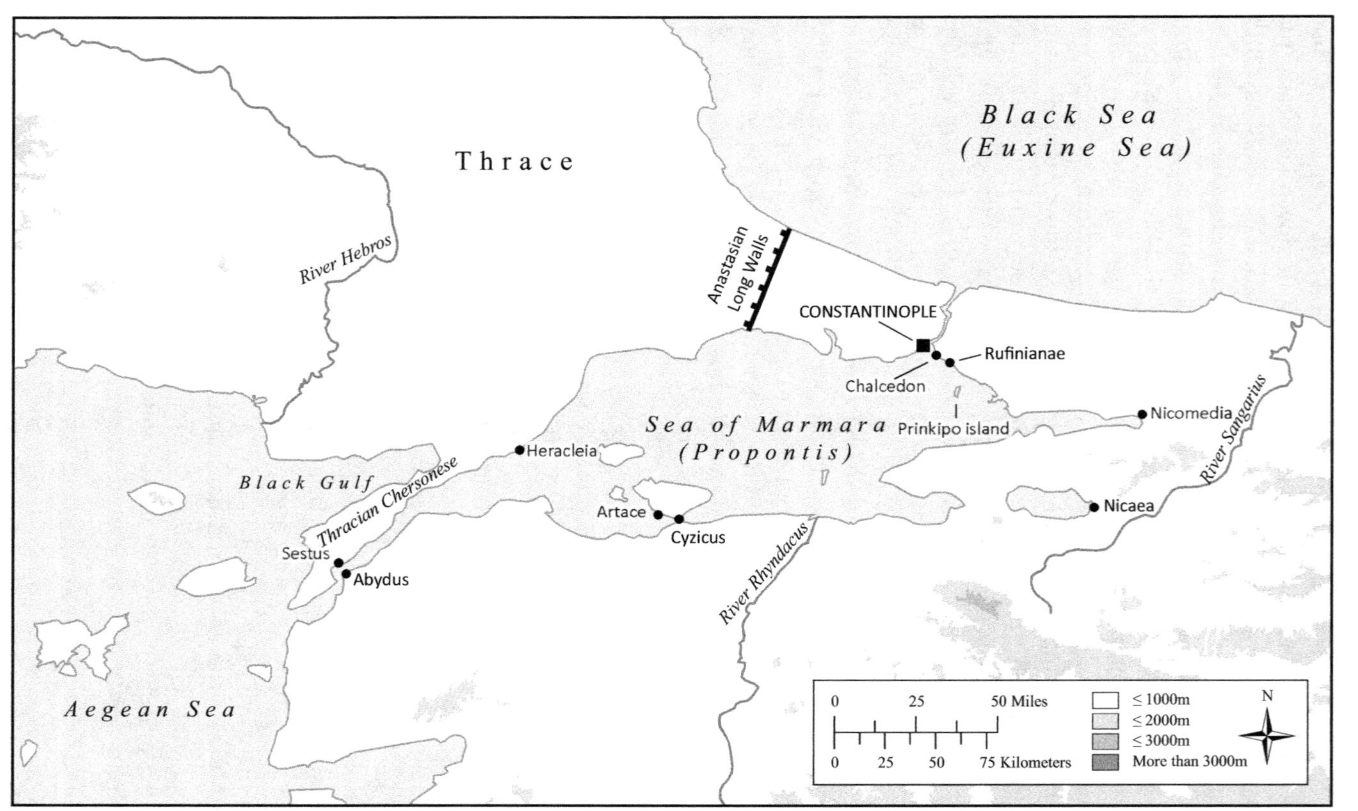

Figure 23   Constantinople and its Environs

empress accused John to her husband of making an attempt at usurpation. She sent the eunuch Narses and Marcellus, the commander of the palace guard, to Rufinianae with a large number of soldiers to find out what was going on, and if they found John attempting rebellion, they were to kill him on the spot and then come back.[220] (25) They set out on this mission. They say that when the emperor heard of this, he sent one of John's friends to him to tell him not to meet Antonina secretly. (26) But John was fated to come to a bad end, and disregarding the emperor's advice, he met Antonina in the middle of the night, near a stone wall behind which she had posted Narses and Marcellus with their troops so that they could hear what was said. (27) Then John agreed unreservedly to the attack and was binding himself with the most solemn oaths when Narses and Marcellus suddenly attacked him. (28) In the confusion that resulted, John's bodyguards, who were stationed nearby, came to him at once. (29) One of them struck Marcellus with his sword, not knowing who he was, and as a result John was able to escape with them; he reached the city with all speed. (30) If he had had the courage to go at once to the emperor, I do not think that he would have come to any harm from him, but as it was he took refuge in a church and gave the empress the chance to prosecute her plot against him at her leisure.

(31) So then, after being a prefect, he became a private citizen. He left that church and was brought to another, in a suburb of the city of Cyzicus called by the Cyzicenes Artace.[221] There, much against his will, he put on the garb of a priest – not that of a bishop, but the priest they call a 'presbyter'. (32) But he would not perform the office of a priest, so that he might have no hindrance to returning to office, for he would not abandon his hopes. His property was immediately assigned to the public treasury. (33) The emperor allowed him a large share, for he was still inclined to be clement to him. (34) There John was able to live, untroubled by any dangers and in the enjoyment of great wealth – what he had concealed himself and what remained to him by the will of the emperor – to live in luxury without hindrance and to believe, if he reasoned sensibly, that his present circumstances were fortunate. (35) Accordingly, all the Romans simply loathed the man, for he was indeed the wickedest of all demons and yet undeservedly enjoyed a life that was even more fortunate than before. (36) But God, I think, could not endure that John's punish-

---

[220] On Narses see 1.15.31. On Marcellus, *comes excubitorum*, 'count of the excubitors', a palace guard, see *PLRE* 3, Marcellus 3, *ODLA*, Marcellus.

[221] Artace, today's Erdek, lies 7 km from Cyzicus. They lie across the Sea of Marmara from Constantinople.

ment should amount only to this and was preparing vengeance against him on a large scale. This is how it came about.

(37) There was a bishop in Cyzicus called Eusebius, who was very harsh towards all those with whom he came into contact, including John. This man the Cyzicenes accused before the emperor and called to trial. (38) But when they achieved nothing, for Eusebius could get around them through his considerable influence, some young men plotted together and killed him in the forum in Cyzicus. (39) John happened to be greatly at odds with Eusebius and as a result suspicion for the attack fell on him. (40) So men were sent by the senate to discover the truth about this heinous crime. First they threw John into prison and then they stood this man up naked – a man who had been such a powerful prefect, enrolled among the patricians, and who had reached the dignity of the consulship, the greatest honour in the Roman state. He stood like a robber or a common thief, and they flogged his back with many strokes and forced him to tell of his past life.[222] (41) John had not been convicted of Eusebius' murder, yet the justice of God seemed to be exacting on him the vengeance of the world. (42) Then they took away all his property and put him naked on a ship, with one cloak, and that of the coarsest material, bought for a few obols. His escort told him to go and beg for bread or obols from passers-by where the ship anchored. (43) And so, begging everywhere on the way, he was taken to the city of Antinous in Egypt.[223] This is the third year that they have been guarding him there in prison,[224] (44) yet in spite of his misfortunes he has never abandoned hope of the throne and actually resolved to denounce some Alexandrians for owing money to the treasury. So John the Cappadocian was overtaken ten years later by punishment for his political career.

Chapter 26

(1) Then the emperor again appointed Belisarius *magister militum per Orientem* and sent him to Libya and got control of the land, as I shall recount later.[225] (2) When the news reached Khusro and the Persians, they were very aggrieved and already regretted having made peace with

---

[222] Mal. 18.89 provides further details of the proceedings, including the names of the investigating senators.

[223] The city of Antinous is also known as Antinoöpolis, named after the Emperor Hadrian's lover, cf. *ODLA*, Antinoopolis.

[224] John probably spent about three years in Artace before the trial (541–4), which would mean that Procopius wrote this passage in 546/7.

[225] In 533. Procopius narrates the reconquest of North Africa from the Vandals in the *Vandalic Wars*.

Rome, since they realised that Rome's power was growing. (3) Khusro sent envoys to Byzantium, declaring that he shared in the Emperor Justinian's rejoicing and jokingly asking for a part of the spoils of Libya, on the grounds that he could never have conquered the Vandals if the Persians had not made a treaty with him. (4) Then Justinian gave Khusro a gift of money and not long afterwards sent back the ambassadors.[226]

(5) But in the city of Dara the following event happened. There was a certain John stationed there among the regular infantry.[227] This man, with the support of a few of the soldiers, not all of them, got control of the city, aiming at seizing power for himself. (6) He sat in the palace as if in an acropolis, strengthening his tyranny every day. (7) Had it not been that the Persians were observing a peace treaty with the Romans at that time, Rome would have suffered irreparable harm. But as it was, the agreement was already in existence, as I have related, and prevented it. (8) On the fourth day of the tyranny the soldiers agreed among themselves and on the advice of Mamas the priest of the city[228] and Anastasius, a respected citizen, they went up to the palace at full noon, each man hiding a sword under his cloak. (9) First they found a few guards at the door of the courtyard and killed them at once. Then they went into the hall and laid hands on the usurper. But some say that the soldiers were not the first to do this: while they were still hesitating in the courtyard and shrinking from the danger, a sausage-seller who was with them rushed in with his cleaver, came up to John and struck him, taking him by surprise. (10) And John, not fatally wounded, fled in panic, and fell suddenly into the hands of these soldiers. (11) So they laid hands on the man and at once set fire to the palace and burnt it down, so that the revolutionaries should have no further hope from that direction, and they put him in chains and carried him off to prison. (12) And there someone, fearing that the soldiers might let the tyrant survive and bring trouble to the city a second time, killed John and in this way put an end to the disturbance. This then was the end of this usurpation.

---

[226] Ps.-Zach. 9.17c confirms the presence of Persians at Belisarius' triumph in Constantinople in 534.

[227] Marc. *com. addit.* (the continuation of Marc. *com.*) a.537 calls him John Cottistis, cf. *PLRE* 3, Ioannes Cottistis 24 and Ps.-Zach. 10.1c. See *REF*, 101.

[228] In other words, the bishop.

Book II

Chapter 1

(1) Not long afterwards Khusro, learning that Belisarius had begun to take over Italy for the Emperor Justinian, could no longer control his thoughts, but wanted to think up an excuse so that he could break the treaty for a fair-seeming reason.[229] (2) He consulted al-Mundhir about these matters and bade him furnish him with grounds for a war. (3) He in turn accused al-Harith of using force against him over a boundary issue and entered into hostilities with him despite the peace; he also began to invade Roman territory on this pretext.[230] (4) He claimed that he himself was not violating the treaty between the Persians and the Romans because neither side had written him into it. (5) And this was indeed the case, for there was absolutely no mention of the Saracens in the treaties because they were subsumed under the name of the Persians and Romans. (6) This land, which was then the subject of the dispute between the Saracens of both sides, is called Strata and lies to the south of the city of Palmyra.[231] It yields neither tree nor any useful cereal crop, since it is scorched exceedingly by the sun, but it has long been given over to flocks of sheep for grazing. (7) Al-Harith therefore insisted that the territory belonged to the Romans, adducing as evidence the name applied to it by all for a long time – for a paved road is called in the Latin language *strata* – and he cited the testimony of men of old. (8) Al-Mundhir for his part saw absolutely no reason to dispute the name, but claimed rather that the owners of the flocks that grazed there had long paid him rent. (9) Justinian accordingly confided the resolution of

148

149

---

[229] Procopius refers to the late 530s: the Persian attack came in spring 540.

[230] Eastern sources also connect rivalries between al-Harith and al-Mundhir to the renewal of hostilities. See Tabari, 252–3, with *REF*, 102–3, *RPLA*, 171, *AEBI*, 243–4.

[231] This road, stretching from Sura (on the Euphrates) in the north to Damascus in the south, via Palmyra, is often referred to as the Strata Diocletiana because some parts of it at least were built under Diocletian. See *ODLA*, Strata Diocletiana.

the dispute to Strategius, a patrician who ran the imperial treasury, an intelligent and well born man, and to Summus, who had commanded the soldiers in Palestine.[232] (10) Now Summus was the brother of Julian, who a little earlier had been on an embassy to the Ethiopians and Homerites.[233] (11) Of the two, Summus held that the Romans should not relinquish the territory, but Strategius begged the emperor not to hand the Persians, who were spoiling for a fight, pretexts for war because of a small and utterly worthless piece of land, which was completely infertile and barren. The Emperor Justinian therefore considered these matters, while much time was spent in settling this issue.

(12) Khusro, the king of the Persians, asserted that the treaty had been broken by Justinian: the emperor had shown numerous signs of treachery towards his family recently, in particular by attempting to foster relations with al-Mundhir during peacetime. (13) For Summus had indeed recently come to him, supposedly to settle matters, but, according to Khusro, he had deceived him with offers of great sums of money if he should come over to the Romans. He also provided a letter in which the Emperor Justinian wrote to al-Mundhir about these matters. (14) He further insisted that Justinian had written a letter to certain Huns, urging them to invade Persian territory and to inflict damage as widely as possible on the villages there. He stated that the Huns themselves, who had come to see him, had handed the letter over to him.[234] (15) With such accusations against the Romans Khusro was intending to break the peace treaty. Whether he was actually telling the truth, however, I am unable to say.

Chapter 2

(1) Meanwhile Vitigis, the leader of the Goths, already beaten in war, despatched two ambassadors to Khusro to urge him to campaign against the Romans.[235] So that his plans might not immediately come to nothing, should the envoys be discovered, those whom he sent were not Goths, but Ligurian priests, induced to this business by generous sums of

---

[232] Strategius was the son of Apion (mentioned at 1.8.5) and *comes sacrarum largitionum*. See *PLRE* 3, Strategius 9.

[233] See *PLRE* 2, Summus: he had been *dux* of Palestine. On his brother Julian see 1.20.9.

[234] See further Proc. *Anecd.* 11.12, where he adds that they were Persian allies and is more explicitly critical of Justinian. They may well have been Sabir Huns. Khusro raises the allegation again at 2.10.16.

[235] The embassy of Vitigis (Witigis) was sent in 538 or 539 as Gothic fortunes in Italy declined. Procopius describes the embassy in similar terms at *Wars* 6.22.17–20. On the king see *PLRE*, Vitigis, *ODLA*, Vitigis.

money. (2) The one of the two who seemed more distinguished took on the appearance and title of a bishop, although he had not earned them, and led the embassy, while the other followed him as his servant. (3) *En route* through the villages of Thrace they recruited a local man to be an interpreter for the Greek and Syriac languages for them and, escaping the notice of the Romans, they reached Persian territory. Since peace then prevailed, they were not strictly guarding the region. (4) Coming before Khusro, the envoys spoke as follows:[236]

'It is generally the case, O King, that all ambassadors undertake their embassy for their own benefit, but Vitigis, the king of the Goths and the Italians, has sent us to speak on behalf of your own kingdom. Consider him now to be present with you and speaking these words. (5) If someone were to summarise the situation, O King, by saying that you had abandoned your own kingdom and all men to Justinian, he would be right.[237] (6) Since he is by nature an innovator and enamoured of things that certainly do not belong to him, and incapable of abiding by established norms, he has formed the desire to seize the whole world and is eager to gain control of every kingdom. (7) Consequently, since he was not strong enough alone to attack the Persians nor able to campaign against others if the Persians opposed him, he decided to trick you with a smokescreen of peace and to enlist by force other great powers against your kingdom. (8) He has thus already destroyed the kingdom of the Vandals and subdued the Moors while the Goths stood aside for him in the name of friendship, then he came against us bringing to bear tremendous resources and manpower. (9) It is obvious that if he manages to eliminate the Goths completely, he will march against the Persians with us and those already enslaved, giving no thought to the name of friendship nor blushing at any of his oaths. (10) So while you still have a hope of safety, do us no further wrong and do not suffer any yourself. Instead, see in our misfortunes what will imminently happen to the Persians and bear in mind that the Romans can never be well disposed towards your kingdom: once they have grown in power they will not hesitate to display their hostility to the Persians. (11) Therefore take this opportunity in good time, so that you will not seek for it once the time has passed. For once the critical moment has gone, it is not naturally inclined to return. It is better to be safe through acting in advance than to miss the opportune moment and to suffer the most shameful fate at the hands of one's enemies.'

---

[236] *RPLA*, 106–7, offers some comments on the speech.
[237] An echo of the Corinthians' speech to the Spartans at Thuc. 1.70.9.

(12) When Khusro heard these words, he thought that Vitigis offered good advice and he was still keener to break the treaty. Gripped by envy of the Emperor Justinian, he completely failed to take into account the fact that the speech had been made by men completely hostile to the Emperor Justinian. (13) Instead, he willingly allowed himself to be persuaded to do what he wanted. He behaved likewise in regard to the speeches of the Armenians and Lazi, which will be related by me very shortly.[238] (14) Yet the sort of accusations brought against Justinian were rather the sort of things that would more reasonably be the subject of panegyrics for a noble emperor, in that he was eager to make his own empire greater and much more glorious. (15) For someone could bring the same accusations against Cyrus, the king of the Persians, or Alexander the Macedonian. But justice is not accustomed to live with envy. For these reasons Khusro was intending to break the treaty.

Chapter 3

(1) In the meantime something else of the following type occurred. The Symeon who handed over Pharangium to the Romans persuaded Justinian, while war was still raging, to bestow on him certain Armenian villages.[239] (2) Having become the master of the villages he was killed in a plot by their former owners. (3) In the wake of the crime, the perpetrators of the assassination fled to Persian territory. They were two brothers, sons of Peroz. When the emperor heard of this, he handed over the villages to Amazaspes, the nephew of Symeon, and appointed him as ruler for the Armenians.[240] (4) Over the course of time one of his relatives, Acacius by name, brought accusations against this Amazaspes to the Emperor Justinian, claiming that he was mistreating the Armenians and wanted to hand over Theodosiopolis and other fortresses to the Persians. (5) Acacius, having made these assertions, slew Amazaspes by treachery with the emperor's approval and then received himself the rulership of Armenia by gift of the emperor.[241] (6) Being naturally wicked, he displayed his character whenever he had the chance. Thus he became the cruellest of all men towards his subjects. (7) He plundered their wealth

---

[238] At 2.3.32–53 and 2.15.14–30.

[239] See 1.15.27–30 on Symeon's defection (in 530).

[240] Amazaspes was probably governor of Armenia Interior before Justinian's reorganisation of the government of the Armenian provinces in 536, on which see *REF*, 100. See *PLRE* 3, Amazaspes.

[241] *NovJ.* 31.1 (of 536) confirms Acacius' role as governor; his rank was then raised as he became governor of the newly created province of Armenia I. See *PLRE* 3, Acacius 1.

without justification and levied an unprecedented charge of four *cente-naria*. But the Armenians, who could no longer stand him, made common cause and killed Acacius, then sought refuge in Pharangium.

(8) The emperor therefore despatched Sittas against them from Byzantium, for he had been spending his time there since the Romans had concluded their treaty with the Persians. (9) When he came to Armenia he at first acted with circumspection as regards the conflict, striving rather to soothe the inhabitants and to bring them back to their previous temper, promising to persuade the emperor to annul the new levy for them. (10) But when the emperor, led on by the accusations of Adolius, the son of Acacius, reproached him for the delay and rebuked him, Sittas then at last prepared for war. (11) Accordingly, he first sought to rally and recruit some of the Armenians by promises of many advantages, so that the subjugation of the remainder might be easier and less troublesome. (12) And the clan known as the Aspetiani,[242] a large and numerous population, wished to come over to him. (13) They made contact with Sittas and asked him to give them written pledges that, should they abandon their compatriots and join the Roman ranks, they would remain immune from all burdens, retaining their own property. (14) He gladly wrote to them and gave the pledges they sought in a brief document, and, having sealed the letter, he despatched it to them. (15) Emboldened by the prospect of a bloodless victory in the war with their aid, he went forth with his entire force to the village of Oenochalakon,[243] where the Armenians had encamped. (16) But by some chance those bearing the document took another route and did not manage to reach the Aspetiani. (17) Moreover, a section of the Roman army came upon some of them, and, unaware of the terms of the agreement, treated them as enemies. (18) Sittas himself, having captured some of their women and children in a cave somewhere, killed them, either unaware of what had happened or in anger at the Aspetiani because they had not come over to him as had been agreed.

(19) Already angry, they drew themselves up for battle with all the rest. Now because both sides were situated in rough terrain that was both dangerous and mountainous, they did not fight just in one place, but scattered over the foothills and ravines. Thus it happened that a few of the Armenians and Sittas, with a handful of his followers, came very close to one another, with only a gully between them. Both sides were composed

155

156

---

[242] The Aspetiani may be the Bagratuni family. See *ODLA*, Bagratuni clan.
[243] Location unknown. The later Avnik, 60 km east of Theodosiopolis, has been proposed, but is unlikely.

of cavalrymen. (20) Sittas therefore, with a few followers, crossed the
gully and charged against his opponents. The Armenians withdrew, then
stood their ground, while Sittas stopped his pursuit and remained there.
(21) Suddenly someone in the Roman army, a Herul by birth, who had
set off in pursuit of the enemy, returned at a great pace from his foray to
Sittas and his entourage. Sittas happened to have fixed his spear in the
ground, which the horse of the Herul fell upon in a great rush and broke.
(22) This greatly vexed the general, and one of the Armenians, witnessing
this, recognised Sittas and insisted to all the others that it was him. For it
happened that there was no helmet on the general's head. Hence the
enemy realised that he had come here with just a few men. (23) So when
he heard the Armenian say this, and since, as has been said, his spear lay
broken on the ground, Sittas drew his sword and immediately tried to
cross the ravine. (24) The enemy charged on him with great enthusiasm
and someone caught up with him in the ravine, striking obliquely the top
of his head with his sword. The whole crown of his head was shorn off,
but the iron blade did not touch the bone. (25) Sittas continued to charge
forward even more than before, but Artabanes the Arsacid, son of John,
fell upon him from behind and killed him with a blow from his spear.[244]
(26) And thus Sittas vanished from the world of men for no reason in a
manner unworthy of his valour and his constant deeds against the enemy,
a man remarkably handsome in his physique and competent at warfare,
an excellent general inferior to none of his contemporaries. (27) Some say
that Sittas was not killed by Artabanes, but that Solomon, a singularly
undistinguished man among the Armenians, slew him.

(28) Following Sittas' death, the emperor ordered Buzes to proceed
against the Armenians. Once he arrived nearby, he sent a message to
them promising to reconcile all the Armenians with the emperor and
requesting some of their notables to come to him for discussions on these
matters. (29) Most of the Armenians were incapable of believing Buzes
and refused to accept his proposals. But there was a certain man of the
Arsacid family, John by name, the father of Artabanes, who was particularly friendly with him and had confidence in Buzes since he was his
friend. Together with his son-in-law Bassaces and a few others he came to
him. Now having arrived and made camp in the place where they were
due to meet Buzes on the next day, they realised that they had come to be
encircled by the Roman army. (30) Bassaces, the son-in-law, therefore

---

[244] He later defected to the Romans and fought in the West. See *PLRE* 3, Artabanes 2, *ODLA*,
Artabanes.

urgently besought John to resort to flight. But since he was unable to persuade him, he left him there alone and with all the remainder evaded the Romans and hastened back again along the same road. (31) Buzes, finding John alone, killed him. From this point the Armenians, having no hope of a future deal with the Romans and being unable to overcome the emperor in war, came before the Persian king with Bassaces, an energetic man, as their leader. (32) The leading figures among them then came before Khusro and spoke as follows:

'Many of us, O Master, are descendants of that Arsaces who was no stranger to the kingdom of Parthia, when the Persian state was subject to the Parthians, and who was a distinguished king inferior to none of his contemporaries.[245] (33) We have now all come to you having become slaves and fugitives – not willingly, however, but under severe duress, ostensibly caused by the Roman empire, but in truth as a result of your decision, O King, (34) if indeed the one who gives the power to those who want to commit injustice rightly also bears the blame for those deeds. Our account will go back to events a little earlier so that you will be able to follow all that has taken place.

(35) Arsaces, the last king among our ancestors, resigned his throne in favour of the Roman Emperor Theodosius.[246] This he did willingly on the condition that all the members of his family would henceforth always live as they chose, never subject to any taxes. (36) We kept the agreement until you made this famous treaty, which one would not be wrong to call a general disaster. (37) For from that point, O King, your friend in theory, but in fact your foe, careless of friends and enemies alike, has brought chaos and confusion to all mankind. (38) You will know this soon enough, as soon as he has been able to subjugate completely the peoples of the West. For what has he not done that was up until now forbidden? What well established custom has he not shaken? (39) Has he not imposed on us an unprecedented levy, has he not enslaved our hitherto independent neighbours, the Tzani, and has he not placed a Roman governor in charge of the king of the wretched Lazi?[247] This last is an action neither fitting

159

---

[245] The rulers of the Parthian empire, which preceded the Sasanian Persian empire, came from the Arsacid dynasty; a branch of the dynasty continued to rule Armenia even after the fall of the Parthians in the 220s. See *ODLA*, Arshakuni dynasty.

[246] The Romans took over western Armenia in 387 following a partition with Persia. This was during the reign of Theodosius I, but it is doubtful whether there were any conditions; three years later, when King Arsaces III died, the Romans replaced him with a *comes* (count). Procopius describes the partition also at *Aed.* 3.1.4–5, where he places it in the reign of Theodosius II and alludes to this passage. See *ODLA*, Armenia, partitions of.

[247] Cf. 1.15.20–5 on the Tzani, 2.15.21 on the Lazi.

160 with the nature of the circumstances nor easy to explain rationally. (40) Did he not send generals to the people of Bosporus, the subjects of the Huns, and bring over to himself a city that did not belong to him?[248] Did he not conclude an alliance with the rulers of the Ethiopians, about whom the Romans had hitherto known absolutely nothing? (41) But he has also taken over the Homerites and the Red Sea and added the Palm Grove to the Roman empire.[249] (42) We leave aside here the sufferings of the Libyans and Italians.[250] The entire earth cannot contain the man: it is a trifle for him to seize control of all of humanity at a stroke. (43) He is scanning the heavens and investigating the furthest recesses beyond the ocean, wishing to subjugate another world to himself.

(44) Why then, O King, do you delay? Why do you respect this ill-starred peace? Of course, so that he can make you his final meal after all the others? (45) If you want to learn what sort of man Justinian would be to those that surrender to him, there is an example close to you among our very selves and the unfortunate Lazi. (46) But if you want to know how he is in the habit of treating those unfamiliar with him and who have committed no injustice, consider the Vandals, the Goths and the Moors. (47) We have not yet even reached the main point. Did he not attempt, O most powerful King, during peacetime, to deceive your slave al-Mundhir and to make him revolt from your rule? Did he not recently seek to recruit Huns that had been unknown to him up until then to **161** damage your interests? Yet in all history there has been no conduct more unacceptable than this. (48) For, I think, now that he has realised that the subjugation of the western peoples has all but come to pass, he is already trying to engage you in the East, since the Persian state alone has been left for him as a rival. (49) Hence from his point of view the peace has already been broken by you, while he himself has set an end for the Endless Peace. (50) For it is not those who first take up arms that break a peace, but rather those who are caught plotting against their neighbours in peacetime. (51) The grounds for complaint are furnished by the one who has made the attempt, even if success proves elusive. The direction the war will take is surely clear to all, for it is not those that provide the grounds for war, but rather those that defend themselves against those who provide the grounds, who generally vanquish their foes. (52) And in truth the trial of strength for us will not be on equal terms, for it happens

---

[248] See I.12.6–8.

[249] A maximalist interpretation of what is reported at I.19–20.

[250] In other words, Justinian's wars in North Africa and Italy, described in the *Vandalic* and *Gothic Wars*.

that most of the Roman soldiers are in the most distant parts of the world; of their two best generals one, Sittas, we killed before coming here, while Justinian will never cast eyes on Belisarius again. For he is staying in the West, ignoring the emperor and controlling Italy himself.[251] (53) Consequently, as you go forth against the enemy, no one at all will come to meet you, while you will have us gladly leading your army, as is natural, with our extensive knowledge of the regions.'

(54) When Khusro heard this, he was delighted and summoned the members of the Persian nobility and revealed to all of them what Vitigis had written and what the Armenians had said, seeking advice as to what should be done. (55) Many views were then expressed on either side, but in the end it was decided that they must go to war with the Romans at the start of the spring (56), for it was now autumn in the thirteenth year of the reign of the Emperor Justinian.[252] (57) But the Romans had no suspicions of this, and they did not think that the Persians would break the so-called Endless Peace, even though they had heard that Khusro blamed their emperor for his successes in the West, and brought against him the charges I have just mentioned.

Chapter 4

(1) And then the comet appeared, at first about as long as a tall man, but later even bigger. Its end was to the West, its beginning to the East, and it followed behind the sun itself.[253] (2) The sun was in Capricorn while the comet was in Sagittarius. Some called it 'the swordfish', because it was long and very sharp at its tip, others 'bearded', and it was visible for more than forty days. (3) Experts disagreed over it and gave different interpretations of the meaning of this star. But I simply record what happened and give every man the chance of judging by the results, as he sees fit.

(4) At once a large Hunnic army crossed the river Danube and invaded the whole of Europe, something that had frequently happened before, but had never brought to mankind misfortunes in such numbers or of such magnitude (fig. 24).[254] For these barbarians plundered everything in

[251] The Armenians are supposedly addressing Khusro before autumn 539; it was not until 540 that Belisarius overrode Justinian's orders and captured Ravenna. The accusation is premature but constitutes an impressive final flourish to the address.

[252] I.e. autumn 539.

[253] The comet is reported not only in other Greek sources, but also in Syriac and Chinese accounts. It appeared in November 539 and remained visible until January 540. Such phenomena were generally regarded as significant, like the comet that preceded Napoleon's invasion of Russia in 1812.

[254] The raid took place in December 539 or January 540. The identity of the raiders is uncertain.

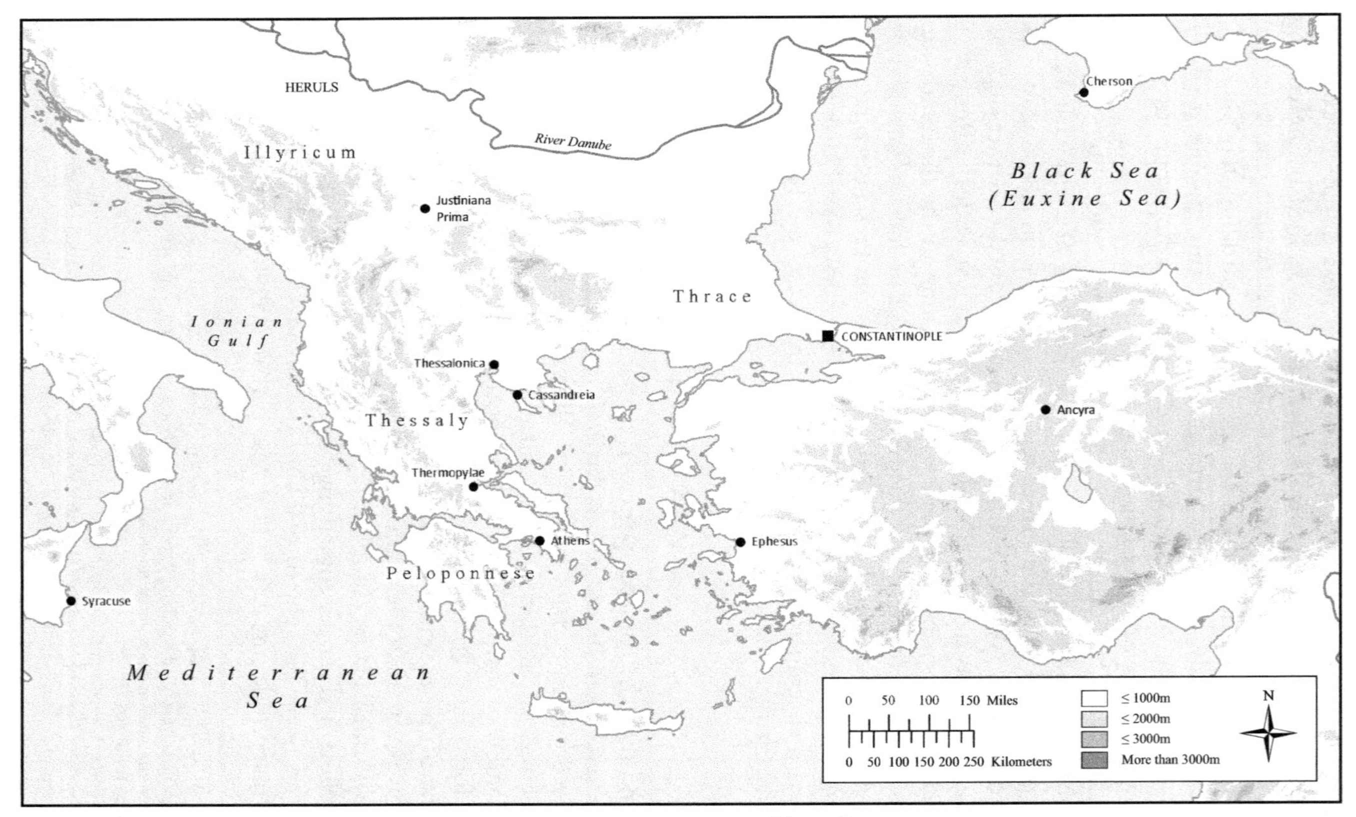

Figure 24   Hunnic Invasions of the Balkans

turn from the Ionian Gulf as far as the suburbs of Byzantium. (5) They took thirty-two fortresses in Illyria, and reduced by force the city of Cassandreia (which the ancients called Potidaea), although, as far as we know, they had never assaulted walls before.[255] (6) Seizing its wealth and carrying off one hundred and twenty thousand prisoners, they all retired home with no resistance being offered.[256] (7) Later they came there often and inflicted unbearable sufferings on the Romans.[257] (8) They also attacked the wall of the Chersonese, forcing the defenders from the wall and ascending the circuit walls through the surf of the sea by the so-called Black Gulf; by this means they came within the Long Walls and fell upon the Romans in the Chersonese, taking them by surprise, killing many, and enslaving nearly all of them.[258] (9) A few actually crossed the strait between Sestus and Abydus, plundered the places on the Asian side, returned to the Chersonese and went home with the rest of the army and all the booty. (10) In another invasion they plundered Illyria and Thessaly and then tried to assault the fortifications at Thermopylae. Since the guards on the walls defended themselves most valiantly, they looked for ways around it and unexpectedly found the path which leads up to the mountain there,[259] (11) and in this way destroyed nearly all of Greece except for the Peloponnese before they went home. (12) But not long afterwards, the Persians broke the truce and did to the Romans in the East what I am about to relate.

(13) When Belisarius had unseated Vitigis, the king of the Goths and Italians, he brought him alive to Byzantium.[260] I will go on to tell how the Persian army invaded Roman territory.

(14) When the Emperor Justinian heard that Khusro was going to make war, he wanted to give him some advice and dissuade him from the undertaking. (15) A man happened to be in Byzantium who had come from the city of Dara, Anastasius by name, who had a reputation for

164

165

---

[255] The text has been emended here: in Haury's edition the 'as far as we know' applies to the city being previously known as Potidaea, which is intrinsically unlikely because the identification was well known. The Ionian Gulf refers to the Adriatic Sea.

[256] The figure is doubtless inflated for effect, cf. *Anecd.* 18 and *Wars* 7.14.6.

[257] Procopius moves on to subsequent raids. The ones mentioned here are likely to have occurred in 544.

[258] The Thracian Chersonese is the Gallipoli peninsula. See *ODLA*, Chersonese. The Black Gulf is today the Gulf of Saros, to the west of the Chersonese. See fig. 23, p. 112.

[259] Echoes of Hdt. 8.216–17: the Persian troops of Xerxes had also been able to turn the pass. See *ODLA*, s.v. walls, defensive, Byzantine, Thermopylae wall; Justinian later strengthened the defences of the pass, Proc. *Aed.* 4.2.2–15.

[260] Cf. *Wars* 7.1.1–2, describing how Belisarius brought the Gothic king with him to Constantinople in 540.

intelligence – the same man as had recently put down the tyranny which had been set up in Dara.[261] (16) So Justinian sent this Anastasius to Khusro with a letter which read as follows: (17) 'Wise men, and men who pay sufficient respect to God, try their hardest to nip off the causes of war as they arise, especially against their particular friends. Unwise men, on the other hand, and those who most lightly bring on themselves the anger of God, manufacture pretexts for fighting and confusion when none exists. (18) Once they have broken the peace treaty, going to war is nothing, since the nature of things makes the wickedest of actions easy for the most dishonourable of men. (19) But when they have made war according to their intention, I do not think it is easy for men to return to peace. (20) Yet you now complain about my letters, which were not written with any ulterior motive, and you have been anxious to interpret them wilfully, not according to our intention in writing them, but as seems most likely to benefit you in your desire to carry out your plans under some covering pretext.

166   (21) But we can show that your own al-Mundhir recently overran our lands during an official peace and did us irreparable harm by capturing cities, seizing property, slaughtering and enslaving men in vast numbers; for this you should apologise, not accuse us. (22) Actions – not intentions – expose to people nearby the crimes of those who have done wrong. Under these circumstances we have decided even so to hold to the peace; yet we hear that you mean to make war on Rome and are fabricating motives that have nothing to do with us. (23) This was only to be expected, for while those who want to preserve the status quo shrug off accusations against their friends even when they are most pressing, those who take no pleasure in the bond of friendship even seek to produce pretexts that have no foundation. (24) But this hardly seems fitting for ordinary men, let alone kings. (25) Leave all this to one side; consider the total losses on both sides in the war, and who will justly bear the blame for what will happen. Think of the oaths that you swore and the money you have received. Consider whether, if you later dishonoured them by unjust tricks and sophistries, you would actually be able to get around them. For God is too powerful to be deceived by any man.'[262]

(26) When Khusro had read this, he made no reply for the present, nor did he send Anastasius back, but forced him to remain there.

---

[261] See 1.26.8.
[262] Perhaps an allusion to Galatians 6:7, 'Be not deceived; God is not mocked' (King James Version).

Chapter 5

(1) When the winter was already ending and the thirteenth year of the reign of the Emperor Justinian was coming to an end, Khusro, the son of Kavadh, at the beginning of spring invaded Roman territory with a large army and conspicuously violated the so-called Endless Peace (fig. 25).[263] He did not advance through the country between the rivers, but with the Euphrates on his right. (2) On the other side of the river is the furthermost Roman fortress, which is called Circesium, a very secure position, since there the large river Khabur flows into the Euphrates, and this fortress stands on the very angle made by the junction of the two rivers. (3) Another long wall outside the fortress cuts off the land between the rivers and makes the shape of a triangle around Circesium.[264] (4) Accordingly Khusro, not wanting to attempt to take such a strong fortress, and not intending to cross the Euphrates, but to attack Syria and Cilicia, did not delay. He advanced his army, and after a journey of about three days for an active man along the bank of the Euphrates, he came upon the city of Zenobia (fig. 26).[265] Zenobia had built this city years before and naturally gave her name to it. (5) Now Zenobia was the wife of Odenathus, the ruler of the Saracens in those parts, who were allies of Rome from of old. (6) This Odenathus restored to Rome the eastern empire when it had fallen to the Persians, although this happened long ago.[266] (7) At this time, Khusro came near to Zenobia and when he heard that the place was unremarkable and found that the land was uninhabited and without any natural advantages, he was afraid in case the time spent there would be wasted and prove a hindrance to great achievements. He tried to take the place by negotiation, but when he met with no success, he drove on his army with all speed.

(8) After a journey of equal length again he came to the city of Sura, which is on the Euphrates, and stopped very near it.[267] (9) There the horse on which Khusro was sitting happened to neigh and stamp the ground.

167

168

---

[263] Procopius thus dates the invasion to before the end of March 540 (when the thirteenth year of Justinian's reign ended).

[264] Circesium, modern Buseira, lies at the confluence of the Khabur and Euphrates and was reinforced already by Diocletian, then later (probably before 540) by Justinian. See Proc. *Aed.* 2.6.1–11, *ODLA*, Circesium.

[265] Zenobia, modern Halabiyya, has been extensively excavated. Justinian improved its defences, probably before this invasion: see Proc. *Aed.* 2.8.8–25 with *ODLA*, Zenobia. Whether the Palmyrene queen Zenobia (r. 266/7–272) actually founded the city is uncertain.

[266] Odenathus (Odaenathus), the Palmyrene ruler, defended the Roman East in the wake of the defeat of Valerian in 260, inflicting several defeats on the Sasanian King Shapur I. See *RPLA*, 160–3, *ODLA*, Odaenathus.

[267] Sura lies just under 100 km along the Euphrates from Zenobia. See *ODLA*, Sura.

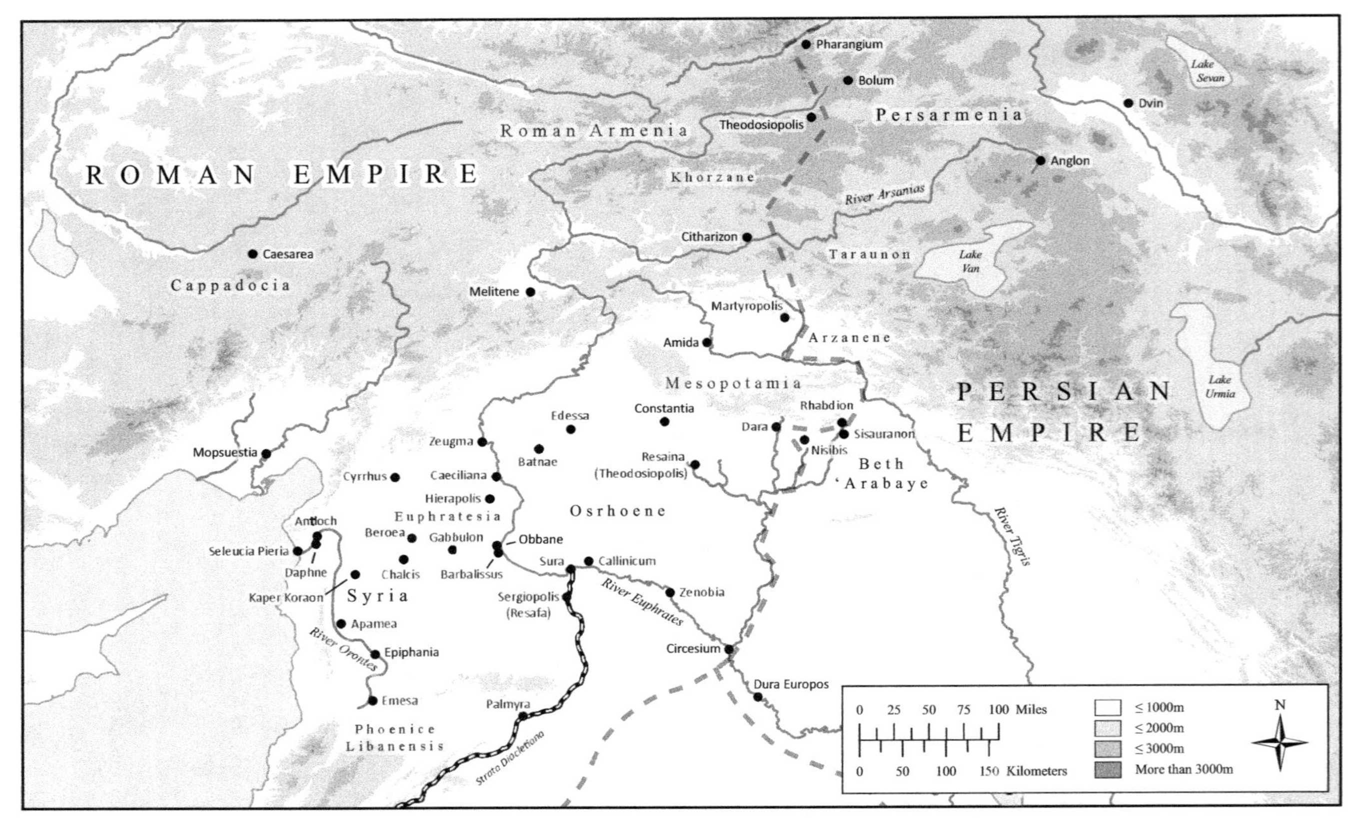

Figure 25　Khusro's Invasions of the Roman East

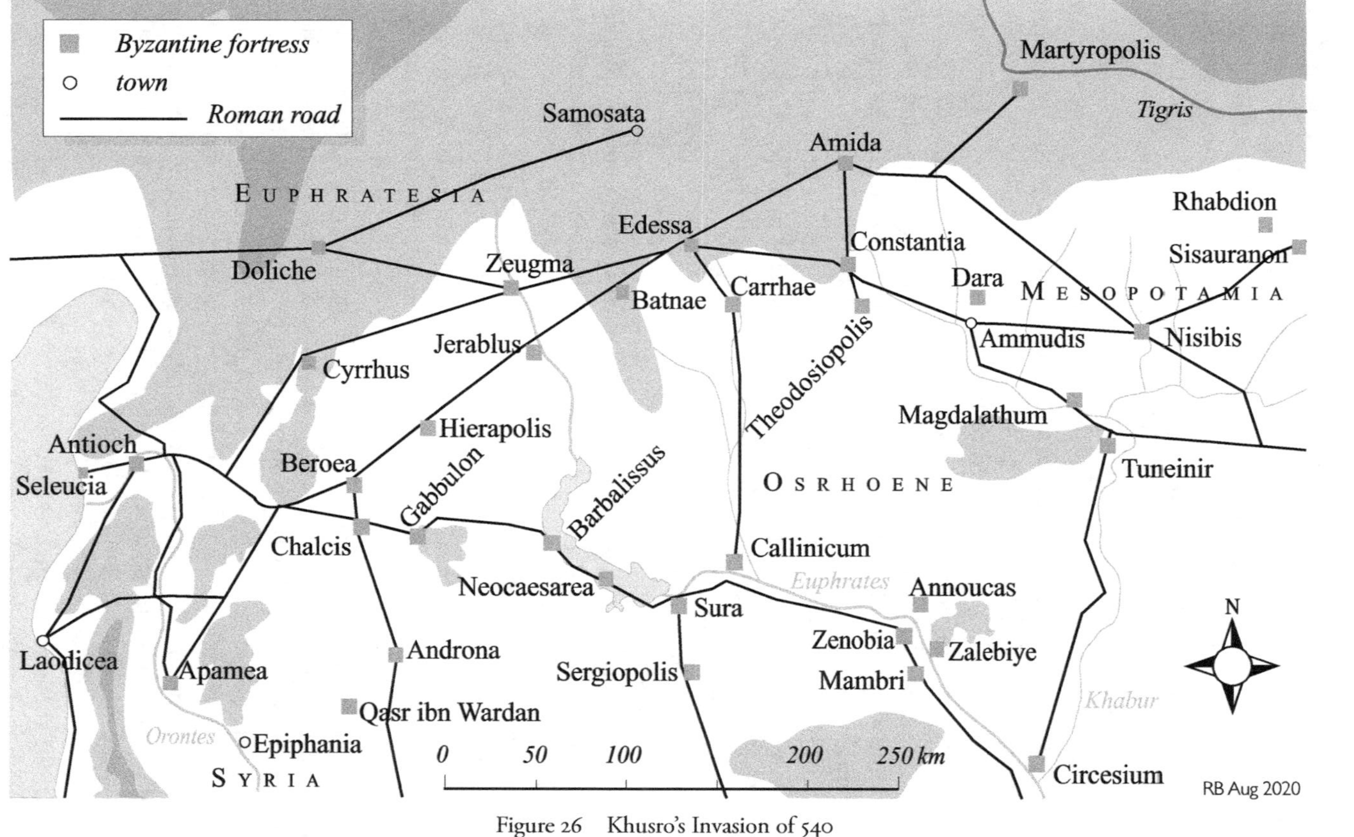

Figure 26   Khusro's Invasion of 540

The magi considered this and announced that the place would be captured. (10) Khusro pitched camp and brought the army up to the outer walls for an assault. (11) There chanced to be a man called Arsaces, an Armenian by birth, in charge of the soldiers there; he posted the soldiers up on the battlements and after fighting from there most valiantly and killing many of the enemy, he was hit by an arrow and killed. (12) Then the Persians retreated to their camp, for it was late in the day, intending to attack the wall again on the following day. But the Romans gave up now that their commander was dead and decided to throw themselves on Khusro's mercy. (13) So on the next day they sent the bishop of the town to plead and to beg for the town to be spared. He took with him some attendants carrying fowl and wine and white loaves, and came to Khusro. Then he threw himself to the ground and, weeping, entreated him to spare the wretched inhabitants and the city that was to the Romans utterly without significance and to the Persians an object of no concern, either in the past or in the future. He promised that the people of Sura would give him a ransom worthy of themselves and of the city in which they lived. (14) But Khusro was angry with the inhabitants of Sura, because it was his first encounter with any Romans, and the people had not received him willingly into the city, but had even dared to raise arms against him and had killed a large number of important Persians. (15) Yet he did not reveal his anger, carefully hiding it by his expression so that he could punish the people of Sura and make himself terrible and invincible to the Romans. In this way he reckoned that all those he came to would yield to him without any trouble. (16) So he raised the bishop up with the greatest friendliness, accepted the gifts, and gave the impression that he would confer at once with the Persian notables about the ransom for the people of Sura and settle their request satisfactorily. (17) He sent off the bishop and his attendants with no suspicion of the plot and sent with him some Persian notables, ostensibly as an escort. (18) He told them secretly to go with him as far as the wall, to talk soothingly to him and raise his spirits with high hopes, so that he and his companions could be seen by the inhabitants to be cheerful and in no fear. (19) When the guards opened the gate and were about to receive them into the city, they were to throw a stone or a piece of wood between the door and the threshold and not allow them to shut it; if anyone tried to shut it, they should try to hold them off for the moment, for the army would follow shortly behind them.

(20) With these instructions to the men Khusro made ready the army and told them to advance at a run to the city when he gave the signal. (21) When they reached the wall, the Persians bade farewell to the bishop

and remained outside, but the people of Sura, seeing that the man was very pleased, and was accompanied with great honour by the enemy, forgot all their problems and opened the whole of the gate, welcoming **171** the bishop and his attendants with applause and congratulations. (22) When they were all inside, the guards pushed the door to close it, but the Persians threw a rock in the way, which they had got ready for the purpose. (23) The guards pushed and struggled still harder, but could not manage to get the door to the threshold. (24) Yet they dared not open it again, since they realised that it was being held by the enemy. Some say that the Persians threw a log, not a stone, into the door. (25) The people of Sura had scarcely realised the plot when Khusro arrived with all his army, and the barbarians succeeded in pushing open the gate, which was soon taken by storm. (26) Khusro, carried away by fury, at once plundered the houses and killed many men, enslaving all the rest, setting fire to the city and razing it to the ground. (27) Then he dismissed Anastasius, telling him to inform the Emperor Justinian where in the world he had left Khusro, the son of Kavadh.

(28) But later, either through kindness or avarice, or else to please a woman whom he took as a prisoner from there, Euphemia by name, whom he had made his wedded wife – he loved her passionately, for she **172** was very beautiful – Khusro decided to do the people of Sura a good turn. (29) He sent a message therefore to Sergiopolis, a city subject to Rome, which is called after the famous saint Sergius and is 126 stades from the captured city, lying to the south of it in the so-called Barbarian Plain, and ordered Candidus, the bishop there, to buy back the prisoners, who were twelve thousand strong, for two *centenaria*.[268] (30) But Candidus openly refused to do it, saying that he did not have the money. Khusro asked him to set down the agreement in a document, promising to pay the money later and thus buy so cheaply such a large number of slaves. (31) Candidus complied and promised that he would give the gold in a year's time, swearing most solemn oaths, and binding himself to this penalty, if he did not give the money at the appointed time, that he would pay double the sum, and that he would no longer be a bishop for having broken his oath. (32) Candidus wrote this down in a document and received all the people of Sura. (33) A few of them survived, but most were unable to withstand the misfortune that had befallen them and perished shortly afterwards. After settling this, Khusro led his army forward.

---

[268] Sergiopolis, modern Resafa, lies some 25 km south of Sura. The city had gained in importance recently, linked to the cult of St Sergius. See *ODLA*, Sergiopolis-Rusafa.

Chapter 6

173 (1) A short time before this it happened that the emperor divided the eastern command into two. He left, at least nominally, the region as far as the river Euphrates to Belisarius, who previously held the whole command, but gave the area from there to the Persian border to Buzes, whom he ordered to look after the whole of the East until Belisarius returned from Italy. (2) And so Buzes with all his army at first remained at Hierapolis. But when he heard what had happened to the people of Sura, he called together the leading citizens of Hierapolis and said:

(3) 'For those who are contending against invaders on an equal basis of strength, it is not unreasonable that they should join battle with the enemy at once. But to those who are by comparison far inferior to their opponents, it will be of more advantage to overcome the enemy by trickery than to take an open stand against them and enter into a danger that they can foresee. (4) You have surely heard how big Khusro's army is. If he wants to take us by a siege, and we fight from the walls, it is likely that our provisions will run out, while the Persians gather all their needs from our land with no opposition. (5) And if the siege is prolonged in this way, I do not think that the circuit wall will be strong enough to **174** resist enemy measures, for it is vulnerable in many places, and thus there will be irreparable harm caused to the Romans. (6) But if we defend the city wall with a part of our army, and the remaining forces occupy the foothills around the city, they can use them as a base from which to overrun both the enemy camp and their foraging parties and to force Khusro to break the siege at once and to make a speedy retreat, for he will not be able either to attack the circuit walls without fear or to find the necessities for such a large army.'[269]

(7) Buzes seemed to be on the right course with this speech, but he did nothing of what was necessary, for he simply chose the best of the Roman army and left. (8) Where on earth he happened to have gone no Roman in Hierapolis nor the enemy army could discover. These things then turned out in this way.

(9) But when the Emperor Justinian heard of the Persian advance, he sent forth his cousin Germanus at once in great confusion with three hundred companions and promised that a large army would shortly follow.[270] (10) When Germanus reached Antioch, he went all around the

---

[269] The logic is sound and reflects the tactics of Sittas and Dorotheus at Satala in 530, cf. 1.15.10–13.

[270] Germanus was Justinian's cousin. See *PLRE* 2, Germanus 4 and *ODLA*, Germanus; he enjoyed a successful military career up to his death in 550. Procopius notes tensions between him and

circuit walls in a circle and found most of them strong (for the river Orontes flows along the part on level ground, rendering it entirely inaccessible to assailants, and the part which is on steeper ground rises up on rocky heights and can hardly be approached by an enemy), but when he came to the peak which the local inhabitants call Orocasias, he found that the wall there was very vulnerable.[271] (11) There is a rock there, which is for the most part quite broad and a little short of the wall in height. (12) He told them therefore either to cut off the rock and dig a deep trench around the wall so that no one could climb from it onto the wall, or to build a larger tower on it and connect its structure with the city wall. (13) But the builders judged that neither of these alternatives should be undertaken. They thought that they could not finish it in such a short time, with the enemy advance so pressing, and that if they began the task and did not complete it they would simply be showing the enemy what point in the wall they should attack. (14) Foiled in this plan, Germanus at first still waited for the army from Byzantium and put his hopes in that. (15) But when after some time no army arrived from the emperor, and none seemed likely to arrive, he grew worried that Khusro might hear that the emperor's cousin was there and consider it more important than anything to capture Antioch and himself, and as a result drop everything else and make straight for it with the entire army. (16) The Antiochenes were of the same opinion, and after a council about it they decided that it would be best to escape their present danger by paying money to Khusro.

(17) So they despatched Megas, the bishop of Beroea, a man of intelligence who happened to be staying with them at that time, to plead with Khusro; he set off and found the Persian army not far from Hierapolis. (18) He came before Khusro and begged him to have pity on men who had done him no harm and were unable to withstand the Persian force. (19) He said it was unseemly above all for a man of royal blood to trample upon and use force against those who retired before him and had no desire to fight him. Not one of the things that he was now doing was a princely or noble act, for without giving the Roman emperor any time to decide whether to strengthen the peace in a way pleasing to both sides or to make preparations for war by agreement in the usual way, he came like this in arms against the Romans, without any consideration, while

Justinian in 548–9 when certain conspirators sought to involve him in a plot against the emperor, *Wars* 7.31–2.

[271] Procopius refers probably to the Parmenius massif north of Mt Silpius where Gunnar Brands has recently identified a rock close to the city walls that corresponds to Procopius' description here.

their own emperor did not yet know what situation they were in. (20)
On hearing this Khusro could not, in his boorishness, control his
conduct by intelligent reasoning, but rather was even more excited in his
intentions than before.[272] (21) He threatened that he would lay waste all
Syria and Cilicia, and, ordering Megas to follow him, he led the army to
Hierapolis. (22) When he reached it and pitched camp, and had seen that
the wall was strong and heard that it had a considerable garrison of
soldiers, he demanded money from the people of Hierapolis, sending to
them the interpreter Paul. (23) This Paul had been reared in Roman territory and went to school in Antioch; he was said to be a Roman by birth.
(24) But the inhabitants were very much afraid for the walls, which
enclosed a large area of land as far as the mountain which rises there, and
besides, they wished to keep their land unplundered. So they agreed to
pay 2000 measures of silver.[273] (25) And Megas kept on pleading with
Khusro for the whole East, until Khusro agreed that he would accept ten
centenaria of gold and leave the entire Roman Empire.

177

Chapter 7

(1) On that day therefore Megas left there and went on his way to
Antioch, and Khusro took the ransom and went to Beroea. (2) Beroea
lies between Antioch and Hierapolis, two days' journey for an active man
from either place.[274] (3) So Megas, because he was with only a few men,
went faster, whereas the Persian army could consistently cover only half
as much ground. (4) On the fourth day he came to Antioch, while the
army came to the suburbs of Beroea. (5) Khusro at once sent Paul and
tried to extort money from the Beroeans – not merely what he had taken
from the people of Hierapolis, but double this amount, for he saw that
their wall was vulnerable in many places. (6) The Beroeans eagerly agreed
to pay it all (for they had no confidence in their walls), but after paying
2000 pounds of silver said that they could not pay the rest. (7) Khusro
pressed them for it, and when night fell, they all fled to the fortress which
is on the acropolis, together with the soldiers who were garrisoned there.
(8) On the following day Khusro sent a party to the city to receive the
money, but when they came near the wall, they found that all the gates
were closed and encountered not a single man. They went back and told

178

---

[272] Despite Procopius' assertions, Khusro had a reputation as a wise and enlightened ruler. See *RPLA*,
    263–5.
[273] The 'measures' are probably pounds, as also at 2.11.24.
[274] Beroea is known today as Halab or Aleppo. See *ODLA*, Aleppo (ancient Beroea).

the king of their experience. (9) He told them to bring ladders up to the **179**
wall and try the ascent, and they acted accordingly. (10) Since no one
opposed them, they got inside the circuit walls, opened the gates at their
leisure, (11) and let into the city Khusro himself and the entire army.
Then the king, already in a great rage, burnt nearly the entire city. He
went up to the acropolis and decided to lay siege to the fortress. (12)
There the Roman soldiers, defending their position bravely, killed some
of the enemy, but Khusro received a great stroke of good fortune from
the foolishness of the besieged, who had not come alone to this fortress,
but had taken refuge with their horses and other animals. By this thrifti-
ness they were put at a disadvantage and came into danger, (13) for there
was only one spring there, and when the horses and mules and other
animals had been mistakenly allowed to drink from it, the water dried
up. This then was the situation of the Beroeans.

(14) When Megas reached Antioch and told them what he had agreed **180**
with Khusro, he could not by any means persuade them to fulfil their
part of the deal. (15) The Emperor Justinian had sent on an embassy to
Khusro John, the son of Rufinus, and Julian, his private secretary; the
Romans call this office *a secretis*, for they traditionally call secrets
secreta.[275] (16) They reached Antioch and stayed there. Julian, one of the
envoys, forbade them outright to give money to the enemy or to sell the
emperor's cities, and he accused the chief priest Ephraem to Germanus of
wanting to surrender the city to Khusro.[276] (17) And so Megas went back
without success. But Ephraem, the bishop of Antioch, was afraid of the
Persian advance and went to Cilicia. (18) Germanus arrived there not
long afterwards with a few men, leaving the majority behind.

(19) Megas quickly came to Beroea and was very upset at what had **181**
happened. He accused Khusro of treating the Beroeans disgracefully by
sending him to Antioch on the pretext of making peace, and then plundering money from the citizens, who had in no way harmed him, and
forcing them to shut themselves in this fortress, and then setting fire to
the city and wantonly burning it to the ground. (20) To this Khusro
replied as follows: 'But you yourself are responsible for this, my friend, by

[275] Julian was the former ambassador to southern Arabia, cf. 1.20.9. John was the son of the Rufinus
who had frequently acted as ambassador to Khusro. See *PLRE* 3, Iulianus 8, Ioannes 7. The *a
secretis* were secretaries that dealt with the business of the imperial consistory, the council of the
highest officials. See *ODLA, a secretis*.
[276] Ephraem, having served earlier as *comes Orientis*, count of the East, became patriarch of Antioch
in 527. He had raised funds to ransom prisoners from the Persians in 531 and had collaborated
with them to track down the anti-Chalcedonian bishop John of Tella (Constantia) in the 530s,
both of which may have made him suspect in Julian's eyes. See *ODLA*, Ephrem of Amida.

forcing us to waste time here. You have now come not at the appointed
time, but rather after a lengthy delay. (21) What need is there for anyone
to discuss at length the strangeness of your fellow citizens, good sir? They
agreed to pay us a fixed sum of silver for their safety, yet they think that
even now they need not fulfil their agreement. They simply put their
trust like this in the strength of the place and hold us in contempt, so
that we are obliged to set about besieging the fortress, as you no doubt
see. (22) With the help of the gods I hope to have vengeance upon them
later and to punish those guilty of the needless deaths of my Persians
before this wall.'

(23) These were Khusro's words, and Megas replied as follows: 'If
anyone reflected that you, a king, are making these charges against
wretched and miserable men, he would have to agree without protest
with what you have said. For power over speech naturally follows from
other types of authority. (24) But if it were possible to disregard the other
factors and choose the true story, you would not be able justly to
reproach us, O King. Listen in peace to all that I have to say. (25) After I
had been sent to tell the Antiochenes what you ordered, I arrived before
you on the seventh day (how could anything be faster than that?) and
found that you had done this to my native town. (26) These men have
already lost all their precious possessions and now face only the struggle
for their lives. They are now, I think, in too strong a position to pay you
the money in the future, (27) for there is no way by which a man can pay
what he does not possess. (28) The names of qualities have long ago been
well distinguished by men. Among them is the following: lack of strength
is distinguished from lack of sense. (29) The one, when through lack of
restraint it is moved to opposition, is hated; but when the other is driven
to the same thing because it cannot perform a service, it naturally wins
pity. (30) We have been granted a most miserable lot, O King; allow us
therefore to have this consolation at least, not to seem responsible
ourselves for what has happened to us. (31) Consider the money that you
have received sufficient; do not judge it by your own high position, but
with consideration for what Beroea can offer. (32) Do not force us further,
in case you should seem incapable of carrying out your undertakings; for
excess is always punished by confrontation with insuperable obstacles,
and it is best not to attempt the impossible. (33) Let this therefore be my
plea for these men for the present. But if I could only meet these
wretches, I should have something else to say which has now escaped me.'

(34) At these words from Megas, Khusro let him go to the acropolis.
When he reached it and heard all about the spring, he went back to

182

183

Khusro in tears and lay down on his face, assuring him that Beroea had no money left whatever, and beseeching him only to spare the men's lives. (35) Khusro was moved by the man's laments and granted his request; he swore an oath and gave pledges to all those on the acropolis. (36) The Beroeans, who had come to such a point of danger, left the acropolis without coming to any harm, and each went wherever he wished. (37) A few of the soldiers followed them, but most of them willingly deserted to Khusro, complaining that the treasury owed them their wages for a long period, and they later went with him to Persia.

184

Chapter 8

(1) But Khusro, who had been informed by Megas that he had been quite unable to persuade the Antiochenes to pay any money, advanced against them with all his army (fig. 27). (2) Some of the Antiochenes left the city with their money, and each man fled as best he could. All the rest were planning to do the same, had not the commanders of the troops in Lebanon arrived in the meantime – Theoctistus and Molatzes – with 6000 men.[277] The hope that this force inspired stopped them. (3) Not long after this the Persian army also arrived. They all pitched their tents there and encamped next to the river Orontes.[278] (4) Khusro sent Paul up to the wall and demanded money from the Antiochenes, saying that for ten *centenaria* of gold he would leave – and it was clear that he would accept even less than this for his withdrawal. (5) Then the ambassadors came to Khusro and said much about the breaking of the peace; they returned after listening to a long response from him. (6) On the next day the Antiochene populace (who are not serious-minded, but are unduly devoted to jokes and unruliness) insulted Khusro from the battlements and jeered at him with inappropriate laughter.[279] (7) When Paul came near the wall to advise them to ransom themselves and the city for a small amount of money, they shot at him and would have killed him had he not anticipated this and taken precautions. And so Khusro, boiling with rage, decided to storm the wall.

(8) On the next day he brought all the Persians up to the wall and told some to attack the wall from different points on the river, while he with

185

---

[277] They must have been summoned earlier, having covered a distance of at least 180 km to reach Antioch: Phoenice Libanensis lies to the south-east, and the nearest base from which they might have come is Emesa. See *PLRE* 3, Molatzes, Theoctistus 2, on the commanders.

[278] The Greek has the rather pleonastic 'by the river Orontes, not far from it'.

[279] The frivolity of the Antiochene populace was well-known, cf. 1.17.37.

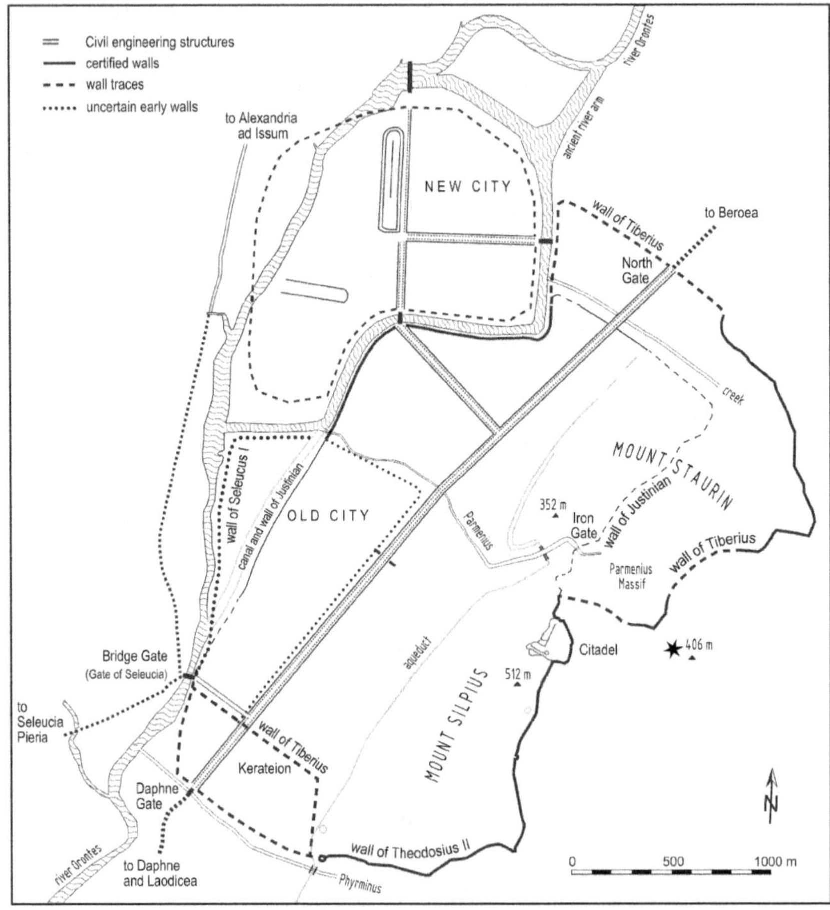

Figure 27   Antioch

the larger and best part set about attacking the heights. For here, as I said
before, the wall was at its most vulnerable.[280] (9) Here the Romans
devised this plan, for the structure on which they would be standing to
fight was very narrow. They bound together long beams and hung them
between the towers, in this way making the area much greater, so that
even more men would be able to fight off the assailants from there. (10)
So the Persians pressed hard from all sides, despatching thick volleys of
arrows especially down from the heights of the hill. (11) But the Romans,

[280] See 2.6.10 and the star on fig. 27.

not only the soldiers, but also many very bold youths from among the populace, fought them off with all their might. (12) And it appeared as though the assailants were joining battle there with their opponents on an equal footing, since the broad high rock which seemed to be drawn up against the wall made the combat just like one on level ground. (13) If **186** someone from the Roman army had had the courage to come outside the wall with three hundred men and take the initiative by seizing this rock and fighting off the attackers from it, I do not think that the city would have been in any danger from the enemy. (14) For the barbarians would not have had a base from which to make an assault on the wall – assailed by arrows from above, as they would have been, from the rock and from the wall. But as it was (for the Antiochenes were fated to be destroyed by this Persian army) no one thought of this. (15) So the Persians, inspired by the presence of Khusro, who was shouting loud encouragements to them, were fighting beyond their power and giving the enemy no chance to see or to take cover from the flying arrows, while the Romans were defending themselves still more strongly, in great numbers and shouting all the time. But the ropes with which the beams were bound could not bear the weight and suddenly broke; all those who were standing on them fell to the ground together with the beams with a great crash. (16) When the other Romans fighting from the adjacent towers heard this, they could not guess what had happened. Thinking that the wall had been broken there, they turned to flee, (17) but a large number of young men from the populace, who formerly used to fight each other in the hippodromes, stayed there after coming down from the wall instead of fleeing.[281] But the soldiers under Theoctistus and Molatzes immediately mounted the horses that were ready to go. They rode off to the gates, **187** shouting that Buzes had arrived with his army and that they wanted to let them into the city quickly and fight with them against the enemy. (18) At this, many men of Antioch and all the women with their children rushed to the gates. In the narrow space they were trampled by the horses, and many fell. (19) But the soldiers, caring nothing for what was happening, rode over the bodies even more ruthlessly than before, and there was great carnage there, especially at the gates themselves.

(20) The Persians, now that there was no opposition, brought up scaling ladders to the wall and climbed up onto it easily. They were soon on the battlements and for a long time would not descend. They seemed to be looking around, not knowing what to do. I suspect that they

---

[281] Procopius refers to the circus partisans, described in negative terms at 1.24.2–6.

thought that the rough ground was full of ambushes laid by the enemy, (21) for the part inside the wall which goes straight down from the heights is an uninhabited area for the most part, full of very high crags and rocky places. (22) Some say, however, that the Persians' hesitation was by Khusro's orders. (23) When he realised the difficulty of the terrain and saw the fleeing soldiers, he was afraid that they might for some reason have to turn back from their flight, make trouble and perhaps hinder him from taking an ancient and famous city, the leading Roman city in the East in wealth and size and population and beauty and every other blessing. (24) It was, evidently, because of this fear, since he considered everything else less important, that he wanted to give the Roman soldiers a chance to flee at their leisure. Consequently the Persians waved at them as they fled, urging them to go as quickly as possible. (25) So the Roman soldiers and their commanders all left through the gate that leads to Daphne, the suburb of Antioch.[282] (26) All the rest of the gates had been captured, and this was the only one which the Persians had left alone. A few of the populace fled with the soldiers. (27) But when the Persians saw that all the Roman soldiers were going, they came down from the heights and entered the city centre. (28) There many young Antiochenes came to fight them, and they seemed at first to be getting the best of the conflict. Some of them were in full armour, but most were without arms, relying only on throwing stones. (29) And they pushed back the enemy and sang the paean, shouting 'The Emperor Justinian triumphs in glory', as if they had won the battle.

(30) But in the meantime Khusro, who was sitting on a tower on the height, sent for the ambassadors, wanting to say something to them. Zabergan, one of the officers,[283] thinking that he wanted to speak to the envoys about a settlement, hastily came before the king and said: (31) 'You do not seem to think, my lord, in the same way as the Romans do about the safety of these men. For even before they came into danger they insulted your monarchy, and now that they are defeated they are attempting the impossible and doing terrible damage to the Persians, as if they are afraid that you might still have some reason left for showing them kindness. Yet you want to take pity on men who do not wish to be saved, and you are eager to spare them when they have no wish for it. (32) They have laid ambushes in a captured city for the victors and are destroying them, even though all their soldiers have long since fled.'

---

[282] The opulent suburb of Daphne lies 6 km south-west of the city.
[283] On Zabergan see 1.23.25.

(33) On hearing this Khusro sent many of the best men against them, but they returned soon after, saying that nothing untoward had happened. (34) For already the Persians struggling against the Antiochenes had routed them because of their superior numbers, and great slaughter had taken place there. For the Persians spared no age group and were killing all before them, from the youngest to the oldest. (35) They say that the wives of two prominent Antiochenes then came outside the wall, but when they found that they would fall into the hands of the enemy (for they were already clearly visible everywhere they went), they ran to the river Orontes, and, terrified that the Persians might rape them, they hid their faces with their veils, threw themselves into the flowing river and disappeared from sight. Thus every kind of misfortune encompassed the Antiochenes.

Chapter 9

(1) Then Khusro said to the envoys: 'I consider not far from the truth the old saying that God does not give men an unmingled share of good, but first mixes it with evil.[284] (2) For this reason we do not even laugh without tears; and some calamity is always linked to blessings, and pain to pleasures, never allowing a man to enjoy the genuine happiness that is given to him. (3) This city, the most remarkable in the Roman empire in reputation and in actuality, I have managed to take very easily – for God has contrived this victory for us, as of course you see. (4) But when I see so many men slaughtered and the victory soaked in so much blood, no feeling of pleasure comes to me from the achievement. (5) The wretched Antiochenes are responsible for this, since they could not repel the Persians when they stormed the wall. Although the Persians were already victorious and had captured the city without a blow, they resolved to resist, dying in irrational recklessness. (6) So all the leading Persians pestered me with demands to sweep the city and kill all those captured, but I told the fugitives to retreat still faster, so that they might win safety as soon as possible.[285] For it is not righteous to trample upon prisoners.'

(7) This was the fanciful and deceitful tale that Khusro told the envoys, but the reason why he gave the chance to the fleeing Romans did not escape them, (8) for he was the cleverest man alive at telling lies and concealing the truth and putting the blame for his own crimes on those

190

191

---

[284] An allusion probably to Homer, *Il.* 24.527–34.
[285] By 'sweeping the city' Khusro means surrounding it with his men and massacring all those found within, cf. Hdt. 6.31.

whom he had wronged. Besides, he was ready to agree to anything and guarantee his agreement with an oath, but he was readier still to forget what he had only just agreed to and sworn to. And for money he did not shrink from lowering his soul to any kind of pollution; he was a past master at feigning piety by his expression and making excuses to evade the responsibility for his actions.

(9) After treacherously getting the better of the people of Sura, who had before this done him no harm at all, and destroying them in the manner which I have related,[286] he saw as the city was being captured a lovely woman of high station being dragged violently along by the left hand by a barbarian. She, not wanting to abandon the child which she had only just released from her breast, dragged it along with her other hand. The child had fallen to the ground, unable to keep up with this enforced run. Then Khusro displayed his real nature. (10) They say that he pretended to groan, giving the impression to those present, who included Anastasius the ambassador, that he was weeping; and he prayed to God to take vengeance on the man guilty of this crime. (11) He meant to imply that this man was the Roman Emperor Justinian, though he knew very well that he himself was the most responsible for all that had happened.[287] (12) Endowed with such an extraordinary nature, Khusro became the king of Persia (for a divine power mutilated Zames' eye, and he was next in line for the throne after Kaoses, for whom Kavadh had an irrational hatred),[288] easily overcame those who revolted against him, and accomplished without difficulty whatever acts of hostility he planned against the Romans. (13) For when Fortune wants to exalt a man, she does what she has decided upon at the appropriate times, with no opposition to the momentum of her will, without giving any thought to the man's rank nor caring that undesirable results should be prevented, nor that many men will curse her for this and jeer at her for going beyond the worth of the man who has lighted on her favour. She has no other thought in mind whatever, if only her plans can be fulfilled. But let this be as God wishes.

(14) Khusro told his army to take the surviving Antiochenes alive and enslave them, and to seize all their money. He himself went down from the heights with the envoys to the temple that they call a 'church'.[289]

---

[286] See 2.5.14–27.
[287] Cf. 2.1.15, ambivalent, and *Anecd.* 11.12, where Procopius accuses Justinian of being responsible for the outbreak of the war.
[288] See 1.11.4–5, 1.23.4–5 on Zames.
[289] Perhaps the octagonal church built by Constantine, recently rebuilt after the earthquake of 528.

(15) There Khusro found such a vast quantity of gold and silver treasures that even though he took nothing but this treasure for booty he still went away vastly enriched. (16) He took many wonderful pieces of marble from there and ordered them to be put down outside the wall so that they **193** could take these, too, to Persia.[290] (17) Having obtained these riches, he told the Persians to burn the entire city. The envoys begged him to leave the church alone, for which he had taken a sufficient ransom, (18) and he agreed to the envoys' request, giving orders to burn everything else.[291] Leaving behind a few men to burn the city, he himself returned with all the rest to the camp where they had previously pitched their tents.

Chapter 10

(1) Some time before this calamity God gave a portent to the inhabitants and indicated what was to happen. The standards belonging to the soldiers who had long been posted there turned of their own accord to the East (they had previously faced the West), stayed in that position, and then turned back again to their former position, without anyone touching them. (2) The soldiers pointed this out to many who were present, including the steward in charge of the camp finances, while the standards were still swinging around. This man, who was called Tatian and came from Mopsuestia, was very intelligent.[292] (3) Yet even so, those who saw this omen did not recognise that the power over the place would pass from the emperor of the West to the emperor of the East. Obviously this was so that those who were fated to suffer this, as did actually happen, could not in any way escape it. (4) For my part I grow dizzy at recording so great a disaster and handing it on to the memory of posterity; I do not know what God's will can be in raising up on high the **194** fortunes of a man or a place and then casting them down again and wiping them out for no reason apparent to us. (5) For it is wrong to deny that He always does everything according to some plan, though at that time He endured to see Antioch brought to the ground by the most impious of men, a city whose beauty and splendour in every way have not even now been wholly obscured.

---

[290] Joh. Lyd. *De Mag.* 3.54.5 also mentions these depredations, tr. in *REF*, 105, as does (e.g.) Ps.-Dion. ii, 64, tr. in *REF*, 107.

[291] The *Life of Symeon the Stylite the Younger*, ch. 57, claims that the whole city was not destroyed. The holy man, who lived on a mountain west of the city, beheld a vision of the sack before it happened and sheltered some who fled the city. See *REF*, 104–5, for a tr. of the chapter.

[292] Probably an *actuarius* or *optio*, a sort of quartermaster, not otherwise known.

(6) Once the city had been destroyed, only the church was left therefore, thanks to the labour and diligence of the Persians to whom the task was entrusted. (7) But many houses were also left around the so-called Kerateion, not through the forethought of any individual, but because they were on the farthest edge of the city and, since there were no adjoining buildings, the fire could not reach them.[293] (8) The barbarians burnt the areas outside the wall too, except for the sanctuary dedicated to St Julian, and the houses that are situated around this sanctuary, (9) for it happened that the envoys lodged there. The Persians left the wall completely alone, however.

(10) Shortly afterwards the envoys came to Khusro again and said: 'If we had not spoken to you in person, O King, we would never have believed that Khusro, the son of Kavadh, had come under arms into Roman territory, in violation of the oaths which you recently swore, something that would seem to be the utmost and surest guarantee among men of their loyalty and truthfulness to one another, and in violation of the treaty, which is the only hope that remains to those whose lives are endangered because of the wickedness of war. (11) One might say that this amounted to exchanging civilised life for that of beasts. (12) For when no treaties are made, we are left with endless war, and war that has no end always alienates those who engage in it from their true nature. (13) What did you want by writing not long ago to your brother monarch saying that he was guilty of breaking the treaty? Is it not clear that this constitutes an admission that breaking the truce is a great evil? (14) If then he did not break it, you are now advancing against us unjustly. But if it should be that your brother monarch has done something of this kind, let your complaint be carried this far and no farther, so that you might be seen to be in the stronger position. For whoever is defeated in adverse conditions may justly gain the upper hand in better ones. (15) Yet we know for certain that the Emperor Justinian has never acted contrary to the peace, and we ask you not to do such wicked deeds to the Romans, which bring no advantage to the Persians, and to you this benefit only – that you have wantonly done irreparable harm to those who have just recently made a treaty with you!'

These were the words of the envoys. (16) When Khusro heard this, he insisted that the truce had been broken by the Emperor Justinian. He recited the grounds for war that the emperor had provided, some of them

---

[293] The Kerateion, the quarter of the Carob trees, lay on the south side of the city, where the city had expanded beyond the walls built by Tiberius. Theodosius II had built further walls to incorporate the district. Tiberius' walls may therefore have protected it from the conflagration.

having some degree of plausibility, but others weak and fabricated with no logic. He decided to show the letters written by Justinian to al-Mundhir and the Huns which, as I related earlier, were the greatest cause of the war.[294] (17) But that a Roman had invaded Persian territory or engaged in any hostile act he could neither claim nor prove. (18) The envoys, on the other hand, partly attributed the causes not to Justinian, but to certain of his subordinates, and partly opposed what he had said on the grounds that it was not a true description of what had happened. (19) But eventually Khusro demanded that the Romans should give him a large amount of money, warning them that they should not aim to secure the peace forever simply by giving him the money on the one occasion, (20) for friendship bought by men for money is generally spent with the money as it is used up. (21) Consequently the Romans must pay a fixed yearly sum to the Persians. 'For in this way', he said, 'the Persians will keep the peace safe for them, guarding the Caspian Gates themselves, and no longer harbouring a grudge against them because of the city of Dara, in exchange for which the Persians will themselves be in their pay forever.'

    (22) 'It is clear', replied the envoys, 'that the Persians wish to reduce the Romans to the rank of tribute-paying subjects.' (23) 'No', said Khusro, 'the Romans will have the Persians as their own soldiers in future and will be paying them a fixed sum for their service. You give an annual payment to some of the Huns and Saracens, not because you are their subjects but so that they can keep your land from ever being plundered.' (24) This was the exchange between Khusro and the envoys; later they agreed that Khusro should receive from the Romans for the present fifty *centenaria*, and that if he received a permanent yearly tribute of five more he would do them no further harm. After taking hostages from the envoys for this agreement, he would make the journey home with all his army, and then the envoys should go to the Emperor Justinian and make a final settlement about the peace for the future.

                                    197

                                    198

Chapter 11

(1) Then Khusro went to Seleucia, a seaside city one hundred and thirty stades from Antioch, but did not find a single Roman there and did no harm.[295] Alone, he washed himself in the water of the sea, sacrificed to the

---

[294] See 2.1.13–14, 2.3.47.
[295] Seleucia Pieria, near modern Samandağ in Turkey today, the port city of Antioch. See *ODLA*, Seleucia Pieria.

sun and whatever other gods he wished; he called upon the gods many times and then went back. (2) When he came to the camp he said that he wished to see the city of Apamea, which lay in the neighbourhood, simply out of curiosity. (3) The envoys reluctantly agreed to this also, but only on condition that when he had seen the city and had taken from it one thousand pounds of silver he should come back without doing it any further harm. (4) It was clear to the envoys and to everyone else that Khusro was only going to Apamea in order to plunder it and the surrounding country on some flimsy pretext. So then he went up to Daphne, the suburb of Antioch. (5) There he greatly admired the grove and the springs of water, for both are certainly sights to be seen. (6) He left after sacrificing to the nymphs, doing no harm except for burning the sanctuary of the archangel Michael and some other buildings, for the following reason.

(7) A Persian horseman, a leading man in the Persian army, known to Khusro the king, came with some others to a rocky place near the so-called Tretus, where there is the sanctuary of the archangel Michael, which is the work of Euaris. (8) This man noticed one of the young Antiochenes on foot and alone, hiding there, and went after him away from the others. The youth was a butcher called Aeimachus.[296] (9) He was on the point of being caught when he turned around suddenly and with a stone hit his pursuer on the temple, penetrating to the eardrum. The Persian fell to the ground at once and Aeimachus drew his opponent's sabre and killed him. (10) He stripped him at his leisure of all his armour and gold and anything else that he happened to be wearing, jumped on his horse and rode on. (11) Either by chance or because he knew the country he was able to evade the enemy and make a complete escape. (12) When Khusro heard this, he was very upset at what had happened and told some of his attendants to burn down the shrine of the archangel that I mentioned before. (13) They thought that this was it and burnt it down with the buildings around it, believing that they had carried out Khusro's orders. This was how this resulted.

(14) Khusro went with all his army to Apamea. There is a piece of wood in Apamea a cubit long, part of the Cross on which it is agreed that Christ willingly long ago underwent his punishment in Jerusalem, and which had been brought there secretly in ancient times by a Syrian.[297]

---

[296] The name means 'constant fighter', which has led to suspicions that the episode is invented; it recalls the biblical story of David and Goliath.

[297] This fragment of the cross in Apamea is attested in other sources. Half of it was later brought to Constantinople, while the other half was seized by the Persians in 611, then returned by Heraclius. On the city, see *ODLA*, Apamea.

(15) The men of those days believed that it would be a great defence for them and for the city. They had a wooden chest made for it, which they decorated with gold and precious stones. They gave it into the care of three priests to keep in complete safety, and on one day every year they bring it out and the people do homage to it. (16) At this time, when the people of Apamea heard that the Persian army was advancing against them, they were thrown into great fear. And when they heard that Khusro was a great liar, they came to Thomas, the chief priest of the city,[298] and asked him to show them the wood of the Cross so that they might do homage to it once more before they died. (17) He acted accordingly. Then a sight was seen there beyond explanation and belief. As the priest carrying the wood was displaying it, there rose above it a tongue of fire, and the part of the ceiling around him was illuminated with an extraordinary light.[299] (18) As the priest walked all over the temple, the flame went with him and before him, keeping all the time to the place above him in the ceiling. (19) Consequently the people of Apamea, such was their delight at the miracle, were amazed, rejoiced and began weeping, all of them already confident of their safety. (20) But when Thomas had gone all around the temple, he put the wood from the Cross into the chest and covered it up, and the flame was suddenly quenched. When he heard that the enemy army was very near the city, he went to Khusro in great haste. (21) Khusro asked the priest if the people of Apamea wanted to make a stand against the Persian army from the walls, to which Thomas replied that nothing of this kind had entered their minds. (22) 'Then', said Khusro, 'receive me and a few companions into the city with all the gates open.' (23) 'Certainly', said the priest, 'it was to invite you to do this that I came.' So all the army pitched their tents and encamped in front of the circuit wall.

(24) Khusro selected two hundred of the best Persians and rode into the city. But when he was inside the gates, he was quite ready to forget what he had agreed upon with the envoys, and he ordered the bishop to give him not just one thousand measures of silver, nor even ten times that, but actually all the treasures that were there – all of gold and silver and of remarkably large size. (25) I think that he would not have shrunk from enslaving and plundering the whole city as well, had not some divine force manifestly prevented him; (26) to such an extent was avarice driving him out of his senses and desire for fame twisting his mind. (27) For he

201

202

---

[298] Thomas was the bishop of Apamea and the metropolitan (ecclesiastical head) of Syria II. At 11.24, Procopius uses the normal term for a bishop, *episkopos*.

[299] The miracle was witnessed by the young Evagrius, as he reports at *HE* 4.26.

thought that enslaving cities was great glory for him, caring nothing if he disregarded treaties and agreements in doing such things to the Romans. (28) Khusro's view was to be revealed by what he undertook at the city of Dara in the course of this retreat, in flagrant breach of his agreement, and what he did to the people of Callinicum a little later during the peace, as I shall recount in subsequent chapters.[300] But God, as was stated, saved Apamea. (29) When Khusro had taken all the treasures and Thomas saw him already drunk with the boundless riches, he brought out the wood from the Cross. He opened the chest, showed the wood and said: 'O most powerful King, this alone is left to me out of all our wealth. (30) We do not begrudge your taking this chest with all the rest – it is decorated with gold and precious stones – but this wood is our salvation and is priceless to us; this, I beseech you and beg you, grant to me.' This was what the priest said. And Khusro agreed to his request and fulfilled it.

(31) But then in his desire for fame he ordered the people to go up to the hippodrome and the charioteers to hold their usual contests. (32) He went there himself with great enthusiasm to watch the events. Since he had heard a long time ago that the Emperor Justinian was extraordinarily devoted to the Venetus colour, that is, the Blue, he wished to oppose him here, too, and wanted to arrange a victory for the Green colour.[301] (33) So the charioteers set off from the starting gates and began the race, and by some chance, the one wearing the Blue colours passed the others and got ahead. (34) The one wearing the Green colours came behind along the same wheel tracks. (35) Khusro thought that this had been done deliberately, and angrily and threateningly shouted that Caesar[302] had unjustly got ahead of the others and gave orders that the horses running in front should be held up, so that from then onwards they would take part in the contest from behind. When his orders were carried out, Khusro and the Green faction thus appeared to win. (36) Then one of the Apameans came before Khusro and accused a Persian of entering his house and raping his daughter, who was a virgin. (37) When Khusro heard this, he boiled with rage and ordered the man to be brought to him, and as soon as he came, he commanded that he be impaled in the camp. (38) When the people heard of this, they shouted with all their might, making a terrible noise, demanding that the man be delivered from the king's anger. Khusro agreed to let the man go, but not long afterwards impaled him secretly. After carrying out such actions there, he headed back with all his army.

---

[300] At 2.13.16–29 and 2.21.30–3.
[301] See Proc. *Anecd.* 7.1–7 on Justinian's support for the Blues.
[302] The Persians referred to the Roman emperor as 'Caesar', cf. 2.21.9.

Chapter 12

(1) When he came to the city of Chalcis, eighty-four stades from Beroea, he forgot his agreement again.[303] Pitching camp not far from the wall, he sent Paul to threaten the Chalcidians that he would take their city by siege if they did not buy their safety by paying a ransom and surrender the soldiers who were there together with their commander. (2) The people of Chalcis were terrified of both rulers and swore that they had no soldiers there, although they had hidden some, including Adonachus, the commander of the forces, in some buildings, so that they were not obvious to the enemy. With some difficulty they managed to gather together two *centenaria* of gold (their city was not particularly rich) and by giving Khusro the ransom they saved their city and their own lives.

(3) From there Khusro did not want to continue his return journey by the way he had come, but he preferred to cross the river Euphrates instead and plunder as much money as possible from Mesopotamia. (4) So he bridged it at Obbane, which is forty stades from the fortress at Barbalissus, then crossed himself, and gave orders for the entire army to cross as quickly as possible, adding that the bridge would be broken on the third day, and fixing even the time of day. (5) When the time came, it happened that some of the army were still left, not having yet crossed, but he did not give this a thought and sent men to break the bridge. (6) Those left behind went home as best they could. Then Khusro was seized with a burning ambition to take the city of Edessa, (7) for a Christian story drove him to it and pestered his mind. They said that it was unconquerable for the following reason.

(8) A certain Abgar was toparch of Edessa in former times (for this was the term by which local kings were known then). This Abgar was the most intelligent man of his generation and as a result greatly honoured as a friend by the Emperor Augustus.[304] (9) He wanted to be allied to Rome, so he went to Rome and in talks with Augustus he so impressed him by his high intellectual qualities that Augustus would not let him leave. Indeed, he became at once passionately devoted to his company,

204

205

---

[303] Chalcis ad Belum, known as Qinnašrīn in Syriac, was the base of the *dux* of Syria I and a significant city. Procopius reports work on the fortifications there by Justinian at *Aed.* 2.11.1, 8, which can be dated to 550/1 through inscriptions translated in *REF*, 243. See *ODLA*, Chalcis ad Belum.

[304] Abgar V Ukkama ('the Black') was a contemporary of Augustus; a correspondence was believed to have taken place between this ruler and Christ, which is reported by various sources, notably in Syriac. The conversion of the small kingdom of Edessa probably took place rather later, during the reign of Abgar VIII (the Great, who reigned from 177 to 212). Procopius' account is similar to that of Eusebius, *Church History*, 1.13, but need not have relied on it entirely. See *ODLA*, Abgar legend.

and whenever he met him, he wished never to be deprived of his presence. (10) Consequently Abgar spent a long time on this visit abroad. When one day he wanted to return home, but could not manage to persuade Augustus to let him go, he devised the following stratagem.

(11) He went into the countryside around Rome ostensibly on a hunting expedition, for he was in fact very fond of this pursuit.[305] As he went around the countryside over a wide area, he hunted down many of the native animals, taking them alive, and from each part of the country he gathered up and took with him some soil. Then he returned to Rome with the animals and the soil. (12) So Augustus went to the hippodrome and sat in his accustomed place, and Abgar came to him and showed him the earth and the animals, explaining to him from which country each bit of soil came and what the various animals were. (13) Then he told him to scatter the earth all over the hippodrome and to gather the animals all together and let them go. (14) So the attendants acted accordingly. Once the animals were separated from each other, they each went to the bit of earth that was from the area where they were caught. (15) Augustus looked hard at this for a long time, surprised that the animals' nature, without training, made them long for their native soil. But Abgar suddenly clasped his knees and said: (16) 'What feelings do you think I have, my Lord? I have a wife and children and a kingdom that, even if small, is at least in my native land.' (17) Augustus, defeated and compelled by the truth of what he said, unwillingly consented to let him go and told him to ask for whatever he wanted. (18) Since Abgar was granted this boon, he asked Augustus to build a hippodrome for him in the city of Edessa, to which he also agreed. In this way Abgar left Rome and returned to Edessa. (19) The citizens asked him if he brought them any benefit from the Emperor Augustus. He answered that he brought to the people of Edessa pain without loss and joy without gain, hinting at the fortunes of the hippodrome.[306]

(20) Sometime later, Abgar, who was now an old man, was seized with a very acute attack of gout. Suffering from the pain and immobility that it caused, he consulted the doctors about it, and collected together the experts on gout from the entire country. (21) But they could not find any cure for his illness, and after a time he abandoned them and, in despair at what to do, lamented the fate that had befallen him. (22) At that time Jesus, the son of God, was incarnate and lived

---

[305] Abgar VIII is known to have visited Rome and to have been an expert huntsman.

[306] A *bon mot* also found (in another context) in the *Patria* of Constantinople, 1.38, tr. A. Berger, *Accounts of Medieval Constantinople* (Washington, D.C., 2013), 23.

among the men of Palestine, clearly revealing by his complete freedom from sin and by his miracles that he was really the Son of God. (23) For he called up the dead and awakened them as if from sleep; he opened the eyes of men born blind, cleansed leprosy from the entire body, removed lameness, and cured all the other ills pronounced incurable by doctors. (24) Abgar heard of this from Palestinians who visited Edessa and was heartened by it; and he wrote a letter to Jesus, asking him to leave Judaea and its unappreciative people and live with him in the future. (25) When Christ received this letter, he wrote back to Abgar, refusing outright to come, but promising him health in the letter. (26) They say that he added also that the city would never be captured by barbarians.[307] Those who composed the history of those times did not know of this ending to the letter, for they did not make mention of it anywhere. But the Edessenes say that it was found with the letter, and they have understandably had the letter inscribed in this form on the gates of the city, in preference to any other defence.[308] (27) But some time later it came under the power of the Persians, not by capture, however, but in the following way.

(28) When Abgar had received Christ's letter, he was shortly afterwards cured of his illness and lived for the rest of his life in perfect health. But after his death the son who succeeded him was the wickedest man on earth. Among the various wrongs that he did to his subjects, he voluntarily defected to the Persians because he was afraid of being punished by the Romans.[309] (29) But very much later the Edessenes murdered the barbarian guards living among them and gave the city up to the Romans[310]. . . it was his objective to win it over, as is attested by the events that took place in my time, as I shall reveal in the appropriate place.[311] (30) It has occurred to me that if Christ did not write what I said, still, since men have come to believe it, he wants by this means to keep the city uncaptured for the following reason: so as never to give them any pretext for error. But may this be and may this be told as is pleasing to God.

208

---

[307] On this correspondence see n. 304.

[308] The text was probably inscribed in the late fifth century; it was also inscribed in other cities, e.g. Philippi in Macedonia. The city was not captured by the Persians until the seventh century.

[309] The son is likely to be Abgar IX Severus, who was removed by the Emperor Caracalla in 212/13. There is no evidence, however, of a defection to the Persians.

[310] There follows a lacuna of nine lines in the manuscript.

[311] It is not certain who is the subject here: it could be Justinian, trying to curry favour with the Edessenes by building projects, or Khusro. The missing lines are likely to have described the flood that struck the city in 525, which is reported by Mal. 17.51 and elsewhere. See also *ODLA*, Edessa.

(31) At this point therefore the capture of Edessa seemed to Khusro a necessary task. When he reached Batnae, a small town of no importance a day's journey from Edessa, he pitched camp there for that night, and as the day broke he set off for Edessa with all his army. (32) It so happened that they lost their way and in their wanderings pitched camp on the following night in the same place – which they say actually happened to them twice. (33) But they say that after Khusro had reached the vicinity of Edessa with such difficulty, a discharge came upon his face and his jaw swelled.[312] Consequently he would not make an attempt on the city, but sent Paul instead, demanding money from the Edessenes. (34) They said that they were not at all frightened for the city, but agreed to give him two *centenaria* of gold to stop him from plundering their land. He took the money and kept the agreement.

Chapter 13

(1) Then the Emperor Justinian also wrote a letter to Khusro, agreeing to accomplish what he and the envoys had settled concerning the peace.[313] (2) When Khusro saw the message, he released the hostages and prepared to depart; he also wanted to ransom all the Antiochene prisoners of war. (3) When the Edessenes learnt this, they displayed an eagerness greater than any attested.[314] There was none who did not bring to the sanctuary a contribution to the ransom for these prisoners, in proportion to their resources, and deposit it there. (4) Some even contributed even well beyond their resources. The prostitutes removed the jewellery that they wore about their persons and threw it in there, while any farmer lacking valuables or silver but possessing an ass or a sheep brought them to the sanctuary with great alacrity. (5) An enormous quantity of gold, silver and other goods was therefore collected, yet none of it was given by way of a ransom, (6) for Buzes happened to be present there, who sought to prevent the transaction, supposing that there would be great profit for him arising from this. Consequently Khusro marched on, leading all the prisoners. (7) The inhabitants of Carrhae met him and offered large sums, but he responded that it would not be appropriate for him to take

---

[312] An Arab chief with Kavadh died from a headwound that flared up during an attack on Edessa in 503, Ps.-Josh. 58 reports.

[313] Cf. 2.10.24.

[314] Cf. Mal. 18.59 for similar generosity on the part of the Antiochenes in 531, who had laid out their possessions on a carpet put out by the patriarch Ephraem to ransom prisoners taken by al-Mundhir.

them, given that most of them were not Christians, but rather adherents of the old faith.[315]

(8) On the other hand, he accepted the money that the inhabitants of Constantia offered, although he said that the city belonged to him through his forefathers, for when Kavadh took Amida, he wanted to capture both Edessa and Constantia too.[316] (9) But when he drew near to Edessa, he asked the magi whether the city could be captured by him, and with his right hand he indicated the place to them. (10) They declared to him that the city could not be taken by any means, basing their judgement on the fact that he held out his right hand towards the city, thereby giving a sign neither of capture nor of any other danger to the city, but rather of salvation. (11) When he heard this, he was persuaded and led off his army against Constantia. (12) Having arrived there, he ordered the entire army to encamp in preparation for a siege. (13) The bishop of Constantia at that time was Baradotus, a just man and most dear to God, whose prayers consequently were always fulfilled for whatever he wanted. (14) At that point this Baradotus came to Kavadh   **211** bearing wine, dried figs, honey and white loaves. He begged him not to attempt to take a city that was of little consequence and had been singularly neglected by the Romans, which had no garrison of soldiers nor any other means of protection, but only its inhabitants, people to be pitied. (15) This is what he said, and Kavadh agreed to grant him the city out of goodwill. He further bestowed on him as a gift all the provisions that he had made ready for his army for the siege, of which there was a vast quantity. Thus he left Roman territory. For this reason, then, Khusro claimed that the city belonged to him through his forefathers.

(16) Having arrived at Dara, Khusro laid siege to it (fig. 28). Within the city the Romans and the general Martin, who happened to be there, made preparations to resist.[317] (17) The city is surrounded by two walls, of which the inner one is large and remarkably worth seeing (for each tower rises to a height of one hundred feet, while the rest of the wall reaches sixty feet), but the outer one is much smaller, though otherwise it is both secure and considerable.[318] (18) The space between has a breadth of not less than fifty feet; here the inhabitants of Dara are accustomed to

---

[315] Carrhae (Harran) was associated with paganism still in Islamic times. See *ODLA*, Harran.

[316] Procopius refers to events of 503 that he omitted at 1.8. See Ps.-Josh. 58 with *RPW*, 101–3. Kavadh, moving west, reached Constantia before Edessa, despite the order of events presented here.

[317] Martin had just come from the West, cf. 2.14.9 and 7.1.1 with *PLRE* 3, Martinus 2.

[318] Procopius describes the fortifications and Justinian's improvements at length at *Aed.* 2.1.11–3.26; these had probably been undertaken before this siege.

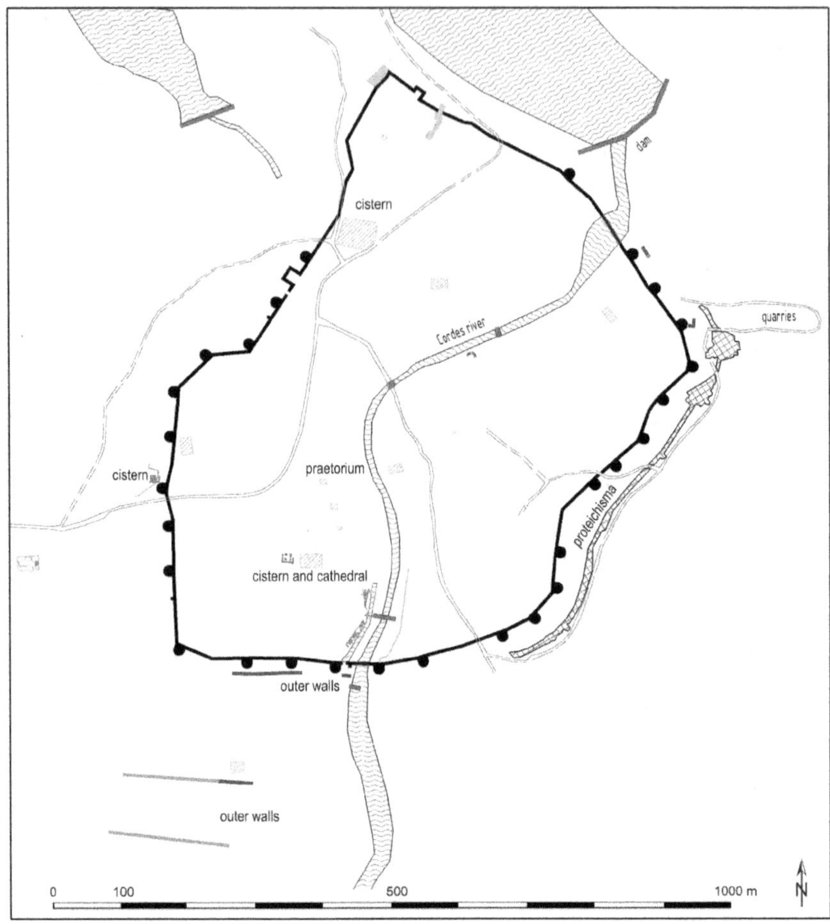

Figure 28   Dara

212 assemble their cattle and other animals when an enemy is threatening them. (19) Khusro therefore first made an attack on the western side of the circuit wall, forcing his way by the volume of missiles, and burnt the gates of the lesser wall. (20) Then he decided to build a tunnel into the eastern section of the city, for only there could the ground be dug up, since the builders had placed all the other parts of the circuit wall on rock. (21) So the Persians began to dig, starting from their trench. Because this was naturally quite deep, neither did the enemy catch sight of them nor did they give any sign to them of what was going on. (22) Consequently they had already penetrated beneath the foundations of the outer wall and were on the point of reaching the zone between the two walls and, soon afterwards, to pass the great wall and capture the city by storm, but – since the Persians were not destined to capture it – one of Khusro's men approached the circuit wall around noon. Whether he was a man or something greater than a man, he gave the appearance to the onlookers that he was gathering the missiles that the Romans had hurled from the walls a little earlier against the barbarian attackers. (23) While doing this and holding out his shield in front of him, he appeared to chat with those on the battlements and, with a laugh, to mock them. Then he declared the entire ruse to them and instructed them all to be alert and to pay the utmost attention to their safety. (24) After providing these indications, he departed, but the Romans gave orders in great turmoil and confusion to dig up the area between the two walls. (25) The Persians, however, knowing nothing of what was going on, applied them-selves to their project nonetheless. (26) While, therefore, the barbarians were constructing a direct path to the city wall underground, the Romans, on the advice of Theodore, a man versed in the science called mechanics, made a lateral trench of adequate depth.[319] Thus it happened that the Persians suddenly fell upon the Roman trench after reaching the middle of the zone between the two circuit walls. (27) The Romans slew the first of them, but those behind swiftly fled to their camp and saved themselves, for the Romans absolutely refused to pursue them in the dark. (28) So Khusro, having failed in this attempt, gave up hope of taking the city in the future by any means, entered discussions with the besieged, and returned to Persian territory after carrying off one thousand measures of silver. (29) When the Emperor Justinian learnt of this, he no longer wished to fulfil the terms agreed, reproaching Khusro for having attempted to capture Dara during a truce. This is what happened to the Romans during the first invasion of Khusro; and the summer then finished.[320]

213

Chapter 14

(1) Khusro built a city in Assyria in the territory of Ctesiphon, a day's journey from the city, and named it 'Khusro's Antioch'.[321] There he settled

---

[319] *PLRE* 3, Theodorus 13, suggests that this Theodore may also have carried out work on the Nea church in Jerusalem.

[320] The end of summer 540. The 'measures' of silver are probably pounds, cf. n. 273 on 6.24.

[321] Veh-Antiok-Khusro, 'the better Antioch of Khusro' lay just south of Ctesiphon. Tabari, 157–8, claims that it was precisely modelled on the original. See *RPLA*, 261–2.

all the Antiochene prisoners, endowing them with a bath-house and a hippodrome and seeing to it that they were entertained with other luxuries too.[322] (2) For he brought with him charioteers and musicians from both Antioch and other Roman cities. (3) Moreover, he consistently fed these Antiochenes at public expense with more consideration than is normal for prisoners and decreed that they be called 'royal', so that they should be subject to none save the king alone. (4) And if some other captive Roman became a runaway and succeeded in seeking refuge in Khusro's Antioch and a resident there declared him to be a relative, then it was no longer permitted for the one who had taken this captive to lead him away, not even if the person who had enslaved him was among the most eminent Persians.

(5) So the omen that occurred during the reign of Anastasius resulted in this outcome. For at that time a strong wind suddenly struck the suburb of Daphne and remarkably tall cypresses there were overturned from their deepest roots and fell to the ground, even though the law prohibited anyone from cutting them down.[323] (6) Thus it was that a little later, when Justin ruled the Romans, a singularly violent earthquake shook down the entire city and instantly levelled most of its buildings, including its most beautiful; it is even said that 300,000 Antiochenes perished at that moment.[324] (7) But in this capture, as I have said, the whole city was destroyed. This then was the tragedy of the Antiochenes.

(8) Belisarius, summoned by the emperor, came to Byzantium from Italy.[325] After he had spent the winter in Byzantium, the emperor despatched him at the start of spring against Khusro and the Persians, together with the commanders who had come with him from Italy, one of whom, Valerian, he ordered to take command of the forces in Armenia. (9) Martin had been immediately sent to the East, and consequently Khusro found him at Dara, as already explained.[326] (10) As for the Goths, Vitigis stayed in Byzantium, but all the others accompanied Belisarius' army against Khusro. (11) At this point one of the two ambassadors of Vitigis, the one who had assumed the title of bishop, died on

---

[322] The hippodrome was still functioning in the seventh century, as the *Miracles of Saint Anastasius* attest.

[323] Cf. e.g. *C.J.* 11.78.1–2.

[324] The earthquake of 29 May 526 is reported by numerous sources. Mal. 17.16 estimates the dead at 250,000. The city had already been struck by a fire in 525; a further earthquake followed in November 528.

[325] In summer 540, cf. *Wars* 7.1.1–2; he therefore set off from Constantinople in early 541.

[326] On Martin see 2.13.16. See 7.1.1 on the commanders that came with Belisarius from Italy.

Persian soil, but the other remained there.[327] (12) The man who had followed them as their interpreter, however, returned to Roman territory and was caught on the edge of the district of Constantia by John, the commander of the forces in Mesopotamia.[328] John brought him to the city and put him in prison, where he revealed, upon being questioned, all that had been done. (13) These things thus turned out in this way. Belisarius swiftly went forth with his followers, keen to anticipate any renewed invasion that Khusro might make into Roman territory.

Chapter 15

(1) In the meantime Khusro led his army to Colchis at the request of the Lazi for the following reason.[329] (2) The Lazi initially used to live in the land of Colchis as subjects of the Romans, not, however, paying tribute, nor subject to any orders from them except that when their king died, the Roman emperor used to send to his successor on the throne the symbols of sovereignty. (3) Together with his subjects, he guarded strictly the frontiers of his country to prevent hostile Huns from the adjacent Caucasus mountains from invading Roman territory through Lazica.[330] (4) For this guard duty they received no money or forces from the Romans, nor did they serve anywhere with the Roman troops, but engaged in continuous commerce by sea with the Romans who lived on the Euxine Sea. (5) For they had themselves neither salt nor cereals nor any other asset and obtained their provisions by supplying skins, hides and slaves.[331] (6) But after the affair of Gurgenes the king of Iberia, which I related earlier in my narrative, Roman soldiers began to be stationed among the Lazi, and these barbarians were annoyed by them, especially with Peter the general, who had a knack for behaving insultingly to those he met.[332] (7) This Peter came from Arzanene, which is on the other side of the river Nymphius, long subject to Persia, and while still a child had

216

---

[327] Cf. 2.2.2 on this mission.

[328] John Troglita was the *dux* of Mesopotamia, on whom see *PLRE* 3, Ioannes 36, and *ODLA*, John Troglita.

[329] Procopius uses the terms Colchis/Colchians and Lazica/Lazi interchangeably.

[330] See 1.11.28 with n.71 on the Lazi. They had rejoined the Romans in 522; they had been aligned with them until the mid fifth century. In this earlier period, it is clear that the Romans were involved in the appointment of the Lazic kings. See *ODLA*, Lazica (Egrisi), *REF*, 56–8, 79–80, 115–16.

[331] Procopius consistently underrates the productivity of Lazica, cf. 1.12.15.

[332] On Gurgenes' defection to the Romans and subsequent flight to Roman territory, see 1.12.4–11. See 1.12.18–19 for the installation of these soldiers, who soon withdrew. Peter's earlier campaigning in Lazica is reported at 1.12.9–14.

been enslaved by the Emperor Justin, when Justin was invading Persia after the capture of Amida with Celer's army. His owner was very kind to him and sent him to school. (8) At first he became Justin's secretary, but when Justin became the Roman emperor on the death of Anastasius, Peter became a general, drifting into greed for money as much as anyone ever had, and used to behave towards everyone with great folly.[333]

217

(9) But later the Emperor Justinian sent out among other commanders to Lazica John, whom they called Tzibus, a man of obscure and undistinguished origins, who had risen to the position of general for the single reason that he was the most wicked man on earth and the best at finding unlawful ways of procuring money.[334] He completely upset and confused affairs, both for Rome and for the Lazi. (10) This man persuaded the Emperor Justinian to build a city by the sea in Lazica, called Petra.[335] There he sat as if he were in an acropolis, plundering the wealth of the Lazi. (11) For the salt and whatever other merchandise seemed essential to the Lazi were not allowed to be imported into Colchis by the merchants or bought from elsewhere. Instead he himself set up in Petra what they call a 'monopoly' and became a trader and overseer of all the activity in this connection, buying up everything and selling it to the Colchians, not in accordance with custom but at the highest price he could.[336] (12) And at the same time the barbarians were annoyed in other ways that the Roman army was quartered with them, to which they had not been previously accustomed. When they could no longer bear it, they decided to go over to the Persians and Khusro, and, unbeknownst to the Romans, they sent envoys to them immediately to organise this. (13) They had been told to obtain pledges from Khusro that he would never give up the Lazi to the Romans against their will, and then to invite him into the country with the Persian army.

218

(14) So when the envoys reached Persia, they had a secret audience with Khusro and said: 'If ever before there have been men who have abandoned their own friends in any way and have wrongfully attached themselves to men who were quite unknown to them, and whom, to their joy, the beneficence of fortune has brought back again to their former friends, consider, great King, the Lazi also to be such. (15) For the

---

[333] See *PLRE* 2, Petrus 27. He was captured during the war narrated by Procopius at 1.7–9.

[334] John is described in similar terms to John the Cappadocian. See *PLRE* 3, Ioannes 20.

[335] Petra (Justiniana) is today Tsikhisdziri in Georgia; it was founded in 535, by which time John must have been in office. It is mentioned in *NovJ.* 28.pr. See *ODLA*, Petra.

[336] The state normally frowned on the creation of monopolies but sometimes exploited them for its own ends. See *ODLA*, monopolies.

Colchians, allies of the Persians since ancient times, did them great good and received the same in return. Of this we have many memorials in writing, while others are preserved up to the present time in your palace. (16) But later it befell our ancestors, either because they were neglected by you or for some other reason (for we cannot find out anything definite about this), to become allied to the Romans. (17) And now we and the king of Lazica bestow upon the Persians ourselves and our land to use as you will. (18) But we beg you to reflect on us in this way: if we have suffered no harm from the Romans and have come to you out of folly, reject this supplication of ours immediately, thinking that the Colchians will never be faithful to you (for when a friendship dissolves, the very process of forming the next one with different people is itself suspect). (19) But if, though friends of the Romans in name, we became in fact loyal slaves and have suffered impious wrongs from men who have behaved tyrannically towards us, receive us, your former allies, and take as your slaves those whom you used to treat as friends, out of hatred for the bitter tyranny that has arisen thus on our borders, and acting worthily of the justice that the Persians traditionally uphold. (20) For the man who does no wrong himself is not just unless, when he has it in his power, he also defends those who are being wronged by others.

(21) We should mention some of the things that the accursed Romans have dared to do to us. They left to our king only the semblance of monarchy and deprived us of control of affairs. The king is in the position of a servant, in fear of the general who gives him orders. (22) They put a huge army over us, not to guard the country from interference (for not one of our neighbours has interfered with us except the Romans), but to keep us virtually in prison and gain control of our possessions. (23) And see, O King, what scheme they have adopted in their desire to accelerate their seizure of what we have. (24) Whatever excess provisions they happen to have, they force the Lazi to buy against their will, and whatever Lazica produces that is most useful to them, they demand to buy from us (that is how they put it), the price in either case being fixed to suit the wishes of the rulers. (25) So they are taking all our gold alongside our basic produce, using the fair name of commerce for it, but in fact oppressing us with all their might. A shopkeeper is set up as our commanding officer, and he has exercised the powers of his office so as to make a business out of our need. (26) Such being the reason then for our defection, it has justice on its side, but we will tell you forthwith what benefits will come to you through receiving the request of the Lazi. (27) You will add to the Persian empire a most ancient monarchy, and the

reputation of your rule will be increased by it; further, you will have access to the Roman sea through our country, and by building ships upon it you will easily be able, O King, to reach the palace in Byzantium since there is no obstacle in the way.[337] (28) One might add that you will have control of the plundering of Roman territory every year by the neighbouring barbarians. (29) For surely you too know well that the country of the Lazi has been up to now a bulwark against the Caucasus mountains. (30) When therefore justice leads and advantage is there as well, we believe that there would be no sense in failing to accept our words.'

221 This was what the envoys said. (31) Khusro was delighted at their words and agreed to help the Lazi; he asked the envoys whether he could go into the land of Colchis with a large army, (32) for he said he had heard from many people before that it was rather difficult country even for an active man, being very rocky and covered over a great expanse by numerous dense forests. (33) But they assured him that the road there would be easy for the entire Persian army, if they cut down the trees and threw them into the ravines by the cliffs. (34) They agreed that they would themselves lead the way and carry out this work for the Persians. (35) Khusro, inspired by this proposal, collected a large force and made ready for the invasion, without revealing his plan to the Persians except only to those with whom he usually shared his secrets, and instructing the envoys to tell no one of what was underway. He was ostensibly setting out for Iberia to settle affairs there, for he put it about that a Hunnic people somewhere there had attacked the Persian empire.[338]

Chapter 16

(1) Meanwhile Belisarius, having arrived in Mesopotamia, was assembling an army from the whole region while sending forth men into Persian territory on spying missions. (2) He himself wanted to confront the enemy there, should they again undertake an invasion of Roman territory. Here then he was organising and equipping the soldiers, who **222** mostly lacked both weapons and armour and were terrified at the very name of the Persians. (3) The spies then returned and announced that

---

[337] There is no evidence for Persian ambitions on the Black Sea. The statement perhaps reflects fears in Constantinople.

[338] Procopius complains at *Anecd.* 30.14 that Justinian's cuts to the intelligence service had the consequence that the Romans fell for the story (cf. 16.3). At *Anecd.* 2.29–31 he mentions a Hunnic incursion organised by Khusro, which was repelled successfully by Valerian, the *magister militum per Armeniam*.

there would be no enemy invasion for the moment, since Khusro was occupied elsewhere by a war against the Huns. (4) Belisarius, having heard this, wished to invade the enemy's territory with his whole army forthwith. (5) In addition, al-Harith came to him with a large army of Saracens, while the emperor wrote a letter to him, commanding him swiftly to invade the enemy's territory. (6) He therefore summoned all the commanders in Dara and spoke thus:

'Since I know, fellow officers, that you all have experience of many wars,[339] I have brought you together now not to fire your resolve against the enemy through a reminder or exhortation – since I do not believe that you need a speech to spur you to boldness – but in order that we might take counsel among us and choose the best possible strategy for the interests of the emperor. (7) For a war tends to be successful above all as a consequence of good advice. Those who are preparing for discussions must free their minds from both modesty and fear.[340] (8) Fear, which always dazes those who have fallen into it, does not permit reason to choose the better option, while modesty, by obscuring better opinions, diverts discussion onto an opposite course. (9) Consequently, if either the great emperor or I myself seem to have taken a decision about the present circumstances, let this not preoccupy you. (10) He is left far removed from events and cannot adjust tactics to opportunities, (11) and so there should be no fear that in undertaking what is advantageous to his interests one might be acting against him. (12) For my part, since I am human and have come here from the West after a long period of time, inevitably some vital point will have passed me by. (13) Consequently, it is incumbent on you to state explicitly what will be to our advantage and that of the emperor without being daunted by my own view. (14) We came here initially, fellow officers, to prevent the enemy from making any incursion into our territory, but now, since things have gone better than we had hoped, it is possible for us to make plans about his territory. (15) Since I gathered you here for this reason, I think it fair that you should declare, without holding anything back, what each of you believes to be the best and most profitable course.'

(16) Such was Belisarius' speech. Peter and Buzes insisted that he lead forth the army against enemy territory without hesitating, and the entire meeting immediately followed their opinion. (17) Rhecithangus and Theoctistus, the commanders of the troops in Lebanon,[341] declared,

223

---

[339] Cf. Thuc. 7.61.3.

[340] One could translate the Greek word *aidōs* equally as 'respect' rather than 'modesty'.

[341] They were then *duces* (dukes) of Phoenice Libanensis. See *PLRE* 3, Rhecithangus and Theoctistus 2.

however, that while they wanted the same as the others as regards the invasion, they feared that, because of their abandonment of the districts of Phoenice and Syria, al-Mundhir would plunder them at his leisure; the emperor would then be angry at them, because they had not protected the lands under their control from plundering. Consequently, they had no desire to join in the invasion with the rest of the army. (18) But Belisarius said that the two men's opinion was far from the truth, since it was then the summer solstice: in this season, he pointed out, the Saracens always dedicate about two months to their god and do not undertake any raid on another's territory.[342] (19) He agreed therefore to release them both with their forces within sixty days and ordered them to follow with the rest of the army. Thus Belisarius was making his preparations for the invasion with great vigour.

Chapter 17

(1) When Khusro and the Persian army had left Iberia and were on the borders of Lazica, with the envoys leading the way, they proceeded without any opposition to cut down the trees (which are thick there and extremely dense and high and, moreover, on rocky ground, making the country quite impassable for the army) and by throwing the trees into the ravines, they made the way completely passable. (2) When they came to the middle of Colchis (where the poets set the tale of Medea and Jason in mythology)[343] Gubazes, the king of the Lazi, came forward and did obeisance to Khusro, the son of Kavadh, as his lord and master, surrendering himself to him, together with his palace and the whole of Lazica.[344]

(3) There is a coastal city in Colchis called Petra, on the so-called Euxine Sea, which had been a poor sort of place before, but which the Emperor Justinian strengthened and made notable with a circuit wall and other buildings.[345] (4) Khusro learnt that the Roman army was here with John, and he sent Aniabedes as general in command of a force against them to take the place at the first shout.[346] (5) But when John heard of the attack, he ordered that no one go outside the fortifications nor show

---

[342] Nonnosus §11 confirms this truce. The truce lasted for two months in the summer.

[343] E.g. Pindar in his fourth *Pythian Ode* or Apollonius Rhodius in his *Argonautica*. Procopius returns to the subject at 8.2.30.

[344] On Gubazes see *PLRE* 3, Gubazes, *ODLA*, Gubaz II.

[345] See 2.15.10.

[346] John is John Tzibus, on whom see 2.15.9. Aniabedes may be a rendering of a Persian title, cf. *PLRE* 3, Aniabedes.

themselves to the enemy from the battlements. He made ready the whole army and stationed it near the gates, telling them to keep quiet, not letting out a sound or a word. (6) So the Persians came near the gates, and when they saw and heard nothing hostile, they concluded that the city was deserted and that the Romans had abandoned it. (7) They therefore came still closer to the wall, meaning to set up scaling ladders at once, as there were no defenders. (8) Hearing and seeing nothing hostile, they sent a message to Khusro, informing him of the situation. (9) He despatched most of his army and told them to make an attempt on the wall from all sides, and he ordered one of the officers to use the device called the ram against the gates. Sitting on the hill that lies very close to the city, he himself became a spectator of the events. (10) But the Romans at once suddenly opened the gates, flung themselves unexpectedly on the enemy, and killed many of them, particularly those stationed with the ram. The rest managed to escape together with their general and were saved. (11) Khusro was seized with anger and impaled Aniabedes for being outgeneralled by John, a shopkeeper and a man without any knowledge of war. (12) Some say that it was not Aniabedes who was impaled, but the officer who was in command of the men working on **226** the ram.

(13) Khusro himself moved with all his army and came up to the wall of Petra and there he pitched camp and began a siege. (14) But on the following day, as he did a tour of the circuit walls, he came to suspect that they were not very defensible and decided to launch an assault. He brought up the entire army there and set about it, ordering them all to shoot at the battlements. (15) The Romans defended themselves with war-machines and all their arrows. So at first the Persians did little damage to the Romans, despite firing very frequently, and suffered much damage at their hands, for they were shooting from a height. (16) But later, since it was fated that Petra should be taken by Khusro, John was by some chance struck in the throat and died, and after this the remaining Romans gave up hope of anything. (17) Then the barbarians retreated to their camp, for it was already growing dark, and on the following day they devised an excavation against the wall in the following way.

(18) The city of Petra is unapproachable partly because of the sea and partly because of sheer rocks that rise up there on all sides. It is from this that it got its name.[347] (19) It has one entrance on level ground, and even this is not a wide one, for precipitous crags overhang it on both sides.

---

[347] The Greek word *petra* means 'rock'.

(20) Here the builders of the city, with forethought to prevent that part of the wall from being assailable, had built long walls stretching for a considerable distance next to each cliff at the entrance. (21) On these walls they built two towers, one on either side, not in the usual way, but with a different technique. (22) They did not leave the space inside the building empty, but made the whole of the towers, from the ground up to a great height, of enormous stones fitting into one another, so that they could not be shaken down by a ram or any other device. This was the nature of the fortifications at Petra.

(23) But the Persians secretly made a trench and got beneath one of the towers. They removed many of the stones from there and put wood in their place, which shortly afterwards they set on fire. (24) The flame gradually rose and broke down the strength of the stones, shaking the entire tower, and suddenly brought it all down to the ground in an instant. (25) But the Romans who were inside the tower realised beforehand enough of what was happening not to fall to the ground with it, but to make their escape inside the city's circuit wall. (26) Now the enemy who were storming the wall on the level ground could capture the city by force without any hindrance. (27) And so the terrified Romans held a conference with the barbarians, and, after receiving pledges from Khusro for their lives and their wealth, made a voluntary surrender of themselves and their city. This was how Khusro took Petra. (28) He found that John had a very sizeable amount of money, which he seized himself, but as for the rest, neither he nor any Persian touched any of it, while the Romans joined the Persian army with their own property.[348]

Chapter 18

(1) In the meantime Belisarius and the Roman army, unaware of what was happening here, were proceeding in good order from the city of Dara to Nisibis. (2) When they were half-way there, Belisarius led the army to the right, where there were sufficient sources of water and a plain large enough for them all to encamp. (3) There he told them to pitch camp about forty-two stades from the city of Nisibis. (4) All the rest were very surprised that he did not want to encamp right against the circuit wall, and some refused to follow him. (5) So Belisarius said to the officers who were around him:

---

[348] Petra thus fell into Persian hands in 541. It was retaken by the Romans in 551 and then razed to the ground. See Proc. 8.11–12 and *REF*, 118–19.

'I did not wish to reveal to everyone what I am planning. For when talk gets around in a camp, it cannot keep secrets, and it gradually spreads until it reaches even the enemy. (6) But I can see that many of you are giving way to indiscipline and that each one of you wants to direct the war himself, so I will now reveal among you what I ought to keep secret, but with this reminder first: when many men in an army give their wishes free rein, it is quite impossible to do what is necessary. (7) It is my belief, then, that Khusro in going against other barbarians has certainly not left his own country without sufficient guard, and especially this city, which is the first to be reached and is set as a defence before his whole land. (8) I know very well that he stationed soldiers inside it in sufficient numbers and of high enough quality to be capable of putting a stop to our attacks. The proof of this you have near at hand. (9) For he put as general over them Nabedes, who, it seems, is first among the Persians after Khusro himself in reputation and standing.[349] (10) For my part, I think that he will test our strength, and will allow our advance only if he has been defeated by us in a battle. (11) So if the engagement should be near to the city, we and the Persians will not be evenly matched. (12) For they will come to the attack from a safe position, and if it should happen that they are successful, they will be greatly encouraged in their offensives, while if they are defeated they will easily escape our onslaught. (13) We shall be able to pursue them for only a little way, and no harm will come to the city from it, for surely you can see that it is impregnable to storm, since it has soldiers defending it. (14) But if the enemy join battle with us here and we defeat them, I have great hopes, my fellow officers, that we shall be able to take the city. (15) For while the enemy flee over a considerable distance, we shall probably either be able to mingle with them and rush inside the gates with them, or else get ahead of them and force them to turn and escape in another direction, making Nisibis easy for us to capture in the absence of its defenders.'

(16) At these words from Belisarius all the others were convinced and remained in the camp with him. But Peter associated with himself John, who was the commander of the regular troops in Mesopotamia and in charge of a not inconsiderable proportion of the army.[350] And coming up not far from the wall, about ten stades away, he waited there. (17) Belisarius stationed those with him for battle, and he told Peter's men to

---

[349] His high standing is confirmed by the poet Corippus. See *PLRE* 3, Nabedes, *ODLA*, Nabed (Gk. Nabedes).

[350] On Peter see 2.15.7, for whom Procopius has a hearty dislike. See 2.14.12 on John Troglita, the *dux* of Mesopotamia.

hold themselves ready for an engagement until he gave the signal and to be aware that the enemy would attack about noon, obviously with the idea that it was their habit to eat in the evening, but the Romans' at noon.[351] (18) This was Belisarius' advice. But Peter's men paid no heed to his orders and in the middle of the day, feeling oppressed by the heat (for the place is very dry), they put down their arms and, without any thought for the enemy, went round the cucumbers that grew there and started eating them, in no sort of order. (19) Nabedes saw this and urged the Persian army upon them at great speed. (20) But the Romans did not fail to see the barbarians advancing upon them from the wall, for they were plainly visible as they came over the flat plain, and they sent a message to Belisarius, asking him to help them, seized their arms and went to meet them in confusion and disorder. (21) Belisarius' men realised from the dust that the Persians were attacking, even though the messenger had not yet arrived, and set off at a run to help. (22) The Persians came upon the Romans, who could not withstand their attack, and turned the Romans to flight without any difficulty, followed them and killed fifty; they also captured and kept Peter's standard. (23) They would have killed them all in this pursuit – for the Romans were giving no thought to valour – had not Belisarius and his army come up and stopped them. (24) For when the Goths charged ahead of all the rest with a dense array of long spears, the Persians could not withstand them and turned to flight.[352] (25) The Romans and the Goths followed and killed one hundred and fifty Persians, for after a short pursuit the rest quickly came within the walls. (26) Then all the Romans retreated to Belisarius' camp, and the Persians on the following day erected Peter's standard on a tower instead of a trophy. They hung sausages on it and jeered and laughed at the enemy, but they no longer dared to attack and guarded the city in safety.

Chapter 19

(1) Belisarius, observing that Nisibis was remarkably secure, had no hope of capturing it and was keen to move forward in order to inflict some damage on the enemy by a sudden incursion. (2) He therefore set off with his army and advanced. After a day's journey they came upon a fortress that the Persians call Sisauranon.[353] (3) Here there was a substantial

---

[351] See 1.8.14, 1.14.34 on these differing mealtimes.
[352] See 2.14.10 on the Goths accompanying Belisarius.
[353] The fortress lies only a few kilometres from Roman territory in the Tur Abdin just to the north, in fact, cf. Proc. *Aed.* 2.4.9 and *ODLA*, Sisauronon.

population and eight hundred cavalrymen, the finest of the Persians, who stood guard, in charge of whom was an eminent Persian, Bleschames by name. (4) The Romans pitched camp very close to the fort and began a siege. Their attack on the circuit wall was driven off with the loss of many men in the fighting, (5) since the wall was extremely strong, while the barbarians there defended themselves very stoutly. Belisarius consequently summoned all the commanders and spoke thus:

(6) 'The experience of many wars, commanders, has allowed us in tough situations to foresee what will happen and to be capable of preferring the better course to the more dangerous. (7) So you understand how great a danger it is for an army to advance into enemy territory leaving behind it numerous fortifications and numerous troops in them. (8) This is precisely what has happened to us in the current circumstances. For should we go forward, certain contingents of the enemy from here and from Nisibis will follow us in secret and probably cause damage to us in places well suited for ambushes or some other scheme. (9) If another army were to meet us in battle somewhere, we would be obliged to draw our forces up against both, and thus we would suffer terrible losses at their hands. I forbear from mentioning that, should we fail in the encounter – were this to occur – we would then have no way of regaining Roman territory. (10) So let us not give the impression of scuppering ourselves by irrational haste and not harm Roman interests by our rivalries. For rash daring brings destruction, but prudent postponement always preserves those who practise it.[354] (11) Let us therefore encamp here and attempt to storm this fortress, while al-Harith is sent with his followers against the districts of Assyria, [355] (12) for the Saracens are by nature incapable of storming a wall but the most adept of all men at plundering.[356] (13) Some of the more battle-ready soldiers will accompany them, so that, if no obstacle presents itself, they can inflict irreparable harm on those who fall upon them, but if the enemy meets them, they will be able to withdraw to us easily and be rescued. (14) And after taking the fortress, if God wills it, let us cross the river Tigris with the entire army with no fear of troublemakers behind us and with a good knowledge of how matters stand in Assyria.'

(15) Belisarius' words seemed to all to be well spoken, and he immediately acted on his plan. He ordered al-Harith to enter Assyria with his followers; with him he despatched 1200 soldiers, of whom the majority

233

---

[354] Echoes of Thuc. 3.82.4, 6.59.1 for 'rash daring', 3.82.4 for 'prudent postponement'.
[355] On Assyria, i.e. Lower Mesopotamia, see 1.17.6.
[356] Cf. Proc. *Aed.* 2.9.3–4 on the Arabs' inability to storm walls, with *AEBI*, 246–7.

234 were drawn from his own guards, while he put in charge of them two bodyguards, Trajan and John, called the Glutton, both experts in warfare.[357] (16) He instructed them to do everything according to al-Harith's commands and ordered al-Harith to plunder everything he came across and thus to return to the camp and report to them on military matters in Assyria. (17) Al-Harith's men therefore crossed the river Tigris and arrived in Assyria. (18) There they found a prosperous land, unravaged for a long time and without protection. They plundered the villages there extensively by a lightning campaign and accumulated a large quantity of goods.

(19) Then Belisarius captured some Persians and learnt that those in the fortress utterly lacked provisions. (20) For unlike at Dara and the city of Nisibis, they were not in the habit of storing the yearly rations in a public granary, but had not anticipated the unexpected onrush of an enemy army by bringing in any of the necessary supplies. (21) Since many people had fled to the fortress, they were naturally afflicted by a shortage of supplies. (22) Once Belisarius learnt this, he despatched George, a highly intelligent man with whom he shared his secrets, in order to test the inhabitants there as to whether he might be able to capture the place through some agreement. (23) By exhortation and by many alluring words to them, George convinced them to accept guarantees for their **235** safety and to hand themselves and the fort over to the Romans. (24) Thus Belisarius captured Sisauranon and released unharmed all its inhabitants, who were Christian and Roman by origin. He sent the Persians with Bleschames to Byzantium and razed the circuit wall of the fort to the ground. (25) The emperor not long afterwards despatched the Persians and Bleschames to Italy to campaign against the Goths.[358] This was the way in which the events relating to the fortress of Sisauranon took place.[359]

(26) But al-Harith, fearing that he might be deprived of his spoils by the Romans, no longer wished to return to the camp. (27) He therefore sent forth some of his followers ostensibly for reconnaissance, but ordered them in secret to return as quickly as possible and to report to them that a large enemy army was stationed at the river crossing. (28) He

---

[357] On these two *bucellarii* of Belisarius see *PLRE* 3, Traianus 2, Ioannes 64.

[358] One of these Persians distinguished himself already in 542 at Verona, a certain Armenian called Artabazes, Proc. 7.3.11.

[359] There is a marked change of time in the following section; it may have been added to respond to criticism of Belisarius subsequently, for which see *Anecd.* 2.18–25: the general was accused of cutting short the whole campaign in order to confront his wife Antonina about her infidelities.

consequently recommended to Trajan and John that they return to
Roman territory using a different route. (29) Hence they did not come to
Belisarius again, but, keeping the river Euphrates to their right, they thus
reached Theodosiopolis on the river Khabur.[360] (30) Belisarius and the
Roman army, having heard nothing about this force, grew concerned,
falling into a state of unbearable and unreasonable fear and suspicion.
(31) Because they had spent a long time on this siege, many soldiers there
happened to be seized by a troublesome fever, for Persian-controlled
Mesopotamia is extremely parched. (32) The Romans, and especially
those who came from Thrace, were unused to this. Since they were quartered in an extraordinarily arid place in stiflingly hot huts, they fell so ill
that one third of the army was lying half-dead. (33) The entire army was
therefore keen to depart from there and to return to their territory as
swiftly as possible, especially the commanders of the troops in Lebanon
and Syria, Rhecithangus and Theoctistus, who realised that the time of
the sacred truce of the Saracens had indeed already expired. (34) At any
rate they frequently came to Belisarius, begging him to release them
immediately, pointing out that, while they sat there for no reason, they
were handing over the villages of Lebanon and Syria to al-Mundhir. (35)
Belisarius therefore summoned all the officers and invited a discussion.
(36) There the first to rise was John, the son of Nicetas, who spoke as
follows:

'Most noble Belisarius, I believe that no other general in all time has
been your equal for both good fortune and courage. (37) This reputation
has taken hold not only among the Romans, but even among all barbarians. (38) But you will maintain this good reputation most firmly if you
should prove able to bring us alive and in safety to Roman territory, for
at present our expectations are not in a happy state. So for my sake take
thought for this army along these lines. (39) The Saracens and the most
battle-ready soldiers, after crossing the river Tigris I am not sure how
many days ago, have come to such a pass that they have not even been
able to send a messenger to us. Rhecithangus and Theoctistus, as you can
clearly see, are on the point of marching away, supposing that right away
the army of al-Mundhir will be in the midst of Phoenice, laying waste all
the villages there. (40) Among those remaining, the sick are so numerous
that there are far fewer people to care for them and bring them back to
Roman territory. (41) Under such circumstances, if any enemy should
encounter us, whether we remain here or are withdrawing, there will be

236

237

---

[360] This is not the Armenian city of this name, but rather Resaina in Osrhoene. See *ODLA*, Resaina.

no one left to report to the Romans in Dara the fate that overtook us. (42) I do not think it possible even to discuss a forward move. So while hope yet remains, it will be useful to plan our return and to take action. (43) For those in danger, and particularly in such danger as this, it is utter madness to consider not one's safety, but plans against the enemy.'

(44) So spoke John, and all the others praised him. In the ensuing disorder they decided to withdraw in haste. (45) Belisarius therefore first placed the sick on pack animals,[361] then led the army behind. (46) When they had quickly regained Roman territory, Belisarius learnt of all al-Harith had done but was unable to impose any punishment on him, since he never came into his sight again. Such then was the conclusion of the Roman invasion.

(47) When Khusro had taken Petra, it was announced to him that Belisarius had invaded Persia, and he was told about the engagement near the city of Nisibis, the capture of the fortress of Sisauranon, and the doings of al-Harith's army across the river Tigris. (48) He posted a garrison in Petra at once and went to Persia with the rest of the army and the Roman prisoners.[362] (49) This happened on the second of Khusro's invasions. And Belisarius was summoned to the emperor in Byzantium and there spent the winter.

Chapter 20

(1) At the beginning of spring,[363] Khusro the son of Kavadh invaded Roman territory with a large army for the third time, keeping the river Euphrates on his right. (2) Candidus, the bishop of Sergiopolis, grew afraid for himself and the city when he heard that the Persian army had come very near.[364] He had not fulfilled what he had agreed with Khusro at the appointed time, and so he came to the enemy camp and begged Khusro not to be angry with him for this. (3) For he said that he had never had any money, and for this reason he had not even wanted to save the people of Sura in the first place, and though he had often made supplications to the Emperor Justinian about them, he had had no success with him. (4) But Khusro put him under guard, tortured him cruelly, and demanded the right to exact from him twice the amount, as

---

[361] The Greek term *hypozygia* could refer equally to wagons, as many translations give.

[362] Proc. *Anecd.* 2.26–37 reports that Khusro had to deal with discontent in his own army in Lazica during his withdrawal from Petra.

[363] The year is 542.

[364] See 2.5.29–32 on Candidus' pledge for the ransoming of the prisoners from Sura in 540.

had been agreed. (5) Candidus begged him to send some men to Sergiopolis and take all the treasures from the church there. (6) When Khusro did so, Candidus sent with them some of his attendants. (7) The people of Sergiopolis therefore received into the city the men sent by Khusro and gave them many of their treasures, assuring them that nothing else was left to them.[365] (8) But Khusro said that this was not enough for him and demanded more than this. (9) So he sent some men ostensibly to examine the city's wealth in detail, but in fact to take possession of the city. (10) Since it was not fated that Sergiopolis should be taken by the Persians, a Saracen called 'Amr, who was a Christian and enrolled under al-Mundhir, came along the city wall by night and told them the whole story, urging them not to receive the Persians into the city. (11) Thus when the men sent by Khusro returned to him with nothing to show for their efforts, he boiled with anger and determined to take the city.

(12) He therefore despatched an army six thousand strong, and ordered the forces to lay siege to it and assault the circuit wall. When they got there, they set to work. (13) The people of Sergiopolis defended themselves strongly at first, but later became discouraged and were frightened by the danger. They decided to surrender the city to the enemy, (14) for they had only two hundred soldiers.[366] But 'Amr came up to the wall again at night and told them that in two days the Persians would raise the siege, since their water was failing them altogether. (15) Accordingly, they did not hold a parley with the enemy, and the barbarians were overcome by thirst and went away, back to Khusro. But Khusro would not now let Candidus go, (16) the reason being, I imagine, that he could no longer be a bishop after he had broken his oath. Such was the course of these events.

(17) When Khusro came to the country of the Commageni, which they call Euphratesia, he did not want to turn to plundering or to capturing anywhere, because in the lands on his way as far as Syria, he had previously captured some places and despoiled the rest, as I have narrated earlier. (18) It was his intention to lead the army to Palestine so that he could plunder it, particularly the treasures in Jerusalem. He had heard that this land was particularly rich and belonged to wealthy inhabitants.

240

---

[365] Among the items seized was a jewelled golden cross that had been presented to St Sergius by Theodora. It was returned in the early 590s by Khusro's grandson, Khusro II, who dedicated a further cross himself. See Evagr. *HE* 6.28 and Th. Sim. 5.13.1–2, both to be found in *REF*, 175–6.

[366] Evagr. *HE* 4.21 reports that Khusro witnessed supernatural defenders protecting the city and therefore withdrew.

241 (19) All the Romans, officers and soldiers, were quite unwilling to meet the enemy or to stop their advance. They each found what places of safety they could and thought it enough to guard these and save themselves.

(20) When the Emperor Justinian heard of the Persian invasion, he sent Belisarius against them again. Riding on the public horses, which they call 'post-horses', since he had no army with him Belisarius very soon arrived in Euphratesia. Now Justus, the emperor's cousin, happened to have taken refuge in Hierapolis with Buzes and some others.[367] (21) When they heard that Belisarius was not far away, they wrote him a letter. (22) This was what the letter made clear: 'Now Khusro, as you doubtless know yourself, has again made war on the Romans, with a far larger army than before. It is not yet clear where he means to go, except that we hear that he is very near. He is not doing any damage to any district, but going steadily forward. (23) Come to us as soon as you can, if you can escape detection by the enemy army, so that you can save yourself for the emperor and help us to defend Hierapolis.'

(24) Such was the content of the letter. Belisarius, not liking what it said, went to the place called Europus, which is on the river Euphrates.[368] (25) From there he sent word all around, collected an army and pitched **242** camp there, and made this reply to the officers in Hierapolis: 'If Khusro is advancing against other peoples, and not Roman subjects, your plan is good and the safest possible. (26) For when men can remain at rest and avoid evils, it is utter madness to incur any unnecessary danger. But if this barbarian, on leaving here, means to strike some other land that belongs to the Emperor Justinian, and that a particularly rich land, with no garrison of soldiers whatever, rest assured that death with valour is in every way better than safety without fighting. (27) For that could not properly be called safety, only betrayal. But come to Europus as quickly as you can, where I have collected the whole army and have hopes of doing to the enemy all that God allows.' (28) When the officers read this, they were encouraged, and leaving Justus with a few men to guard Hierapolis, the others went to Europus with the rest of the army.

Chapter 21

(1) When Khusro heard that Belisarius was encamped with the entire Roman army at Europus, he decided to go no further forwards. He sent

---

[367] On Justus see 1.24.53.

[368] Europus lies 30 km north of Hierapolis, well placed for crossings of the Euphrates. See *ODLA*, Carchemish.

to Belisarius one of the royal secretaries called Abandanes,[369] who had a high reputation for intelligence, to find out what sort of general he was, though ostensibly to complain that the Emperor Justinian had not sent envoys to Persia to treat for peace according to their agreement. When he heard this, Belisarius did as follows. (2) He chose six thousand tall, especially fine-looking men and set out for a hunt, some distance from the camp, telling Diogenes the bodyguard and Adolius, the son of Acacius, an Armenian by birth, who saw to the emperor's tranquillity in the palace on a permanent basis (the Romans call the holders of this office *silentiarii*), but was at that time commanding some Armenians, to cross the river with a thousand horse and move about the bank there, giving the enemy the impression all the time that if they wanted to cross the Euphrates and go to their own country, they would never allow them.[370] They acted accordingly.

(3) When Belisarius had heard that the enemy was very near, he made a tent of some fine cloth, of the sort which it is the custom to call a *papilio*,[371] and sat there as if in a deserted spot, trying to show that he had come without any equipment. He arranged the soldiers like this. (4) On either side of the tent were Thracians and Illyrians, and after them Goths, next to them Heruls, and then Vandals and Moors. They extended far over the plain. (5) They did not wait standing in the same place all the time, but separated from each other and walked about, nonchalantly watching Khusro's envoy without the slightest interest. (6) None of them had either a cloak or any other covering for their shoulders, but they strolled about dressed in linen tunics and trousers, with their belts on top. (7) Each one had his horsewhip, and for weapons one had a sword, another an axe, another an uncovered bow. (8) They all gave the appearance of being intent upon the hunt and unconcerned by anything else. (9) So Abandanes came before Belisarius and said that King Khusro was angry because the Caesar (for this is what the Persians called the Roman emperor) had not sent him the envoys as he had previously agreed, and that as a result Khusro had been forced to bear arms against Roman territory. (10) But Belisarius was not afraid at the thought of so great a number of barbarians being encamped nearby, nor was he thrown into confusion by what the man said, but answered him with a relaxed and

243

244

---

[369] Not otherwise known. See *PLRE* 3, Abandanes.

[370] Diogenes was a long-serving *bucellarius* of Belisarius. Adolius was an Armenian, cf. 2.3.10, the son of Acacius. The *silentiarii* or 'silentiaries' were ushers at meetings of the emperor's ministers, cf. *ODLA, silentiarii*.

[371] The Latin term could be translated as 'butterfly' or 'pavilion'.

laughing expression: 'Men do not usually act in the way that Khusro has just now done. (11) For other men, if a dispute occurs between themselves and any of their neighbours, send spokesmen to them first, and only make war on them if they do not find them reasonable. (12) But he comes into the midst of the Romans and then offers peace talks.' With this he dismissed the envoy.

(13) The envoy came to Khusro and told him to leave as quickly as possible, (14) for he said he had met a general who was the bravest and shrewdest among men, and soldiers such as he had never seen before and for whose orderly behaviour he had the greatest admiration. Further, the stakes in the struggle were not equal for himself and for Belisarius, the difference being that if he himself won, he would be conquering Caesar's slave, whereas if he should chance to be defeated he would bring great shame on the monarchy and the Persian race. The vanquished Romans could easily save themselves in strongholds and in their own land, while of the Persian troops, if they should meet with a reversal, not even a messenger could escape to Persia. (15) Khusro was convinced by this warning and decided to retreat to Persia, but was greatly puzzled as to how to do it, (16) for he believed that the river crossing was guarded by the enemy. He could not go back along the same road, which was completely deserted, because all their provisions which they had earlier brought with them when they invaded Roman territory were already exhausted. (17) Finally, after much pondering, it seemed best to him to risk a battle to get to the opposite bank and make their journey through country that was flourishing with every kind of good thing. (18) But Belisarius knew very well that even a hundred thousand men could never check Khusro's crossing, for the river can be crossed by boat in many places thereabouts for some distance, and in any case, the Persian army was too big to be prevented from crossing by a few enemy. He told Diogenes and Adolius with their men, along with the thousand men, first to move around the bank there, so as to send the barbarians into confusion and perplexity. (19) But after he had frightened the enemy in the way I have related, he was afraid that something might prevent Khusro from leaving Roman territory. (20) It seemed to him a noteworthy achievement to drive out Khusro's army without risking a battle against the myriads of barbarians with soldiers who were very few in number and absolutely terrified of the Persian army. Accordingly, he told Diogenes and Adolius to stay quiet.

(21) Khusro built a bridge with great speed and suddenly crossed the river Euphrates with the entire army. (22) For the Persians can cross any

river without trouble, since they have in their equipment on the march iron hooks with which they fit long beams to each other and improvise a bridge on the spot wherever they want it. (23) As soon as he was on the other side, he sent a message to Belisarius, saying that he had done a favour to the Romans by the retreat of the Persian army, and that he was expecting the envoys from them, who ought to be present very shortly. (24) Belisarius, too, crossed the river Euphrates with the entire Roman army and immediately sent messengers to Khusro. (25) When they reached him, they were full of gratitude for the retreat and promised that envoys would come to him from the emperor forthwith, who would ratify with him the previous agreement about the peace. (26) They asked him to make his way through Roman lands as though it were friendly territory. He agreed to this also, if the Romans would give him an eminent man as hostage for this agreement, so as to guarantee that they would fulfil their undertakings. (27) So the envoys returned to Belisarius and told him of Khusro's words, and he went to Edessa and immediately sent as an unwilling hostage to Khusro John, the son of Basil, by far the most notable of the Edessenes by birth and wealth.[372] (28) The Romans held Belisarius in high regard, and the man seemed to have gained more renown in this affair even than when he brought Gelimer or Vitigis as captives to Byzantium. (29) For it really was a matter for much note and praise that, when all the Romans were terrified and hiding in their strongholds, and when Khusro was in the midst of the Roman empire with a large army, a general should come post-haste from Byzantium with a few men and encamp opposite the Persian king, and that Khusro, in fear either of fortune or of the man's valour, or else deceived by some tricks, should suddenly stop his advance and actually flee, despite his show of wanting peace.[373]

(30) In the meantime Khusro, in defiance of his agreement, took the city of Callinicum, which was completely undefended. For the Romans, seeing that its circuit wall was rotten and could very easily be taken, were engaged in pulling it down in sections and restoring it with a new structure.[374] (31) At this time they had pulled down a portion, but had not yet rebuilt the missing part. When they heard that the enemy were very near,

247

248

---

[372] Procopius gives more details at *Anecd.* 12.6–10: Justinian refused to allow his grandmother to ransom him from Khusro. He died before returning to Edessa. See *PLRE* 3, Ioannes 30.

[373] This achievement drew the attention of later Byzantine chroniclers: Theoph. 219–22 incorporates almost the entire narrative into his chronicle, the only section of *The Persian Wars* he retained. Proc. *Anecd.* 3.30–1 offers a less generous appraisal.

[374] Cf. Proc. *Aed.* 2.7.17 on the reconstruction of the walls.

they removed their most valuable treasures for safety, and the rich inhabitants retreated to other fortresses, but the rest stayed there without soldiers. (32) It so happened that a large number of farmers had gathered there, whom Khusro enslaved, and he razed the whole city to the ground. (33) Not long afterwards he received John, the hostage, and went back to his native land. (34) The Armenians who had gone over to Khusro received pledges from the Romans and came with Bassaces to Byzantium. This was what happened to the Romans on Khusro's third invasion, and Belisarius was summoned to Byzantium by the emperor to be despatched again to Italy, for things were already very bad there for the Romans.[375]

Chapter 22

(1) At about this time a plague occurred, as a result of which all human life was very nearly extinguished.[376] Now for everything that comes from heaven some explanation of its cause can probably be given by daring men, of the sort usually given by the experts in these matters who love to invent an ingenious explanation of what is incomprehensible to man and to fabricate outlandish natural science. They know very well that they are saying nothing sound, but think it enough if they can deceive some of those they meet and convince them by their talk. (2) But for this disaster there is no way of giving a reason or of conceiving one in the imagination, except indeed to refer it to God. (3) For it did not happen in a part of the earth or to certain men only, nor did it observe a season of the year, from which some clever explanations of its cause might be deduced; it was spread over the whole earth and ruined the lives of all alike, however much they differed from one another, sparing neither sex nor time of life. (4) For while people differ from each other by their place of habitation, or mode of life, or natural disposition, or habits, or by any other characteristic, in this disease alone the difference was of no benefit. (5) It attacked some in summer, others in winter, others in the other parts of the year. Let every man, both sophist and astrologer, say as he thinks

---

[375] Bassaces had taken part in the Armenian defection to Khusro, cf. 2.3.31. Procopius underplays the return of the Armenians to the Roman fold here. Belisarius did not return to Italy until 544. See *PLRE* 3, 212.

[376] The first instance of bubonic plague in history, known as the Early Medieval Pandemic (EMP) or Justinianic Plague. It returned at regular intervals after the initial outbreak until the mid eighth century. John of Ephesus offers an equally vivid account as Procopius' at Ps.-Dion. ii, 74–98, cf. Evagr. *HE* 4.29. See *ODLA*, 'Justinianic Plague'. Procopius' account has many echoes of Thucydides' description of the plague that struck Athens in 430 B.C., 2.47–54.

fit about it. For my part, I will go on to say what the origin of this disease was and how it destroyed men.

(6) It began with the Egyptians who live in Pelusium.[377] Once it had divided, part went to Alexandria and the rest of Egypt, and part came to Palestine, on the borders of Egypt, and from there overran the whole earth, always moving forward and travelling at a fixed pace. (7) It seemed to advance according to an established plan and to spend a fixed time in each country, affording no one a merely cursory degree of destruction, but spreading in each direction to the limits of the world, as if frightened that some cranny of the earth might escape it. (8) It left out no island nor cave nor peak inhabited by people, and if by any chance it did pass by a country, either not affecting the inhabitants, or else just lightly touching them, it returned again later, and, not touching the neighbouring people on whom it had previously fallen most severely, it did not leave that country until it had achieved its just and right number of dead to correspond with those who had earlier been destroyed from among those living around there. (9) This disease always began from the coast and then moved up to the country inland.

251

In the second year, in the middle of spring, it reached Byzantium, where it happened that I too was living at the time.[378] (10) This was how it happened. Apparitions of demons were seen by many in every human form, and those who came upon them thought that they were struck by the man they had met in some part of their body, and were instantly seized by the disease at the same time as they saw this apparition. (11) At first those who came upon them tried to turn them away, intoning the most divine names and observing other rites as best each could, but they accomplished nothing at all, since most of them died, even after they had taken refuge in churches. (12) Later they would not even listen to their friends calling to them, and they shut themselves up in their rooms and pretended that they could not hear, even when their doors were being battered, obviously afraid that it was a demon that was calling them. (13) Some were struck by the disease in a different way, seeing a vision in a dream and seeming to suffer the same thing from the apparition standing over them, or else hearing a voice foretelling that they were enrolled among the number of those who were to die. (14) But the majority were seized by the disease without realising in a dream, either while asleep or in waking life, what was going to happen. They were overcome in this

252

---

[377] Whether it originated in East Africa or Asia remains the subject of debate; the former is more probable. It was probably in July 541 that it appeared at Pelusium.

[378] Some have dated its arrival to February 542, but April is more likely.

way. (15) They would suddenly develop a fever, some waking from sleep, others as they walked about, others as they did something else. (16) Their body did not alter its previous hue, nor was it hot, as if a fever had come upon it, nor was there any burning; the fever was so slight from the beginning until the evening[379] that it did not give an impression of danger either to the victims themselves or to a doctor who touched them. (17) So not one of those who had succumbed seemed likely to die of it. But on the same day for some, on the next day for others, and not many days later for still others, a bubonic swelling developed, not only in the place where the part of the body under the stomach is also called the bubo (groin), but also within the armpit, and, in some, beside the ears and in places on the thighs.[380]

(18) So far as this, something similar happened to all of those struck by the disease. But after this I cannot say whether the difference in what happened lay in the difference of bodily characteristics, or whether it was according to the wishes of the bringer of the disease. (19) For some were afflicted by a deep coma, others by violent frenzy, and each suffered the characteristic symptoms of the disease. Those in a coma forgot all their usual habits[381] and seemed as if they were sleeping forever. (20) If anyone tended them, they would eat in their sleep, while some who were neglected died at once for want of food. (21) But those afflicted by the frenzy were seized by terrible sleeplessness and multiple hallucinations; they fell into a panic because they suspected that people were coming against them in order to kill them, and tried to run away, screaming at the top of their voices. (22) Their attendants were kept working continually and had a terrible time throughout. (23) So everyone pitied them as much as the sufferers, not because they were afflicted by the plague from their proximity to it (for it so happened that no doctor or anyone else caught this disease from touching the sick or the dead, since many people throughout this time stood up remarkably to the service of burying or tending even people unrelated to them, while many others died at once from an attack of the disease for no obvious cause), but because they endured great hardship. (24) They had to put their charges back again when they had fallen out of bed and were rolling on the floor, and they forced them back by pushing and dragging them when they tried to throw themselves out of buildings. (25) Where there was water available,

---

[379] Or, parsing the Greek slightly differently, 'up to the end' (as one manuscript has it).

[380] The term 'bubonic' arises from these buboes, swollen infected lymph nodes, usually in the groin, armpit or thigh.

[381] Or perhaps 'their loved ones'.

they wanted to throw themselves into it, not so much because they wanted to drink (for the majority jumped into the sea), but above all because of their mental illness. (26) They also had great difficulty with food, for they did not easily accept it. Many died for want of attention, either overcome by hunger or else flinging themselves down from a height. (27) But in those who were not afflicted either by the coma or by the frenzy, the bubo became gangrenous and they too died, unable to withstand the pain. (28) One might think that the same happened to all the others, but since they were scarcely in their wits, they could not feel the pain, for their sickness of mind took away their sensations.

(29) Some doctors, in bewilderment because of their ignorance of what was happening, thought that the epicentre of the disease lay in the buboes, and they determined to examine the bodies of the dead. After opening some of the buboes they discovered a remarkable sort of carbuncle that had grown inside them.[382] (30) Some of the victims died immediately, others many days later, and in some the body erupted in black blisters the size of a lentil; these did not live even for one day, but all died the very same hour. (31) Many were overtaken by a spontaneous vomiting of blood that caused their immediate death. (32) I can affirm this, however: the most highly respected doctors foretold that many would die who in fact recovered soon afterwards, beyond all expectation, and they were certain that many would recover who were on the point of death at that very moment. (33) And so in this plague there was no explanation that came within human conception, for in all cases the result was usually something unexpected – baths helped some, but harmed others just as much. (34) Many died if they were neglected, but many were saved contrary to all expectation. Again, nursing tended in both directions for those who had it, and to sum it all up, no path to safety was discovered by man, either through taking precautions not to contract the disease, or to survive it once he had contracted it. On the contrary, catching it was inexplicable and recovery spontaneous.

(35) Women who caught the disease while they were pregnant were sure of death. Some miscarried and died, others gave birth and immediately perished with their infants. (36) They say, however, that three survived giving birth, though their children died, and that one died in childbirth, but her child was born and survived. (37) Those in whom the bubo grew and came to the stage of discharge recovered from the disease

---

[382] The carbuncle, *anthrax* in Greek, arises from the fact that the swollen lymph nodes turn dark as a result of haemorrhaging.

256

and survived, since it is clear that in them the peak of the carbuncle had been relieved in this way, and this was generally a sign of recovery. But in the cases of those in whom the bubo remained in its previous form, the ills which I have just described came upon them. (38) In some cases it happened that the thigh withered, in which case the bubo swelled, but did not suppurate at all. (39) Others survived, but with their tongue damaged, living on either lisping or speaking with difficulty and incoherently.

Chapter 23

(1) The plague lasted in Byzantium for four months and was at its peak for about three. (2) At the beginning not many more people died than usual, then the disaster grew greater, and finally the number of dead reached 5000 a day, and then attained 10,000 and even more than this.[383] (3) At first each man took care of the burial of the dead from his own household. They would throw the dead, either by stealth or by force, into the graves of others; but later everything was in confusion everywhere. (4) Slaves remained without masters, men who were formerly very rich were deprived of the service of their attendants, either by their sickness or by their deaths, and many households were emptied of people altogether. (5) Consequently some eminent men remained unburied for many days because of the crisis. Provision for the situation naturally fell to the emperor. (6) So he allotted soldiers from the palace and money for the task and told Theodore to look after it, the man in charge of the

257

imperial responses, who informed the emperor of the requests of suppliants and told them in turn of his wishes. The Romans call this office in the Latin language that of the *referendarius*.[384] (7) Those whose households had not yet been reduced to complete desolation looked after the burial of those who belonged to them themselves. (8) Theodore, on the other hand, spent the emperor's money and some of his own as well in burying the neglected dead. (9) After all the tombs that were there originally had been filled with corpses, they dug up all the areas around the city in turn, and each laid the dead there as best he could and then went

---

[383] The mortality rate remains the subject of dispute: some put it as high as 50 per cent, others as low as 20 per cent. Papyri from Egypt have been interpreted as indicating a decline in population in the capital from 750,000 to 500,000, but some scholars would estimate the population at the outset to have been closer to 500,000.

[384] On Theodore see *PLRE* 3, Theodorus 10. His work is also reported by John of Ephesus in Ps.-Dion. ii, 91–2. On the role of the *referendarii*, legal clerks, see *ODLA, referendarii*.

away. But later the men digging the trenches could not keep up with the number of the dead and went up onto the towers on the circuit walls at Sycae;[385] (10) they tore off the roofs and threw the bodies in there all jumbled together, and piled them up as each one lay there. They filled up virtually all the towers with corpses and then covered them up again with the roofs. (11) As a result a dreadful stench came over the city and did still more harm to the people there, especially if a carrying wind blew from that direction.

(12) At that time all the customary rites of burial were neglected. For the dead were not carried with the customary escort, nor to the sound of the usual music; rather, it was enough if someone carried a dead body on his shoulders and threw it down when he came to the coastal part of the city, where the dead would be thrown onto boats in a heap and carried wherever they might chance. (13) Then even those of the populace that had earlier been partisans forgot their mutual hatred and together tended to the care of the dead, and they buried corpses of those to whom they were unconnected, carrying them themselves. (14) Those who previously delighted in consorting with shame and wickedness shook off the lawlessness of their lives and most zealously practised piety, not because they had now learnt prudence, or because they had suddenly become lovers of virtue – (15) for men's characters, whether fixed by nature or lengthy learning, cannot be changed so easily, except when some benevolent divine force inspires them – but then they were all, so to speak, struck by what was happening and, thinking that they were about to die straight away, were compelled, as was only to be expected, to learn moderation for a time. (16) As soon as they had recovered from the disease and were safe and thought that they were now secure, since the disease had gone to other men, they abruptly reverted again and changed for the worse; they displayed the strangeness of their habits even more than before, surpassing themselves completely in wickedness and lawlessness. It would not then be a lie to assert that this disease, whether by chance or by foresight, carefully selected the most wicked and spared them, though this became clear only later.[386]

(17) At that time it was not easy to see anyone in Byzantium out in public; all those who were healthy sat at home either tending the sick or mourning the dead. (18) If one did manage to see a man actually going out, he would be burying one of the dead. All work was stopped;

---

[385] Across the Golden Horn to the north, the later Galata, cf. *ODLA*, Sycae.
[386] Probably an allusion to Justinian and his entourage, who are termed 'most wicked' in the *Anecd.*

craftsmen abandoned all their crafts and every task that any man had in hand. (19) In a city with a remarkable abundance of good things a harsh famine ran riot. It seemed a struggle, and indeed very worthy of note, to have an adequate supply of bread or anything else. As a result, even to some of the sick the end of their life came to seem premature because of the want of provisions. (20) To sum it all up, it was quite impossible to see anyone dressed in a *chlamys* in Byzantium,[387] especially when the emperor fell ill (for he too had a bubonic swelling);[388] in the city that held the sovereignty over the whole Roman empire everyone was wearing clothes befitting private citizens and staying quietly at home. (21) This was the course of the plague in Byzantium and in the rest of the Roman empire. It also attacked Persian territory and all the other barbarians.[389]

Chapter 24

(1) It so happened that Khusro had come north from Assyria to a place called Adarbiganon, from where he intended to invade Roman territory through Persarmenia.[390] (2) The big fire temple is there, which the Persians honour most of all gods.[391] Magi tend the unquenched fire there and scrupulously perform the other rites, while practising divination for the most important matters. This is the fire that the Romans of former times called Hestia and used to worship.[392] (3) There a man who had been sent from Byzantium announced to Khusro that Constantianus and Sergius would soon reach him as envoys about the agreement. (4) These two men were both rhetors, very intelligent men – Constantianus, an Illyrian by birth, and Sergius, from the city of Edessa, which is in Mesopotamia.[393] (5) Khusro stayed there and waited for them. But on the journey Constantianus fell ill and some time passed, during which it

[387] The *chlamys* was a long woollen cloak worn by imperial officials, fastened at the shoulder, as can be seen in the Ravenna mosaics.

[388] One scholar has suggested that some coins issued at this time show Justinian with a bubo on his neck, but the evidence is doubtful.

[389] The plague spread widely and quickly: already in the mid sixth century it is attested in England.

[390] The reference is to Ādurbādagān, i.e. modern Azerbaijan, also referred to as Media Atropatene. The events described in the following chapters should be dated to 542, not 543; earlier works often assume the latter date.

[391] Procopius refers to the important fire temple at Takht-i Suleyman today, known in antiquity as Ādur Gušnasp, 'The fire of the stallion', where kings often went after their coronation. It was destroyed by Heraclius' forces in 624, Theoph. 307–8 (tr. in *REF*, 200).

[392] The Vestal Virgins tended to the sacred fire (of the goddess Vesta) in Rome. Cf. *ODLA*, Vestal Virgins.

[393] See *PLRE* 3, Constantianus 1, Sergius 3, on the two men. The former was later given a military command, cf. 2.28.2.

happened that the plague attacked the Persians. (6) Accordingly, Nabedes, who at that time held the post of commander in Persarmenia, sent the bishop of the Christians in Dvin by order of the king to Valerian, the general in Armenia,[394] to complain about the slowness of the envoys and to spur the Romans on about the peace as vehemently as he could. (7) He reached Armenia with his brother, met Valerian, and assured him that as a Christian he was himself well disposed to the Romans, and that King Khusro always heeded him on every matter. So if the Roman envoys went to Persia with him no hindrance would stand in the way of arranging the peace as they wished. (8) This is what the bishop said.[395] But the bishop's brother came secretly to Valerian and told him that Khusro had great difficulties, for his son had rebelled,[396] aiming at usurpation, and at the same time he himself and all the Persian army had been overtaken by the plague; this was why he now wanted to come to terms with the Romans. (9) When Valerian heard this he dismissed the bishop at once, and promising that the envoys would soon come to Khusro, he referred what he had heard to the Emperor Justinian. (10) Influenced by this news, the emperor immediately ordered Martin and the other commanders to invade the enemy lands as swiftly as possible, for he knew very well that no enemy would stand in their way. (11) He told them all to join together and make the invasion like this into Persarmenia. When the commanders had read this, they all streamed into the districts of Armenia with their troops.

(12) But already shortly before this Khusro had left Adarbiganon in fear of the disease and gone to Assyria with all his army, where the plague had not yet settled. So Valerian encamped near Theodosiopolis with the troops that accompanied him, while Narses drew up the Armenians and some Heruls that he had with him. (13) Martin, the *magister militum per Orientem*, arrived at the fort of Citharizon with Ildiger and Theoctistus, pitched his camp there and waited.[397] This fort is four days' journey from Theodosiopolis. Peter came there shortly afterwards with Adolius and some other officers. (14) Isaac, Narses' brother, was in command of the army units there. Philemuth and Verus came to Khorzianene with their

261

262

---

[394] Valerian was then *magister militum per Armeniam*, having returned with Belisarius from Italy. See *PLRE* 3, Valerianus 1, *ODLA*, Valerianus.

[395] It is possible that the bishop was trying to stall the Romans, fearing that they would take advantage of the situation revealed by his brother.

[396] An allusion apparently to the revolt of Anasozadus, recounted in greater detail by Procopius at 8.10.8–22, where it is dated to 550 rather than 542. It is hard to work out what is the correct date.

[397] On the important border fortress of Citharizon see *ODLA*, Citharizon. See also fig. 17, p. 71.

Herul followers,[398] not far from Martin's camp. (15) Justus the emperor's cousin, Peranius, and John, the son of Nicetas, with Domnentiolus and John, called the Glutton, encamped at the fort called Phison, which is very near the borders of Martyropolis. (16) In this way the Roman officers encamped with their troops, and the whole army came to 30,000 men. (17) They did not all gather together, nor did they even hold a conference among themselves.[399] The generals enquired about the attack by sending around some of their following to one another. (18) But Peter, without telling anyone, suddenly and without due forethought invaded the enemy country with his troops. Learning of this on the next day, Philemuth and Verus, the leaders of the Heruls, immediately followed. (19) When Martin's and Valerian's men heard of this, they quickly undertook an invasion.

(20) Shortly afterwards they all met in enemy country, except for Justus and his men, who were encamped, as I have said, a long way from the rest of the army; they heard of their invasion later and invaded the enemy country near them with all speed, but could not join up with their fellow officers. (21) But all the rest marched off directly towards Dvin, without plundering or doing any other harm to the Persian territory.

Chapter 25

(1) Dvin is a productive district in many respects, and in particular is well provided with healthy air and water; it lies eight days' journey from Theodosiopolis.[400] (2) There are plains suitable for riding, many densely populated villages close to one another, and many merchants who live and work in them. (3) They import commodities from India and from the Iberians, who live close by, and from virtually all the Persian peoples and from some Romans, and they trade with each other there. (4) They call the Christian bishop the *catholicos* in Greek because he is the one man in charge of the whole area.[401] (5) About a hundred and twenty stades from Dvin, on the right as one goes from Roman territory, there is a mountain that is hard to climb and very precipitous, and a village called

---

[398] Khorzianene is to be identified with the Khorzane mentioned at Proc. *Aed.* 3.3.9–14, situated between Citharizon and Theodosiopolis. On the two commanders, see *PLRE* 3, Philemuth, Verus.

[399] While it was normal procedure not to concentrate forces in enemy territory because of difficulties of supply, the lack of co-ordination was careless.

[400] See *ODLA*, Dvin, on the Persarmenian city in this period, cf. *RPLA*, 174.

[401] The Greek word *katholikos* means 'general' or 'universal'; it can be applied to the main church of a diocese or province. The term came to be used for the head of various churches, among them the Armenian. See *ODLA*, Catholicus (Armenian).

Anglon in a very narrow space in the harsh terrain.[402] (6) As soon as Nabedes heard of the enemy attack, he went there with all his army and barricaded himself in, taking heart from the strength of the position. (7) The village lies at the foot of the mountain,[403] and a strong fortress of the same name as the village lies on the precipices. (8) Nabedes therefore blocked off the entrances to the village with boulders and carts, and made it even harder to reach. (9) In front of it he dug a trench and posted the army there, filling some old huts with foot soldiers by way of an ambush. The Persian army amounted to 4000 men altogether.

(10) This then was accomplished in this way. When the Romans reached a place a day's journey from Anglon, they captured an enemy spy and questioned him about Nabedes' present whereabouts. He said that he had retreated from Anglon with the entire Persian army. (11) When Narses heard this, he was angry and railed at his fellow officers, reproaching them for their hesitation. (12) The others did the same, too, insulting one another, and without further thought for battle or danger they were eager to plunder the area. (13) So they set off without a commander and in no order or formation went forward, without any kind of watchword among themselves as is usual in such enterprises, and without being divided into formations at all. (14) The soldiers were mixed up with the camp followers as they advanced for the easy snatching of large quantities of money. (15) But when they were near Anglon, they sent out spies who returned and told them of the enemy's battle formation. (16) The commanders were taken aback by the unexpectedness of it, but thought that to turn back with an army so large in number would be altogether shameful and cowardly, and so they drew up the army as best they could in the present circumstances in three divisions and advanced straight towards the enemy. (17) Peter had the right wing, Valerian the left, and in the middle Martin's men were positioned. When they were very near to the enemy, they waited, holding to their ranks only in a disorderly fashion. (18) The reason was the extremely rocky and difficult terrain and the fact that they had been drawn up for battle on the spur of the moment. (19) Yet the barbarians were still quietly waiting; they gathered close together, looking to see the strength of their opponents. For Nabedes had told them earlier not to begin the fight, but to defend themselves as best they could if the enemy attacked them.

---

[402] Anglon is the Armenian Angł in the province of Ayrarat on the river Aratsani (Procopius' Arsinus, 1.17.21, the Murat Su today). The whole region is very mountainous.

[403] Others translate as 'the mountain's extreme end', but the Greek, which literally means 'the final part of the mountain', more naturally is taken to refer to the foot, cf. e.g. 6.4.23.

(20) Narses was the first to come to grips with the enemy, with his troop of Heruls and Romans, and, making a strong push, he routed the Persians who opposed him. (21) In their flight the barbarians ran up to the fortress, where they did dreadful damage to each other in the narrow space. (22) Then Narses himself, spurring on his men, pressed against the enemy still more strongly, and the rest of the Romans joined in the combat. (23) But the men set in ambush suddenly emerged from the huts in the narrows, as I have said, and killed some of the Heruls. In their sudden rush they actually wounded Narses on the temple. (24) His brother Isaac rescued him, fatally wounded, from the fighting. Shortly afterwards he died, after giving a brave performance in this engagement. (25) Then naturally a great confusion struck the Roman force, and Nabedes set the entire Persian army upon the enemy. (26) Firing at a large mass of the enemy in the narrows, they killed many without diffi-culty, and especially the Heruls, who had first joined battle against their opponents with Narses and were fighting for the most part without armour. (27) The Heruls have no helmet or corselet or any other protec-tion, save for a shield and a thick cloak, which they wrap around them-selves when they go into battle.[404] (28) But Herul slaves actually go into battle without shields; only when they have shown themselves brave in war do their masters allow them to carry shields before them in engage-ments. Such is the situation of the Heruls.

(29) The Romans could not withstand the enemy and all fled with all their might, with no thought for bravery and with no self-respect or anything valorous in their minds. (30) But the Persians, suspecting that this disgraceful rout was not genuine and that the Romans were somehow ambushing them, pursued them as far as the rough country and then returned, not daring to fight on level ground, for the Romans were few and the others many. (31) The Romans, however, and particu-larly all the generals, thought that the enemy were pursuing them all the time and fled all the more, losing no time and spurring on their galloping horses with whips and shouting, and throwing their corselets and other arms onto the ground in panic and confusion. (32) They had no hope of being able to form up against them if the Persians caught them, and they put their hopes of safety entirely in their horses' hooves. In sum, the flight was such that hardly any of the horses survived: when they stopped their gallop, they immediately collapsed and died. (33) This disaster was

---

[404] On the Heruls in general see *ODLA*, Heruli. Notwithstanding their equipment they were frequently employed by the Romans. Cf. 1.13.19 on Pharas and his Heruls at the battle of Dara.

greater than any that the Romans had suffered before, for many of them perished and still more fell into the hands of the enemy.[405] (34) The enemy captured their weapons and pack animals in such vast numbers that Persia's wealth actually seemed to be increased as a result of this action. (35) Adolius, while passing by a fortress in Persarmenia in this retreat, was struck on the head by a stone thrown by one of the inhabitants, and he died there. Justus' and Peranius' troops invaded the country around Taraunon, and after plundering some of it, they immediately returned.[406]

Chapter 26

(1) In the following year[407] Khusro, the son of Kavadh, invaded Roman territory for the fourth time, leading his army against Mesopotamia. (2) This invasion was made by this Khusro not against Justinian, the emperor of Rome, nor against any other man, but solely against the God whom the Christians worship. (3) For after he had retreated, failing to capture Edessa in his first invasion,[408] he and the magi were seized by dejection at being defeated by the Christian God. (4) To assuage it, Khusro threatened in his palace that he would bring all the Edessenes to Persia as slaves and make the city a pasture for sheep. (5) So he came near to Edessa with the whole army, and he sent some of the Huns who were with him to the circuit wall of the city above the hippodrome with the single intention of seizing some sheep, which the shepherds happened to have placed there in great numbers beside the wall (fig. 29). They put their trust in the strength of the place, because it was extremely sheer, and they thought that the enemy would not dare to come so close to the wall. (6) So the barbarians laid their hands on the sheep, while the shepherds fought hard to stop them. (7) Many Persians came to the aid of the Huns, and the barbarians were able to take away a flock. But when Roman soldiers and townsmen came to attack the enemy, the fighting became hand to hand and the flock spontaneously returned again to the shepherds.[409] (8) One of the Huns, fighting in front of the rest, troubled the Romans more

269

[405] Typical Procopian hyperbole. He uses the same expression with more appropriateness at 7.18.19 about Hannibal's victory at Cannae in 216 B.C.

[406] Taraunon is the region known in Armenian sources as Taron, west of Lake Van.

[407] 543, not 544, as is sometimes supposed. There are a few notices on this siege of Edessa in Syriac sources, cf. *REF*, 113, while Procopius recounts one further anecdote about it at 8.14.35–7.

[408] In 540, cf. 2.12.6, 31–4.

[409] The local population was just as vigorous in its defence of the city in 503, cf. Ps.-Josh. 60, 62, where the feats of their slingers are noted.

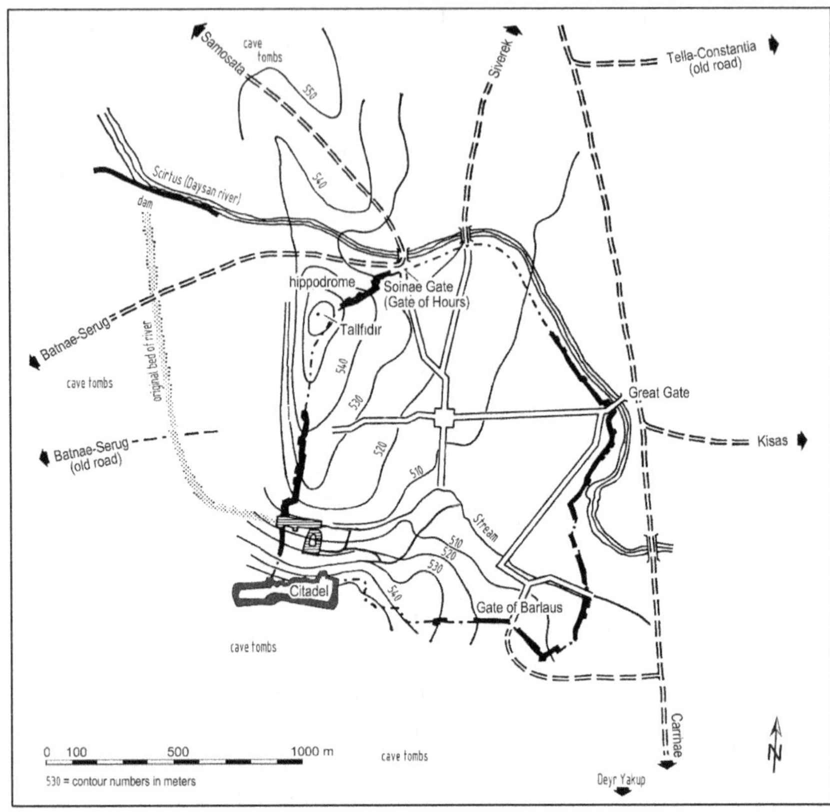

Figure 29   Edessa

than anyone. (9) A peasant hit him on the right knee with a sling, and
when at once he fell flat on his face from his horse to the ground, this
gave more strength than ever to the Romans. (10) The fighting began
early in the morning and ended at midday, when the two sides parted,
each thinking that they had had the better of it. (11) The Romans went
inside the circuit walls, while the barbarians all pitched their tents and
encamped seven stades from the city.

(12) Then Khusro either beheld a vision in a dream or else reflected
that if he could not take Edessa after two attempts great disgrace would
overtake him. (13) Accordingly, he decided to sell the Edessenes his
retreat for a high price. (14) So on the next day Paul, the interpreter,
came to the wall and said that some eminent Romans must be sent to
Khusro. (15) They quickly chose four of the notable men among them

and despatched them. (16) When they arrived at the Persian camp, Zabergan met them at the king's wish, and frightening them with many threats, he asked them which was preferable to them, the course which led to peace or that which led to war.[410] (17) They admitted that they preferred peace to dangers, and Zabergan said: 'Then you must buy it at a high price.' (18) The envoys said that they would give what they had given before, when he had come against them after taking Antioch. (19) Zabergan sent them away, laughing, telling them to deliberate most thoroughly about their safety and then come again to the Persians. (20) Shortly afterwards Khusro sent for them again, and when they came to him, he told them which Roman places he had previously enslaved, and in what manner. He threatened that the Edessenes would suffer worse from the Persians unless they gave them all the money that they had inside the walls, for he said that only in this way would the army go. (21) On hearing this, the envoys agreed to buy peace from Khusro if he did not demand the impossible from them, but they said that no one at all could see the ultimate issue of the danger before the conflict. (22) For war never proceeded for those who waged it according to fixed terms. Khusro at this point therefore angrily told the envoys to leave as quickly as possible.

(23) On the eighth day of the siege he decided to make an artificial hill against the city's circuit wall. He cut down many trees from the nearby districts, leaves and all, and put them together in a square in front of the wall, where no arrow from the city could reach them. Then he heaped a huge amount of earth on the trees and put a vast quantity of stones on top, unsuitable for building, cut in any sort of way, thinking only of raising the hill to a great height as quickly as possible. (24) Between the mound and the stones he inserted long beams, binding the structure together so that it would not be weak as it grew high. (25) But Peter the Roman general (who happened to be there with Martin and Peranius) wanted to repel the builders and sent some of his Hun troops against them.[411] (26) They came upon them suddenly and killed many, the most successful of them in this being one of the bodyguards, a man called Argek, who killed twenty-seven men by himself. (27) After this, however, the barbarians kept strict watch, and no one could attack them. (28) But when the specialists engaged in this task came forward within arrow's range,[412] the Romans fought strongly from the wall, directing slings and

271

272

---

[410] On Zabergan see 1.23.25, cf. 2.8.30.
[411] On Peter see 1.12.9, 2.15.7, on Peranius 1.12.11 and 2.24.15.
[412] The specialists were doubtless siege engineers.

bows against them. So the barbarians devised this solution. (29) They hung thick, broad coverings of goat's hair called 'Cilician' on long beams and kept them in front of those who were working on the *agesta* (for this was what the Romans called what they were making in Latin).[413] (30) Neither flaming arrows nor other projectiles could penetrate here; instead, everything was deflected by the screens and stopped there. (31) Then the Romans in great fear and in utter confusion sent envoys to Khusro. With them went Stephanus, who was famous among the doctors of his day and who had once cured Kavadh, the son of Peroz, when he was ill, and had received a large amount of money from him.[414] (32) When he came with the others to Khusro, he said:

'From ancient times everyone has taken kindness to be the sign of a good king. (33) Most powerful King, if you engage in battle and slaughter and enslave cities, you might perhaps acquire other names, but never will you appear good. (34) Of all cities, Edessa ought least to suffer any ill from you. (35) For it is the city from where I am sprung, I who reared you, knowing nothing of what was to come, and who was your father's adviser and told him to make you his successor on the throne. So I became responsible above all others for your rule over Persia, and for my city's present ills, (36) since for the most part, men bring upon themselves their future misfortunes. (37) But if you have any recollection of such good service to you, do us no further harm and give me this recompense. In return for it you, O King, will avoid the appearance of vicious cruelty.'

This was what Stephanus said. (38) But Khusro said that he would not go unless the Romans surrendered Peter and Peranius to him, because they had dared to join battle against him though they were his hereditary slaves.[415] (39) And if the Romans did not find it pleasing to do this, they must choose one of two things, either to give him five hundred *centenaria* of gold, or to receive into the city some of his lieutenants who would search everywhere and bring to him all the gold and silver that was there, and leave the rest to its owners. (40) These were the options that Khusro threw out to them, in good hopes of taking Edessa without any trouble. But the envoys (for everything that the king had ordered seemed equally impossible to them) did not know what to do and walked back to the city in great distress. (41) When they were inside the circuit wall and had

---

[413] Similar devices had been used in the past, e.g. at the siege of Plataea in 429 B.C., Thuc. 2.75.5, cf. Ps.-Josh. 53 on the siege of Amida in 502–3. Procopius alludes to a Latin word *agesta*, derived from *agger* and *aggestus*, a mound or bank of earth.

[414] Nothing further is known of Stephanus beyond what is here reported. See *PLRE* 3, Stephanus 9.

[415] Peter was from (Persian) Arzanene, cf. 2.15.7, while Peranius was an Iberian prince, cf. 1.12.11.

reported Khusro's demands, the city was filled with confusion and lamentation.

(42) The structure of the hill rose high and advanced with great enthusiasm. The Romans, not knowing what to do, sent the envoys off to Khusro again. (43) When they were inside the enemy camp, they said that they had come to entreat him about the same matters, but were not granted any conference with the Persians. They returned to the city, driven out of the camp with insults and shouting. (44) At first the Romans tried to raise the wall opposite the hill higher by means of another structure, but since the Persian construction was already far higher, they stopped building and persuaded Martin to treat for peace as seemed best to him. He came very near the enemy camp and talked to some of the Persian officers. (45) But they deceived Martin, saying that their king wanted peace, but that he could not persuade the Roman emperor ever to abandon his rivalry with Khusro and make peace with him. (46) Belisarius too, who, as not even Martin himself would deny, was far superior to him in power and rank, had recently persuaded the Persian king when he was in the midst of the Romans to depart to Persia, promising that envoys would soon come to him from Byzantium and ratify the peace on a firm basis,[416] but had fulfilled none of his promises, for he was unable to overcome the wishes of the Emperor Justinian.

Chapter 27

(1) In the meantime the Romans did as follows. They made a trench from the city under the enemy mound, telling the diggers not to stop their work until they were under the middle of the hill. They were planning to set fire to the mound by this means. (2) But as the trench advanced nearly half-way under the hill, a noise reached the Persians standing above. (3) They noticed what was happening, and they began to tunnel from above on both sides of the middle so as to catch the Romans who were causing them problems there. (4) The Romans realised this and stopped, throwing earth into the place they had hollowed out. They worked on the end of the mound, the lower part near the city wall, digging out wood and stones and earth, and they made a sort of hut, throwing dry, readily combustible tree trunks there, drenched with oil of cedar and prepared with sulphur and bitumen in large quantities. (5) While they prepared this, the Persian officers had many meetings with

---

[416] 2.21.25, cf. 2.24.3.

Martin and told him what I have said, giving him the impression that they would listen to peace proposals. (6) But when they had finished the hill and it was near the city's circuit wall and was very lofty, far exceeding the wall in height, they sent Martin away, refusing an agreement outright, and intending henceforth to do battle.

(7) So the Romans at once set fire to the tree trunks that had been prepared for this. The fire burnt a portion of the mound, but all the wood was consumed before it could reach right through it. They kept throwing more wood into the trench, without losing any opportunity.[417] (8) Once the fire was at work throughout the whole mound, smoke could be seen in the night above and all around the hill. The Romans, not wanting to give the Persians any notion of what was happening, devised the following plan.

(9) They filled small pots with charcoal and fire, and threw these, together with flaming arrows, onto all parts of the mound in great quantities. The Persians on guard went around and put these out with great energy; they thought that the smoke was coming from this. (10) As the damage increased, the barbarians came to help in large numbers, but the Romans fired at them from the wall and killed many. (11) At dawn Khusro arrived, and with him the majority of the army, and when he went up onto the hill, he was the first to perceive the problem. (12) He pointed out that the cause of the smoke was from below, not from the missiles shot by the enemy, and he told the whole army to come quickly to help. (13) The Romans took courage and jeered at them, while some of the barbarians threw earth onto where the smoke appeared, others water, hoping to get the better of the danger, but not having any success whatever. (14) For where earth was thrown on, the smoke was naturally checked, but it soon came up again in other places, because the fire compelled it to force an exit where it could. And where the water was thrown on in the largest amounts, it made the pitch and the brimstone work even more, causing them to burn up the wood in the vicinity, and continually forcing the fire forward, since the water could not reach the inside of the mound in sufficient quantity to be able to put out the fire by force of volume. (15) By evening there was so much smoke that it could be seen by the inhabitants of Carrhae and others living far beyond. (16) After many Persians and Romans had climbed to the top of the mound, fighting and shoving broke out there, with the Romans getting

---

[417] Evagr. *HE* 4.27 adds that an image of Christ, 'not made by human hands', was deployed at this point to ensure that the material caught fire. The story is likely to have developed after Procopius was writing. See *ODLA*, Mandylion of Edessa.

the upper hand. (17) Then too the flames burnt brightly and could be seen over the mound, and the Persians abandoned this undertaking.

(18) But on the sixth day after this, at the break of dawn, they secretly attacked a part of the circuit wall with scaling ladders, at the place that is called the Citadel.[418] (19) As the night was drawing to its end and the Romans standing guard there were sleeping peacefully, they brought the ladders to the wall quietly and already were climbing up. (20) Alone of all the Romans one peasant was awake and roused the others by shouting and making a great noise. (21) In a sharp battle the Persians were defeated and returned to the camp, leaving behind the ladders, which the Romans drew up at their leisure. (22) At midday Khusro sent a large part of the army to storm the so-called Great Gate.[419] (23) The Romans met them – not only soldiers, but also peasants and some townsmen – and they completely routed the barbarians after defeating them in battle. (24) While the Persians were still being pursued, Paul the interpreter came into the midst of the Romans from Khusro and told them that Recinarius had come from Byzantium about the peace; and so the two sides separated.[420] (25) But Recinarius had actually arrived at the barbarian camp a few days before. (26) The Persians had breathed not a word of this to the Romans, obviously waiting for the attack on the wall, so that, if they could take it, they would not seem to be offending against the truce, and if they were defeated, as did happen, they could arrange the agreement at the invitation of the Romans. (27) But when Recinarius was inside the gates, the Persians demanded that those who were going to treat for peace should go at once to Khusro, to which the Romans replied that envoys would be despatched three days later, since at the present time their general Martin was ill.

(28) Khusro suspected that their story was not sound and prepared for battle. He then threw a large number of bricks on the mound, and two days later he came to the city's circuit wall with all his army to storm it. (29) Stationing some of the officers and a part of the army at each gate, he thus surrounded the entire wall and brought scaling ladders and siege engines up to it. (30) He drew the Saracens up behind with some Persians, not to attack the wall, but so that when the city was captured, they could sweep the area and catch the fugitives. (31) With these

279

280

---

[418] Probably on the south side of the city, where the Citadel was located. Justinian later strengthened this section of the walls, Proc. *Aed.* 2.7.13–16.

[419] The eastern gate of the city, where Christ's promise to Abgar to protect the city was inscribed (cf. 2.12.26).

[420] Recinarius was an associate of John Troglita, the *dux* of Mesopotamia. See *PLRE* 3, Recinarius.

intentions Khusro drew up his army in this way. The battle began early in the morning, and at first the Persians had the upper hand. (32) For they were many and their opponents very few; for most of the Romans were unaware of what was happening and were totally unprepared. (33) But as the engagement went on, the city was filled with confusion and disturbance, and all the men hastened up to the wall, even with their wives and children. (34) The men of military age fought the enemy very bravely alongside the soldiers, and many peasants performed amazing deeds of valour against the barbarians. (35) The children and the women, together with the old men, collected stones for the fighters and helped in other ways. (36) Some even filled a large number of cauldrons with oil, and after heating them on the fire all around the wall for a sufficient time, they poured the oil, boiling vigorously, onto the enemy by means of a sprinkler and hurt them even more as they approached the wall. (37) So the Persians now refused to fight and flung down their weapons, coming to the king and saying that they could not endure the struggle any longer. (38) But Khusro was seized by a violent anger and urged them all forward against the enemy with threats and commands. (39) With shouts and a great uproar they brought towers and other engines against the wall, to take the city at the first blow. (40) But when the Romans fired rapidly and defended themselves with all their might, the barbarians were utterly routed, and the Romans tauntingly invited Khusro to storm the wall as he retreated.

(41) Only Azarethes was still fighting with his men at the gate called Soinae, at the place they call Tripyrgia.[421] (42) The Romans there were no match for them and were indeed giving way before their attacks. The barbarians had already torn down the outer wall, which they call the outwork, in many places and were pressing hard the defenders from the main wall, until Peranius sallied out against them with many soldiers and some Edessenes, overcame them, and drove them out. (43) The fight for the wall began early in the morning and ended in the evening, and both sides kept quiet for that night, the Persians afraid for their palisades and for themselves, and the Romans collecting stones for the battlements and making everything else completely ready to fight the enemy on the next day when they attacked the wall. (44) On the following day not one barbarian came to the walls, but on the one after, part of the army at Khusro's order attacked the gate named after Barlaus.[422] They were,

---

[421] The reference is to the 'Gate of the Hours' on the north side of the city. The Tripyrgia is not otherwise known but presumably refers to three towers in close proximity.

[422] The gate of Barlaus is the south gate of the city (leading towards Carrhae).

however, met by the Romans and defeated decisively in battle and soon returned to their camp. (45) Then Paul, the Persian interpreter, came to the wall and called for Martin to make the peace terms. (46) So Martin held a conference with the Persian commanders, and they came to an agreement. Khusro, taking five *centenaria* from the Edessenes, left them an agreement in writing that he would do no further harm to the Romans; after burning all his palisades, he returned home with all his army.[423]

Chapter 28

(1) Around this time two Roman commanders died, Justus the emperor's cousin and Peranius the Iberian. Justus perished through illness, but Peranius fell from his horse while hunting and suffered a fatal fracture. (2) In their stead the emperor consequently appointed other generals, sending Marcellus, his own nephew,[424] who had recently come of age, and Constantianus, who had a little earlier been despatched to Khusro with Sergius. (3) Then the Emperor Justinian sent Constantianus and Sergius as envoys to Khusro to treat for peace.[425] (4) They came upon him in Assyria, where the two cities of Seleucia and Ctesiphon lie, founded by the Macedonians who reigned over the Persians and the other peoples there after Alexander, son of Philip.[426] (5) The river Tigris divides the two cities, for there is no other territory between them. (6) There the ambassadors met Khusro and demanded that he return the districts of Lazica to the Romans and ratify definitively the terms of the peace treaty. (7) But Khusro replied that it would not be easy for them to negotiate with one another, unless they first suspended hostilities and thus could travel back and forth between one another continuously without worry. They would then resolve their differences and arrange a peace treaty that would be secure for the future. (8) The Roman emperor, he added, must give him money for the ongoing truce and send him a doctor, Tribunus by name, to spend a specified time with him, (9) for it happened that this doctor had cured him earlier of a severe illness and as a consequence had become

283

---

[423] Jord. *Rom.* 377 credits Martin and Constantianus (cf. 2.24.3 and 28.2) with the conclusion of the peace.

[424] On whom see *PLRE* 3, Marcellus 5. He had a successful career under Justinian and Justin II, his elder brother.

[425] See 2.24.3 for their initial mission, which had been held up when Constantianus fell ill.

[426] Seleucia was founded on the right bank of the Tigris by Seleucus I around 300 B.C.; Ctesiphon lay opposite. While Seleucia had declined by this point, it had been succeeded by another important city, Veh-Ardashir (also known as Kōkhē). See *ODLA*, Ctesiphon, Kokhe, Seleucia ad Tigrem.

a friend whose company he dearly missed.[427] (10) When the Emperor Justinian heard this, he immediately sent Tribunus and the money, which amounted to twenty *centenaria*. (11) Thus was concluded a five-year truce between the Romans and Persians in the nineteenth year of the reign of the Emperor Justinian.[428]

284 (12) A little later al-Harith and al-Mundhir, the chiefs of the Saracens, engaged in war against one another on their own, with neither the Romans nor the Persians providing any assistance. (13) Al-Mundhir, having seized one of al-Harith's sons pasturing horses in a lightning raid, immediately sacrificed him to Aphrodite,[429] as a result of which it was recognised that al-Harith was not betraying the Roman cause to the Persians. (14) The two sides subsequently met in battle with their entire armies; al-Harith's forces gained a decisive victory, routing their enemies and slaying many. Al-Harith came close to capturing alive two sons of al-Mundhir, but did not quite succeed.[430] This then was the situation among the Saracens.

(15) It became clear, however, that the Persian king Khusro had concluded the truce with the Romans with treacherous intent, so that he might catch them relaxing their guard because of the peace and strike an intolerable blow against them. (16) For in the third year of the truce he contrived the following plan.[431] Among the Persians lived two brothers, Vahriz and Yazdgushnasp, who held the highest offices there and were generally thought to be the most wicked of all Persians; they also enjoyed a great reputation for cunning and malice. (17) Having therefore decided to seize the city of Dara by a sudden attack and to expel all the Colchians

285 from Lazica and replace them with Persian settlers, Khusro chose these two men to help him execute both projects. (18) It seemed to him that it would be a significant boon to take control of the land of Colchis and to hold it securely, since he reasoned that it would be an asset to the Persian kingdom in many respects. (19) They would then henceforth hold Iberia securely, since the Iberians would find no one at all with whom they might seek refuge following a rebellion: (20) ever since the most

---

[427] Cf. *Wars* 8.10.11–6 on Tribunus' activities at the Persian court. Ps.-Zach. 12.7p also describes his services. See *PLRE* 3, Tribunus 2.

[428] The truce was concluded probably in April 545: see *REF*, 113.

[429] Probably the Arabic deity al-ʿUzzā, cf. Ps.-Zach. 8.5a, another human sacrifice of al-Mundhir.

[430] A late Syriac source, Michael the Syrian, reports a signal victory won by al-Harith over al-Mundhir in June 554 in which one of al-Harith's sons was killed. See *REF*, 129. Some have wanted to connect the two battles mentioned here with this report, but it is usually thought that the first seven books of the *Wars* were completed and published by 550/1, which makes the link problematic.

[431] I.e. in 547–8, cf. *RPLA*, 248.

distinguished among these barbarians had set their sights on revolt, as I reported earlier,[432] the Persians no longer allowed them to appoint a king for themselves, while the Iberians proved unwilling subjects of the Persians. The two sides thus viewed one another with great suspicion and distrust. (21) It was clear that the Iberians most strenuously objected to their condition and would soon revolt, provided that they could seize an opportune moment.

(22) In addition, he reckoned that the Persian kingdom would never again be plundered by the Huns who live close to Lazica, while it would be easier and more convenient to despatch them against the Roman empire whenever he should be so inclined; for to him Lazica was nothing other than a bulwark against the barbarians that inhabit the Caucasus. (23) Above all, he hoped that the annexation of Lazica would benefit the Persians through the fact that they would be able to set out from there and effortlessly overrun, by both land and sea forces, the districts of Cappadocia next to the so-called Euxine Sea,[433] as well as seize the adjoining provinces of Galatia and Bithynia and with no resistance to take Byzantium by a lightning strike.[434] (24) For these reasons Khusro wished to take over Lazica, but he could not place any trust in the Lazi, since (25) once the Romans had evacuated Lazica, the majority of the Lazi had naturally resented Persian rule, because the Persians are single-minded beyond all others and excessively rigid in their daily routines. (26) Among them the laws are baffling to all people, while their regulations are absolutely unbearable. The contrast in outlook and in way of life was always especially marked in the case of the Lazi, however, because the Lazi are more Christian than anyone else,[435] but the Persians take an opposite approach to the whole issue of religion. (27) Even apart from these matters, salt is found nowhere in Lazica, nor even do wheat, vines or any other useful crop grow there. (28) Everything is brought to them by ship from Romans on the coast, and for these products they offer to the traders not gold, but skins, slaves and anything else that happens to be abundant there.[436] (29) Henceforth cut off from this trade, the Lazi were naturally aggrieved. Aware of this, Khusro was keen to make a move in advance and in security, before they rose in revolt against him. (30) It seemed to him in his deliberations that the most advantageous plan was

286

---

[432] At 1.12.2–5.
[433] I.e. the Black Sea.
[434] As the Lazi suggested to Khusro in 540, cf. 2.15.27.
[435] Procopius describes the Iberians similarly at 1.12.3.
[436] Procopius repeats more or less what he had reported earlier at 2.15.5.

287 to remove Gubazes, the king of the Lazi, as quickly as possible, and to uproot the Lazi from there in their entirety so that Persians and other peoples might live together in this country.

(31) Once he had formed this plan, Khusro sent Yazdgushnasp to Byzantium ostensibly on an embassy, and he despatched with him five hundred Persians selected for their valour. These he instructed to get within the city of Dara, to take lodgings in many houses, and to set all of them on fire in the night. While all the Romans were naturally occupied with this fire, they were to open the gates at once and receive the remainder of the Persian army into the city. (32) Earlier the commander of the city of Nisibis had been told to keep in readiness, hidden somewhere nearby, a mass of soldiers. Thus did Khusro suppose that the Persians would effortlessly destroy all the Romans, capture the city of Dara, and hold it securely in the future. (33) But someone who knew well what was going on, a Roman man who had come to the Persians as a deserter a little earlier, reported the whole matter to George, who was staying there at the time; I mentioned him previously for having persuaded those besieged in **288** the fortress of Sisauranon to give themselves up to the Romans.[437] (34) George therefore met this ambassador on the border between Roman and Persian territory and stated that he was not acting according to the norms of an embassy and that never had such a large mass of Persians taken up quarters in a Roman city. (35) He must therefore leave all the others in the village of Ammodius, while he himself, with a few companions, would be allowed into the city of Dara. (36) Yazdgushnasp consequently grew angry and appeared put out because he had been insulted gratuitously, even though he was on a diplomatic mission to the Roman emperor. (37) But George, ignoring his fury, saved the city for the Romans by receiving Yazdgushnasp within it with only twenty men.

(38) So this barbarian, following the failure of his enterprise, came to Byzantium as an ambassador, bringing with him his wife and two daughters (since this was his cover for the throng that accompanied him). When he came before the emperor he was unable to say to him anything important or trivial about serious matters even though he spent no less than ten months on Roman territory. (39) However, he presented to the emperor gifts from Khusro, as is customary, and a letter, in which Khusro asked the Emperor Justinian to report as to whether his physical health was as excellent as it could be.[438] (40) Yet the Emperor Justinian regarded

---

[437] 2.19.22–3.

[438] These aspects of the ceremonial involved in high-level diplomatic missions to Constantinople are confirmed in the *De Ceremoniis*, 1.89, which describes how Persian ambassadors presented gifts to the Roman emperor and asked after his health. See *REF*, 124–8, esp. 127, *RPLA*, 245–8.

this Yazdgushnasp with a greater fondness than any other ambassadors **289** we know of and treated him with considerable honour, (41) such that, whenever he entertained him, he invited Braducius, who followed him as an interpreter, to recline with him on the couch, a gesture with no precedent at any time.[439] (42) For no one had ever beheld an interpreter sharing a table even with a relatively lowly official, and indeed certainly not with an emperor. (43) Justinian nonetheless received and dismissed this man more magnificently than a normal ambassador even though he had undertaken the embassy for no purpose, as I have reported. (44) For if someone were to add up the emperor's expenses and the presents that Yazdgushnasp carried away from there upon his departure, he would find that they reached a total of more than ten *centenaria*. Such then was the outcome of Khusro's plot against the city of Dara.

Chapter 29

(1) Khusro first sent a huge mass of timber, suitable for ship-building, to Lazica, but told no one for what reason he was sending it; the word was given, rather, that he was despatching this material for the construction of devices on the circuit wall of Petra. (2) Then he selected three hundred battle-ready men, along with Vahriz, whom I mentioned recently,[440] and despatched them under his command, having instructed him to kill Gubazes as discreetly as possible, while he himself organised the following steps. (3) When the timber was then brought to Lazica, it was **290** suddenly struck by chance by lightning and reduced to ashes. Vahriz, having arrived in Lazica with the three hundred men, made preparations to fulfil Khusro's instructions concerning Gubazes. (4) It happened that one of the Colchian nobles, Pharsanses by name, had clashed with Gubazes and incurred a great hatred on his part, such that he did not dare at all come into the king's presence. (5) When Vahriz learnt of this, he summoned Pharsanses and, having revealed to him the whole matter, sought his advice, asking the man how he should go about executing his mission. (6) They decided therefore, following their joint deliberations, that Vahriz should go to the city of Petra and summon Gubazes there, so as to announce to him what the king was deciding about the future interests of the Lazi. (7) But Pharsanses secretly reported these plans to Gubazes. Consequently Gubazes did not come to Vahriz, but rather

---

[439] Braducius fell under suspicion as a result and was later executed by Khusro, as Procopius reports at 8.11.8–9.

[440] At 2.28.16.

openly set his sights on revolt. (8) Vahriz instructed the other Persians to
assure the defence of Petra with all their strength and to prepare most
carefully for a siege, while he himself, with his three hundred men,
returned home, his mission unaccomplished. (9) Gubazes reported his
situation to the Emperor Justinian and begged him to forgive the Lazi for
their previous actions and to defend them, who now wished to be free of
Persian rule, with all his might, since, left to themselves, the Colchians
could not ward off the Persian forces.

(10) When Justinian heard this news, he was overjoyed and sent 7000
men and the commander Dagisthaeus with one thousand Tzani to assist
the Lazi.[441] (11) When they arrived on Lazic soil they encamped with the
Lazi and Gubazes around the circuit wall of Petra and laid siege to it. (12)
But because the Persians there defended themselves very stoutly from the
circuit wall, much time was consumed in the prosecution of the siege; for
the Persians happened also to have stored up sufficient food supplies for
themselves. (13) Shaken by these events, Khusro despatched against them
a substantial army of both cavalry and infantry, appointing Mihr-Mihroe
as commander. Gubazes, when he learnt of this, consulted with
Dagisthaeus and acted as follows.

(14) The river Boas rises very close to the frontiers of Tzanica among
the Armenians that inhabit Pharangium.[442] At first it flows mostly to the
right as a shallow stream, easily fordable by anyone, until it reaches a
place where the boundaries of Iberia lie to the right and the Caucasus
mountains terminate opposite. (15) There live various peoples, among
them the Alans and Abasgi, who have long been Christians and friends of
the Romans;[443] also the Zekhi, and beyond them Huns known as
Sabirs.[444] (16) When this river reaches the place where lie the boundaries
of the Caucasus and Iberia, it is joined there by other waters and swells to
a much greater size. From that point, known as the Phasis rather than the
Boas, it flows on, becoming navigable for ships as far as the so-called
Euxine Sea, where it has its mouth, and on either side of it lies Lazica
(fig. 30). (17) But on the right, the whole territory is inhabited on a large
scale by the local population as far as the border of Iberia, (18) for all the

---

[441] Procopius describes Dagisthaeus as young and inexperienced, 29.33. He was probably Valerian's
successor as *magister militum per Armeniam* and arrived in 548.

[442] Procopius returns with greater accuracy to Caucasian geography at 8.2–4. On the Boas see 1.15.20–
30. Here Procopius mistakenly identifies it with the Phasis.

[443] The Abasgi, Procopius means, had long been Roman allies. On the Alans see 1.15.1.

[444] The Zekhi lived beyond Pityus and the territory of the Abasgi on the Black Sea Coast. On the
Sabirs see 1.15.1.

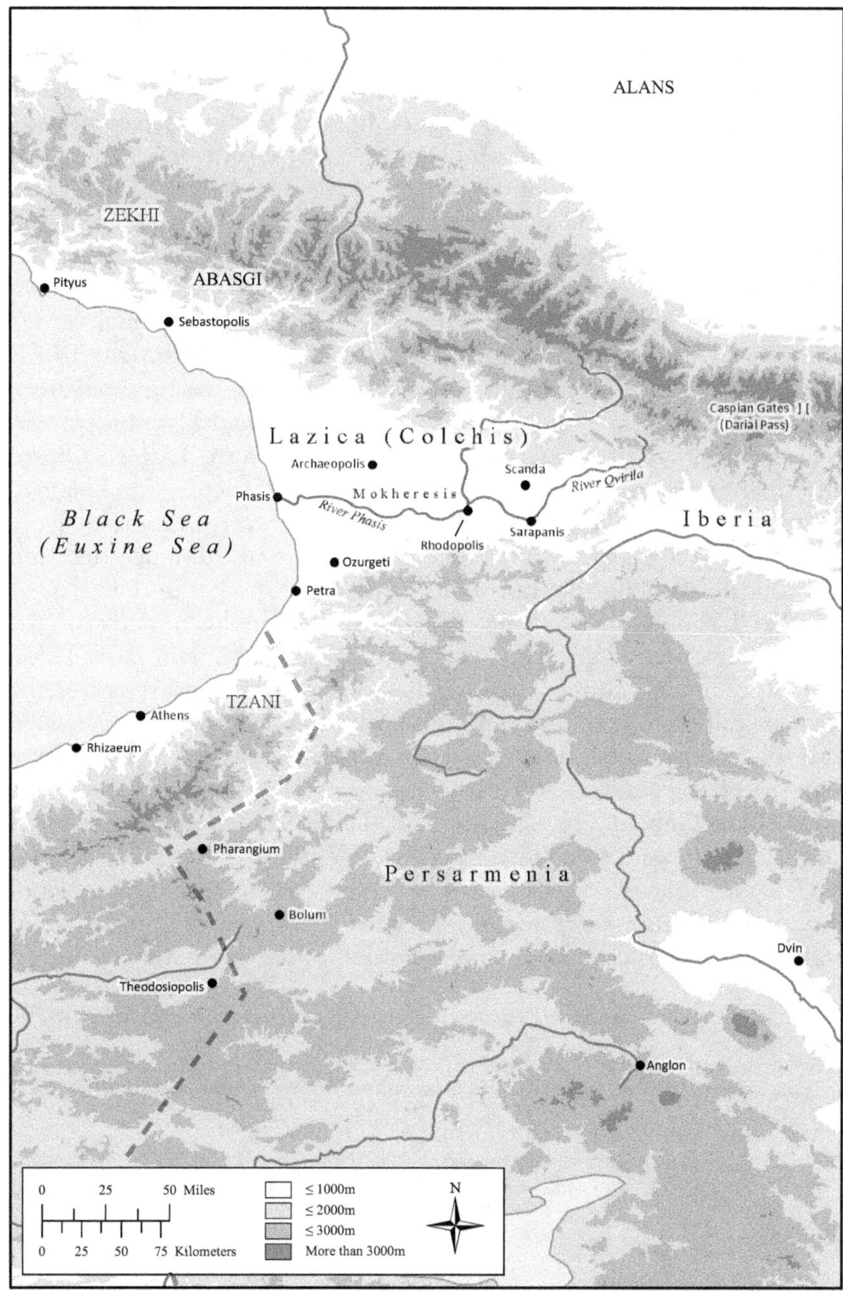

Figure 30   Lazica and Iberia in the 540s

Lazic villages lie here, on this side of the river,[445] as well as towns built by them here long ago, among which is Archaeopolis, a very secure place.[446] Here also lie Sebastopolis and the fortress of Pityus,[447] as well as Scanda and Sarapanis on the border with Iberia.[448] The most notable cities here, however, are Rhodopolis and Mokheresis.[449] (19) On the left of the river, for the distance of a day's journey for an active man, lie the Lazic borderlands, which are devoid of human habitation. The Romans known as Pontic inhabit the adjacent land. (20) In the Lazic borderlands, where no people live, the Emperor Justinian founded the city of Petra in my own day. (21) Here John, known as Tzibus, set up a monopoly, as I related earlier in my narrative,[450] and caused the revolt of the Lazi. (22) To the south of the city of Petra the Roman borderlands start immediately, where there are densely populated villages, as well as Rhizaeum, Athens and various others as far as Trapezus.[451] (23) So when the Lazi led Khusro into their territory, they crossed the river Boas and, keeping the Phasis to their right, came to Petra. They claimed that this was a measure to avoid being obliged to be ferried across the Phasis at the cost of much time and effort, but in fact they did not want to show their homes to the Persians. (24) Yet Lazica is inaccessible from all sides, whether on this or the further side of the river Phasis, (25) since massive mountain peaks lie on each side of the country, creating here extremely lengthy passes; the Romans call such roads *kleisourai* in Greek.[452] (26) But at the time when Lazica happened to be unprotected, the Persians very easily reached Petra with their Lazic guides.

(27) Now Gubazes, once he learnt of the Persian approach, instructed Dagisthaeus to send some men to guard very stoutly the pass that lies on the far side of the river Phasis[453] and at all costs not to raise the siege until they could capture Petra and the Persians there. (28) He himself went with the entire Colchian army to the borders of Lazica in order to protect

[445] The northern side of the river, which Procopius places in Europe, following earlier writers. See 8.2.27–33.

[446] Archaeopolis, the modern Nokalakevi in Georgia, is a well defended hilltop site on the river Tekhuri. See *ODLA*, Archaeopolis. Cf. the list of cities of this region in the preface of *NovJ.* 28 of 535.

[447] Roman ports on the Black Sea coast. See *ODLA*, Sebastopolis, Pityus.

[448] Already alluded to at 1.12.15: they had been returned to Roman hands by the Eternal Peace in 532.

[449] Rhodopolis, modern Vardtsikhe, lies in eastern Lazica in the fertile region of Mokherisis. The city of Mokherisis lies just to the west. See *ODLA*, Rhodopolis.

[450] Cf. 2.15.10–12.

[451] Procopius surveys the same region at 8.2.3–5, 10. All these places are ports along the Black Sea coast. See *ODLA*, Trebizond.

[452] Derived from the Latin *clausura*.

[453] The southern side of the river, lying in Asia: see n. 445. The pass may be near today's Ozurgeti.

the pass there with all his might. (29) It happened that much earlier he   **294**
had invited the Alans and the Sabirs to an alliance; they had agreed, in
exchange for three *centenaria*, not only to protect the land unharmed for
the Lazi, but even to make Iberia so deserted that it would no longer be
possible for the Persians to come from there. Gubazes promised that the
emperor would give them the money. (30) He himself reported the deal
to the Emperor Justinian and implored him to send the money to the
barbarians and to offer some consolation to the sorely afflicted Lazi. (31)
He added that the treasury owed him ten years' salary, since he was
enrolled among the *silentiarii* of the palace,[454] but he had received
nothing of it from the moment that Khusro entered the land of
Colchis.[455] (32) The Emperor Justinian meant to fulfil his request, but
because some pressing business arose, he did not send the money at the
appointed time. These, then, were Gubazes' actions.

(33) But Dagisthaeus – for he was a young man by no means competent to prosecute a Persian war – did not react appropriately to the
circumstances. (34) So although it was surely necessary to send the bulk
of the army to the pass, and perhaps even attend to this task himself, he
sent only one hundred men, as though managing some trifle. He himself,
besieging Petra with his entire army, accomplished nothing despite the
small numbers of the enemy. For although at the outset they had
numbered no fewer than 1500, (35) during the lengthy battle from the   **295**
walls in which they displayed a courage greater than that of anyone we
know of, they were struck by missiles of the Romans and Lazi, from
which many died; and so they were reduced to a very small number
indeed. (36) The Persians therefore fell into despondency and perplexity
and remained quiet, while the Romans dug a trench next to the wall for a
small stretch. Immediately the circuit wall collapsed here. (37) But it
happened that there was a house in this space right next to the circuit
wall that extended for the whole length of the collapsed section (38)
which replaced the wall for the besieged and made them no less secure
than before. (39) This was not enough to shake the Romans at all,
however, for they knew well that by doing the same thing elsewhere they
would capture the city very easily, and so they grew still more hopeful.
(40) Dagisthaeus therefore reported the developments to the emperor,
proposing that prizes be prepared for him for his victory and indicating

---

[454] On the post see 2.21.2.

[455] Payments would naturally have been interrupted after Khusro's invasion in 541, but that had taken
place seven years earlier. The figure is therefore problematic; perhaps there had been delays in
paying his salary even earlier.

what presents the emperor should give to him and his brother, since he would shortly take Petra. (41) So the Romans and Tzani launched a very fierce assault, but the Persians unexpectedly resisted, despite being reduced to a very small number. (42) When the assault proved ineffective, the Romans turned again to digging. They reached such an advanced stage in their work that the foundations of the circuit wall no longer rested on the ground but rather stood for the most part over empty space, right on the point of collapse in all likelihood. (43) And if Dagisthaeus had wanted immediately to set fire to the foundations, I think that the city would have fallen to the Romans forthwith. But now, waiting for encouragement from the emperor, hesitating constantly and wasting time, he remained quiet. Such then was what occurred in the Roman camp.

Chapter 30

(1) Mihr-Mihroe, when he had passed the borderlands of Iberia with the whole Persian army, continued to advance, keeping the river Phasis on his right. He had absolutely no desire to go through the villages of Lazica in case an obstacle to him arose there. (2) He was keen to save the city of Petra and the Persians there, even if a part of the circuit wall had suddenly collapsed, (3) since, as I had mentioned, it was suspended in the air. Some fifty volunteers from the Roman army got within the city and acclaimed the Emperor Justinian gloriously triumphant. (4) Their leader was a young man of Armenian birth, John by name, the son of Thomas, whom they called Guzes.[456] (5) This Thomas had built many of the fortifications around Lazica on the emperor's instructions and commanded the soldiers there, since he seemed to the emperor to be a prudent man. (6) Now John, when the Persians engaged his men, was wounded and immediately withdrew to the camp with his followers since no one else from the Roman army came to defend him. (7) A Persian man, Mirranes by name,[457] who held command of the garrison in Petra, fearful for the city, instructed all the Persians to maintain the strictest guard while he himself went to Dagisthaeus. He proffered flattering and deceptive words, agreeing to hand over the city shortly with no struggle. Thus he was able to mislead him, so that the Roman army did not immediately enter the city.

---

[456] John Guzes died during the Roman capture of Petra in 551. See *PLRE* 3, Ioannes *qui et* Guzes 44.
[457] On the name see 1.13.16 and n. 95.

(8) When Mihr-Mihroe arrived at the pass, the Roman garrison there, one hundred strong, came to oppose them, defending themselves vigorously, and they pushed back those making an attempt on the entrance to the pass. (9) But the Persians, far from withdrawing, constantly replaced the dead and marched on, forcing the entrance with their entire strength. (10) More than one thousand Persians died, but the Romans left off their slaughter and withdrew in the face of the masses pressing them, and, by running up to the peaks of the mountains there, they were saved. (11) Once he learnt of this, Dagisthaeus raised the siege at once, and, without issuing any orders to his army, hastened to the river Phasis; and all the Romans followed him, abandoning their possessions in the camp. (12) The Persians, when they noticed these developments, opened the gates, went out and came up to the enemy tents in order to seize the camp. (13) But the Tzani, who happened not to have followed Dagisthaeus, came forth at a run to protect the camp and routed the enemy with no difficulty, killing many of them. (14) The Persians therefore fled and returned within the circuit walls, while the Tzani plundered the Roman camp and marched directly to Rhizaeum. From there they went to Athens and returned home through the territory of Trapezus.

(15) Mihr-Mihroe and the Persian army arrived there on the ninth day after the withdrawal of Dagisthaeus. Here they found three hundred and fifty of the Persian garrison wounded and unfit for service and only one hundred and fifty unharmed, since all the others had died. (16) The survivors had not thrown the bodies of any of them outside the circuit wall. Rather, despite being suffocated by the awful stench, they put up with it against all expectation, so as not to provide the enemy with any encouragement in their prosecution of the siege from the sheer number of those killed. (17) Mihr-Mihroe mockingly declared that the Roman state merited tears and lamentations since it had reached such a weak point that it was unable by any means to capture one hundred and fifty men with no defensive wall. (18) He was keen to rebuild the section of the circuit wall that had collapsed, but since for the moment he did not have any lime or other building material ready to hand, he contrived the following solution. (19) He filled with sand the linen sacks in which the Persians had transported their supplies to Colchis and laid them in the place of the stones so that, once inserted there, they replaced the wall. (20) After selecting 3000 battle-ready men, he left them there, providing them with food for a short period and instructing them to see to the building of the circuit wall; he himself hastened back with all the remainder of the army.

(21) Because there were no supplies to be had if he went from there by the same road as he had come, and given that he had left everything that the army had brought from Iberia in Petra, Mihr-Mihroe decided to take a different route through the mountains there, where he learnt that people lived, so that they could live off their plunder. (22) On this journey a noble among the Lazi, Phubelis by name, set an ambush for the Persians when they were encamped. Having brought up Dagisthaeus with 2000 Romans, they slew some of the Persians, who were grazing their horses, in a lightning attack, and after seizing the horses they quickly withdrew. In this way Mihr-Mihroe left with the Persian army.

(23) Gubazes, though informed about what had happened to the Romans at Petra and at the pass, was not fearful nonetheless, nor did he relax his guard of the pass in his care, believing that here lay their main source of hope. (24) For he was well aware that, even if the Persians had forced their way through the Romans beyond the Phasis, crossed the pass and reached Petra, from there they could inflict no harm on Lazic territory because they had no means of crossing the Phasis, particularly in the absence of any ships. (25) For this river is no less deep than any other while also being extremely wide. (26) Such is the strength of its current, furthermore, that when it flows into the sea, it proceeds as a distinct stream for a very long distance, not merging at all with the surrounding waters. For those sailing these waters it is indeed possible to draw fresh water in the middle of the sea. (27) The Lazi had nonetheless built fortresses on the near side of the river[458] so that, should enemies be carried across by ship, it would be impossible to land.

(28) The Emperor Justinian sent the agreed sum of money to the Sabir people as well as bestowing other sums on Gubazes and the Lazi. (29) Much earlier he had sent another considerable army to Lazica, which happened not yet to have arrived. Its commander was Rhecithangus from Thrace, an intelligent man and expert in warfare.[459] This was then the state of affairs.

(30) Once Mihr-Mihroe reached the mountains, as I reported, he was keen to fill Petra with supplies from there, for he believed that the food that they had brought with them was nowhere near sufficient for a garrison of some 3000 men. (31) But since what was to hand was scarcely enough for the maintenance of this army, which numbered no fewer than 30,000 men, they were unable therefore to send anything substantial to

---

[458] See n. 445: this is the north bank.
[459] No more is known of this force. On Rhecithangus see 2.16.17.

Petra. Upon reflection, he found that the best course for them was to   **301**
dismiss the bulk of the army from Colchis while a few remained, who
would then transport most of the provisions that they came across to the
garrison in Petra; for them what was left would suffice. (32) Accordingly
he selected 5000 men and left them there, for whom he appointed as
commanders Vahriz and three others. (33) For it did not seem necessary
to him to retain more there, given the complete absence of the enemy.
He himself went with the rest of the army to Persarmenia and rested in
the villages around Dvin.

(34) The 5000, when they drew near to the borders of Lazica, all
encamped next to the river Phasis, and from there went around in small
groups plundering the villages there. (35) Gubazes, when he noticed this,
instructed Dagisthaeus to bring help there urgently because it would be
possible for them to inflict great damage on the enemy. (36) He acted
accordingly and came nearby with the entire Roman army, keeping the
river Phasis to his left, until he reached the place where the Lazi were
encamped on the opposite bank of the river. (37) It so happened that
here the Phasis was fordable, which neither the Romans nor the Persians
remotely suspected because of their lack of experience of the districts
there. The Lazi, however, being aware of this, crossed over here suddenly
and joined up with the Roman army. The Persians selected one thousand
notable men from their ranks and sent them forth in case anyone should   **302**
come against their camp to damage it. (38) Two of the Persians, who had
gone in advance on reconnaissance and stumbled across the enemy
contrary to their expectations, reported the whole plan. (39) The Romans
and Lazi therefore made a sudden attack on the one thousand, of whom
not one managed to flee. Rather, most were killed, while some were taken
alive, and Gubazes and Dagisthaeus were able to learn the size of the
Persian army and its distance from them by road, as well as how matters
stood with them at the time. (40) So they broke camp with the entire
army and went off against them, reckoning that they would fall upon
them late at night; their own forces numbered 14,000 men. (41) The
Persians, with no thoughts of the enemy, were enjoying a lengthy sleep,
believing the river to be impassable and their one thousand men to be a
long way ahead with no opposition. (42) The Romans and Lazi fell upon
them unexpectedly at the break of dawn. Some they found still in the
grip of sleep, others just awake and lying on their beds defenceless. (43)
Consequently not one of them had any thought of valour, but most were
caught and killed; others their enemy captured, among whom was one
commander, while a few escaped in the darkness and were saved. (44)

The Romans and Lazi took the camp and all the standards, seizing as booty numerous weapons and large sums of money, as well as a great number of horses and mules. (45) They made a pursuit of the enemy over a very long distance and penetrated deep into Iberia. There they came upon some other Persians and killed many of them. (46) Thus the Persians left Lazica, while the Romans and Lazi, once they discovered there a huge quantity of various supplies, including flour, which the barbarians had brought in from Iberia in order to transport it to Petra, burnt it all. (47) They left many of the Lazi at the pass so that it would no longer be possible for the Persians to transport supplies to Petra, then returned with the remainder of the booty and the prisoners. (48) This was the end of the fourth year of the Romans' truce with the Persians and of the twenty-third year of the reign of the Emperor Justinian.[460]

(49) In the previous year John the Cappadocian was summoned by the emperor and went to Byzantium, for at this point the Empress Theodora had reached the last day of her life.[461] (50) He was unable, however, to recover any of his former offices, but remained a priest, an honour that he held against his will. Yet the man had often dreamed of reaching the imperial power, (51) for the divine power, which is naturally disposed to adopt a glorious appearance among men, loves to keep in suspense with grandiose and lofty hopes those whose intentions happen not to be founded on a solid character. (52) To this man John soothsayers continually foretold many fantasies, including a tale that he was fated to put on the robe of the Augustus. (53) But there was a priest called Augustus in Byzantium who guarded the treasures of the church of Sophia.[462] (54) Now when John was deemed worthy of the priesthood and forcibly tonsured, he had no garment suitable for a priest, and so he was obliged by those in charge of the business to put on the cloak and tunic of this Augustus, who was near at hand.[463] Thus, I believe, the prophecy found its fulfilment for him.

---

[460] The end of March 549, although the last events described are more likely to have occurred in late summer 548.

[461] The empress died in June 548.

[462] Perhaps a *skeuophylax*, a sacristan, or a *keimēliarkhēs*, 'treasurer'.

[463] Described already at 1.25.31, where the events are placed at Cyzicus.

Appendix: Nonnosus

Nonnosus on Roman Missions to Southern Arabia

Introduction

The brief summary that the ninth-century patriarch Photius gives of Nonnosus' work provides a fascinating glimpse of a series of Roman embassies to southern Arabia and Ethiopia. Some of the details concern people mentioned by Procopius, notably the phylarch Caïsus (Qays), which is why we offer here a full translation of Photius' notes. In order to follow his account, however, it is necessary to examine more closely the relationship between three diplomatic missions he mentions and the ones mentioned by Procopius and Malalas. The embassies may be presented as follows.

Embassies Described by Nonnosus

A. Abrames' (Abraham's) first mission to Qays, the grandson of Ḥarith, who ruled over the Kindites and Maʿadd (§4). Abraham made a treaty with him and brought his son Muʿāwiya back to Constantinople as a hostage.
B. Nonnosus' mission to Qays and Kālēb (§5): his brief was to persuade Qays to come to the Emperor Justinian, which he failed to do, and to visit Kālēb (Nonnosus' Elesbaas) and the Ḥimyarites.
C. Abraham's second mission to Qays (§8), in which he succeeded in convincing him to come to Constantinople himself, leaving his kingdom to his two brothers, ʿAmr and Yazīd. Qays, who had come with many of his own retainers, was then made phylarch of 'the Palestines'.

Procopius' Embassy (i.20.9–11)

D. The envoy Julian was instructed to persuade Sumuyafaʿ Ashwaʿ
    (Esimiphaeus) to restore Qays to his chiefdom over the Maʿadd and
    to urge the Ethiopian ruler to help the Romans reduce their
    dependence on the Persians for imports, particularly of silk.

Malalas' Embassy (18.56, cf. Theophanes, 244–5)

E. Theophanes' version of Malalas gives the envoy's name as Julian; this
    emissary visited the court of the Ethiopian ('Indian') ruler, i.e. Kālēb,
    and successfully persuaded him to open hostilities with the Persians.
    The account contains a detailed description of the Axumite court.

The difficulty lies in determining the relationship between these various
diplomatic missions. Many chronologies have been proposed; here we
follow that proposed by Joëlle Beaucamp.[1]

Procopius' embassy takes place during the reign of Sumuyafaʿ Ashwaʿ,
i.e. after 525 and before Abraha seized power, i.e. some time in the early
530s. Though Beaucamp insists that it must have taken place in 531, since
it is placed in his account between the Roman defeat at Callinicum and
Kavadh's death in September that year, this places undue weight on the
historian's chronology; more cautiously, it may be placed in 530 or 531, at
any rate before the war with Persia ended in 532. Given that Malalas
mentions Julian in his account, it is most likely that the mission he
describes derives from his report; the account even slips into the first person on occasion. Missions D and E would thus be one and the same. The
date of Julian's embassy is not clear in Malalas, but is likely to be 530 or
531. Although one has the impression from Malalas that Julian's visit to
the Ethiopian court was a remarkable success, given the willingness of the
king immediately to declare war on Persia, this is only an apparent dis-
crepancy with Procopius' more critical portrayal of the mission's outcome: much was promised, as Julian no doubt proudly reported, but in
the end, as Procopius describes, little delivered.[2]

How then do Nonnosus' three missions fit with that of Julian
recounted by Procopius and Malalas? The most plausible scenario is to
envisage that Nonnosus and his father undertook their missions to Qays

---

[1] J. Beaucamp, 'Le rôle de Byzance en mer Rouge sous le règne de Justin: mythe ou réalité?' in J.
Beaucamp, F. Briquel-Chatonnet and C. Robin, eds., *Juifs et chrétiens en Arabie aux Ve et VIe siècles:
regards croisés sur les sources* (Paris, 2010), 197–218.

[2] See *RPW*, 237–8, Beaucamp, 'Le rôle de Byzance', 198–203.

following the conclusion of the Eternal Peace with Persia, or even somewhat later, after the resumption of war with Persia in 540. By this point he had evidently become an important ruler in central Arabia who might, Justinian reasoned, be of more use to the empire within it than operating on its margins.

The translation that follows uses the text in R. Henry, ed. and tr., *Photius*, Bibliotheca, vol. 1 (Paris, 1959), 4–7. His French translation has been taken into account, as has that of J.H. Freese, *The Library of Photius*, vol. 1 (London, 1920) and that of N. Wilson, *Photius: The Bibliotheca* (London, 1994), 27–9. Richard Burgess made important improvements to our original translation. Bevan offers a partial translation in *AEBI*, 238–9. The paragraph numbers are our own insertion for ease of reference.

Nonnosus

(1) Read: a *History* of Nonnosus, in which is recounted his embassy to the Ethiopians and Amerites (Homerites) and Saracens, very powerful peoples at that time, as well as to other eastern peoples.

(2) Justinian governed the Roman empire at this time and the phylarch of the Saracens was Caïsus (Qays), a descendant of Arethas (al-Harith), who had himself been phylarch.[3] Nonnosus' grandfather was sent to Arethas by the then Emperor Anastasius and concluded a peace treaty with him.[4] (3) Moreover the father of Nonnosus, whose name was Abrames (Abraham),[5] also went on an embassy to Alamundarus (al-Mundhir), the phylarch of the Saracens, and rescued two Roman commanders, Timostratus and John, who had been captured according to the rules of war.[6] This rescue of the commanders was undertaken for the Emperor Justin.

(4) Now Caïsus, to whom Nonnosus was sent, was the leader of two of the most notable peoples among the Saracens, the Khindeni (Kindites)

---

[3] This is Procopius' Qays at 1.20.9. The al-Harith in question is a Kindite leader allied to Rome who had been killed by the Nasrid al-Mundhir in 528, which is reported by Mal. 18.26. See *AEBI*, 221, 232–3.

[4] Nonnosus' grandfather was called Euphrasius, *PLRE* 2, Euphrasius 3. On the treaty he arranged c. 502, probably with both Kindite and Jafnid leaders, see *REF*, 51–2, *ODLA*, Nonnosus.

[5] *PLRE* 2, Abramius; he was a priest, as is clear from Ps.-Zach. 8.3a.

[6] See *PLRE* 2, Ioannes 70, Timostratus, cf. *REF*, 79. They were captured perhaps in 523, perhaps a little earlier, then released the following year. See Proc. 1.17.44 and Ps.-Zach. 8.3a.

and the Maadēni (Ma'add).[7] But before Nonnosus was chosen as ambassador, his father too had been sent to this Caïsus by the Emperor Justinian and made a peace treaty with him, the result of which was that he took the son of Caïsus, who was called Mavias (Mu'āwiya), as a hostage and brought him back to Justinian in Byzantium.[8]

(5) Nonnosus subsequently went on an embassy with the following two objectives: to bring Caïsus to the emperor, if possible, and to reach the king of the Auxomitae (Axumites), whose ruler at this time was Elesbaas ('Ella 'Aṣbeḥa). In addition to these two (aims), he was also to visit the Homerites.[9]

(6) Auxumis (Axum) is a very large city and is a sort of capital for the whole of Ethiopia; it lies to the south and east of the Roman empire.[10]

(7) Nonnosus survived many plots of foreign peoples, as well as many dangerous animals on his journey; he also encountered rugged terrain and frequent crises. Nevertheless he accomplished his mission and was able to return home safely.

(8) [Nonnosus says] that, after Abrames went on another embassy to him, Caïsus divided his phylarchate between his brothers Ambrus ('Amr) and Iezidus (Yazīd) and came to Byzantium.[11] He obtained from the emperor the chieftainship of the Palestines for himself and brought a vast contingent of his own subordinates with him.[12]

(9) He says the ancients used to call what are now called sandals *arbylae* (boots) and a turban a *phasōlis*.

(10) [He says] that most of the Saracens, both those in Phoinikōn (the Palm Grove) and those beyond the Palm Grove and the mountains called Taurēnoi,[13] regard a particular place as sacred because it is dedicated to

---

[7] The Kindites and Ma'add were important groups in the centre of the Arabian peninsula. See *AEBI*, 238–9 and R. Hoyland, *Arabia and the Arabs from the Bronze Age to the Coming of Islam* (London, 2001), 49–50.

[8] This embassy probably took place after the Eternal Peace of 532.

[9] Elesbaas is Procopius' Hellesthaeus (1.20.1) i.e. Kālēb. The Homerites are the Ḥimyarites.

[10] On Axum see Proc. 1.19.22.

[11] Given the uncertainty as to the identity of Qays, that of his brothers is likewise unclear. A Yazīd, brother of Qays b. Salama led an expedition against the Naṣrid ruler al-Mundhir, but another Qays, a nephew of al-Harith (§2), revolted against the Ḥimyarite king Abraha and is referred to by the Mārib dam inscription of 547.

[12] It is uncertain how Qays' phylarchate, apparently wide-ranging in nature, impacted on the phylarchate of Palaestina III earlier granted to Abū Karib (see Proc. 1.19.10).

[13] Not otherwise known, though it could refer to Mt Sinai.

one or other of their gods and they gather there twice every year.[14] (11) One of these festivals lasts an entire month, concluding almost in the middle of spring, when the sun crosses Taurus. The other festival lasts for two months and is celebrated after the summer solstice.

(12) He says that during these festivals they are all at peace, not only with one another, but also with all the people living among them. They say that even the animals live in peace with men, and even among themselves. He also recounts many other surprising things, hardly different from myths.

(13) [Nonnosus says] that Adulis is fifteen days' journey from Axum.[15] As they were leaving Axum, Nonnosus and his companions witnessed an amazing spectacle near a place called Awē, which lies between Axum and Adulis:[16] a not inconsiderable herd of elephants, almost five thousand in number. These elephants were feeding in a large plain. It was not easy for any of the inhabitants to approach them nor to keep them away from their feeding grounds. This spectacle did indeed happen to them en route.

(14) It is necessary also to mention the climate changes[17] between Awē and Axum, which lead to opposite experiences of summer and winter. For when the sun is crossing Cancer, Leo and Virgo,[18] as far (south) as Awē summer and the dryness dominate the air, as they do for us, but from Awē to Axum and the rest of Ethiopia stormy weather takes over. It does not last for the whole day, but rather begins each day in the afternoon, when it clouds over and the countryside is inundated by violent rainstorms. It is right at this point that the Nile reaches its peak, flooding Egypt and irrigating the land. But when the sun is crossing Capricorn, Aquarius and Pisces,[19] the land of the Adulitans as far (south) as Awē is conversely inundated by rain, while for those from Awē as far as Axum and the rest of Ethiopia it is summer, and the land at that time provides them with seasonal crops.[20]

---

[14] Cf. Proc. 2.16.18 with Hoyland, *Arabia and the Arabs*, 161–3, on such periods of sacred truce.

[15] Cf. Proc. 1.19.22.

[16] Cosmas Indicopleustes, *Christian Topography*, ii.60 refers to a people called Awa/Ava, conquered by an unnamed Axumite king (in his transcription of an inscription from Adulis), which ought to correspond to the place mentioned here.

[17] Literally, 'the mixing of airs'.

[18] I.e. June, July and August.

[19] I.e. December, January and February.

[20] The Ethiopian climate varies greatly between regions, depending especially on the elevation.

(15) [Nonnosus says] that the following thing happened to him – it is a wonder just to hear about it – when he was sailing from Farsan and had reached the last of the islands.[21] He encountered certain beings with a human shape and appearance, but very short and with black skin and thick hair all over their bodies. Women of similar appearance followed the men, as did the children, who were even shorter than the men among them. They were all naked, except that both adult men and women alike covered their private parts with a small piece of skin. They displayed no wildness or savagery, but instead had human speech, a language utterly unknown both to all their neighbours and even more so to Nonnosus' entourage. They lived off shellfish and fish that are thrown up by the sea onto the island. They had no courage, but rather, upon seeing the men with us, cowered under (the bushes) as we do when we see particularly large animals.

---

[21] The Farasan islands, lying off the Arabian coast north-east of Adulis, occupied by the Romans already in the second century A.D.

Index of Persons and Titles

A

Abandanes, royal secretary of Khusro,
ii.21.1–14

Abraham (Abrames), father of Nonnosus;
despatched by Justin I to al-Mundhir to
rescue two captured Roman commanders,
§2; sent on another embassy to Qays, §8

Abramus, king of the Homerites, i.20.3–8;
hollow commitment to Justinian to invade
Persia, i.20.13

Abu Karib, ruler of the Saracens inhabiting the
Arabian Palm Groves, i.19.10–13

Acacius, appointed governor of Armenia after
denouncing and killing his predecessor,
ii.3.4–5; killed by subjects because of his
cruelty and avarice, ii.3.6–7; father of
Adolius, ii.21.2

Adergudunbades, appointed *kanarang* by
Khusro, i.6.15–18; foils Khusro's plan to
murder Kavadh; betrayal by his son leads to
his death, i.23.7–22

Adolius, son of Acacius; slanders Sittas's
handling of the Armenian campaign, ii.3.10;
formerly a *silentarius*, made joint commander
of a cavalry detachment, ii.21.2, 18–20;
arrives at Citharizon in preparation for
invasion of Persarmenia, ii.24.13; killed in
Persarmenia, ii.25.35

Adonachus, commander of Roman forces
stationed at Chalcis, ii.12.2

Aeimachus, Antiochene youth who kills Persian
noble, ii.11.8–11

Agamemnon, father of Iphigenia, i.17.11

Aigan, Massagetae commander; serves with
the Romans at the battle of Dara, i.13.20;
i.14.39, 44

Alexander, member of embassy despatched to
Khusro, i.22.1

Alexander the Macedonian, son of Philip;
construction of the Caspian Gates along with
a nearby fortress, i.10.9; comparison with

Justinian and Cyrus, ii.2.15; foundation of
Seleucia and Ctesiphon and Macedonian
dominance over region, ii.28.4

Amazaspes, nephew of Symeon; appointed
ruler of the Armenians by Justinian; later
denounced and murdered by his relative
Acacius with the approval of the emperor,
ii.3.3–5

Ambazuces, a Hun; friendly to the Romans
and in possession of the fortress and
Caspian Gates; offer to cede control of the
aforementioned to Anastasius I politely
refused, i.10.9–12

'Amr, a Saracen Christian under al-Mundhir's
command; betrays the Persians by foiling
their attempts to capture Sergiopolis,
ii.20.10–14

'Amr (Ambrus), brother of Qays; receives half
of Qays' phylarchate, §8

Anastasius I (Roman emperor, 491–518),
refuses Kavadh's request for a loan to pay
the king of the Hephthalites; his generosity
towards the Amidenes following the sack of
their city by Kavadh, i.7.1, 35; despatches
Roman army to aid Amida prior to its
fall; among those accompanying the army
are Justin I and Vitalian, the former his
successor, the latter a usurper, i.8.1–3;
declines offer from Ambazuces to purchase
control of the Caspian Gates and its nearby
fortress; his fortification of Dara draws
the ire of Kavadh, whom he successfully
placates; fortifies Theodosiopolis as well,
i.10.9–19; succeeded not by a relative, but
by Justin I; embassy despatched to Kavadh
includes his nephew Hypatius, i.11.1, 24; his
nephew Probus sent to Bosporus to recruit
Huns, i.12.6; Justinian's *magister officiorum*,
Hermogenes, was previously the *assessor* of
the Vitalian, a usurper during Anastasius'
reign, i.13.10; Kavadh refers to Anastasius I's

Germanus (Roman commander), present at the battle of Dara, **i.13.21**

Germanus (Justinian's cousin), sent by Justinian to meet the Persian advance; discovers vulnerability in the circuit wall of Antioch; realizes that Justinian's promise of a large army is unlikely to materialize and fears that his very presence is detrimental to the city's safety, **i.6.9–14;** hears accusation of treason against Ephraem, the bishop of Antioch; leaving the majority of his men in Antioch, he flees to Cilicia, **ii.7.16–18**

Glones, a Persian; in charge of the garrison left at Amida, **i.7.33;** his son surrenders Amida to the Romans as Glones had died; digression follows, detailing how Glones was led into a trap and killed; under Glones' command no structure within or without Amida is deliberately destroyed; Glones' strict rationing; food shortage of the Persians apparent only after the Romans pay the garrison to return Amida, **i.9.4–23**

Godidisclus, a Goth; experienced in military matters; accompanies army despatched to Amida by Anastasius I, **i.8.3**

Gubazes (Lazic king), surrenders himself and his people to Khusro, **ii.17.2;** Khusro plots to have him killed, **ii.28.30;** attempt by Vahriz to kill Gubazes thwarted by the Lazic nobleman Pharsanses; in response, Gubazes revolts and begs for Justinian's forgiveness and aid; Justinian sends a force under the command of Dagisthaeus to assist Gubazes; upon Dagisthaeus' arrival, both men lay siege to Petra; Gubazes plans to continue the siege of Petra while also addressing the threat of Mihr-Mihroe's approaching Persian army, **ii.29.2–13, 27–32;** despite Dagisthaeus' setbacks, Gubazes remains unperturbed, believing the terrain to be in his favour; Gubazes receives Justinian's promised financial aid, but further help does not arrive; Gubazes and Dagisthaeus join forces and destroy Persian force left on the Lazic border by Mihr-Mihroe, **ii.30.23–45**

Gurgenes (Iberian king), following Kavadh's order to comply with Persian customs, the king seeks an alliance with the Romans; unable to withstand the Persian army sent against him, he flees along with the leading Iberians to the borders of Lazica, **i.12.4–13;** reference to the revolt of Gurgenes, **ii.15.6**

Gusanastades, Persian general or *kanarang*; advises the usurper Blases to execute Kavadh, **i.5.4–6;** following Kavadh's resumption of the throne, he is killed; his relative Adergudunbades, the first Persian to swear allegiance to Kavadh, assumes Gusanastades' office, **i.6.12–18**

H

al-Harith, son of Jabala; ruler of the Saracens in Arabia; made king by Justinian over many tribes in order to match the strength of the Persian-allied al-Mundhir; unable to prevent al-Mundhir's incursions into Roman territory, **i.17.47–48;** his forces join Belisarius' army and are present at the battle by the Euphrates river; suspected of treachery, **i.18.7, 26–35;** boundary dispute with al-Mundhir, **ii.1.3–7;** leading a large Saracen force, he joins Belisarius in Mesopotamia, **ii.16.5;** sent by Belisarius to plunder Assyria and to assess the military situation therein; fearing the loss of his plunder, he avoids rejoining Belisarius and returns to Roman territory via another route; escapes punishment despite Belisarius' learning of his disobedience; Khusro informed of al-Harith's depredations, **ii.19.11–30, 46–47;** engages in a war with al-Mundhir, gaining a victory over the latter, **ii.28.12–14;** his descendant Caïsus (Qays); receives Nonnosus' grandfather and concludes a peace treaty, **§2**

Hellesthaeus (Elesbaas), Christian king of the Ethiopians; launches expedition against the Homerites to prevent planned persecution of Christians; defeats Homerites in battle and places a Christian Homerite, Esimiphaeus, on the throne as his client king; Esimiphaeus soon deposed, and despite multiple attempts, Hellesthaeus is unable to restore him; agrees to aid Justinian against the Persians by providing an alternative source for the purchase of silk; unable to keep his promise, **i.20.1–12;** king of the Auxomitae (Axumites), **§5**

Hermogenes, *magister officiorum* under Justinian; formerly *assessor* of Vitalian; sent by emperor to Dara to assist Belisarius and his army; prepares for and participates in the battle for Dara, **i.13–14;** returns to Byzantium, **i.16.10;** supports Belisarius in his desire to avoid battle with the Persians by the Euphrates, **i.18.16;** following the battle at the Euphrates, he unsuccessfully treats with Khusro concerning peace, **i.21.1;** despatched on another embassy, he accompanies Sittas' army as it marches

of Hierapolis; Khusro eventually agrees to leave Roman territory for a fixed sum of gold, **ii.6.17–25**; unable to persuade the Antiochenes to pay any money to Khusro; chastises Khusro for his cruel treatment towards the Beroeans and convinces him to spare the survivors from further harm, **ii.7.1–34**; informs Khusro of the Antiochenes' refusal to pay any ransom, **ii.8.1**

Mihr-Mihroe, a Persian; commander of army tasked with invading Roman-controlled Armenia; camp in Persarmenia attacked and plundered by Roman forces; invades Roman territory and defeated at Satala, **i.15.1–17**; shares command of Persian army that invades Mesopotamia, **i.21.4**; leads Persian army to lift the siege of Lazic Petra, **ii.29.13**; having defeated the Roman force guarding the pass to Petra, he arrives to find the siege abandoned; after reinforcing the garrison and ordering the repair of the circuit wall, he departs with the remainder of his army by a different route; some of his troops ambushed by Phubelis and Dagisthaeus; having selected a force to supply the garrison with sufficient provisions, he withdraws from Lazica with the bulk of his army, **ii.30.1–33**

mirranes, Persian name for the rank of 'commander in chief'; held by the Persian Peroz at the battle for Dara; **i.13.16; i.14.1ff**; the *mirranes* Peroz punished by Kavadh for his failure to defeat the Romans at Dara, **i.17.26–33**; reference to the battle at Dara, **i.18.6**

Mirranes, a Persian; commander of the garrison at Petra; deceives Dagisthaeus into believing that he will surrender the city, **ii.30.7**

Molatzes, shares command with Theoctistus of the troops in Lebanon; arrives at Antioch to provide assistance againt Khusro; flees with soldiers during the siege, **ii.8.2, 17**

Mu'āwiya (Mavias), the son of Qays; sent as a hostage to Byzantium, **§4**

al-Mundhir, son of Sakkike; leads Saracens accompanying Persian army; king of the Saracens; advises Kavadh on invasion route into Roman territory; description of personality, **i.17.1, 30–48**; invades and withdraws from Roman territory along with Persian army, **i.18.1ff**; dispute with rival al-Harith over territory; sought as ally by Justinian, **ii.1.2–13; ii.3.47**; allegedly violates the peace between Rome and Persia, **ii.4.21**; poses ongoing threat to Syria and the Levant,

ii.16.17; ii.19.34; engages in conflict with his rival al-Harith, **ii.28.12–14**; phylarch of the Saracens in possession of two captured Roman commanders, **§2**

Mundus, *magister militum per Illyricum* under Justinian; along with Belisarius, assists in suppressing the Nika revolt, **i.24.40–43, 52**

N

Nabedes, general of the soldiers stationed in Nisibis; second only to Khusro in reputation and standing; defeats a Roman force near the city, having caught them ill-prepared to fight, **ii.18.9, 16ff**; holds post of commander in Persarmenia; despatches the bishop of Dvin to press the Romans on the matter of peace, **ii.24.6**; hearing of the Roman invasion of Persarmenia, Nabedes entrenches his forces at Anglon; inflicts defeat upon the Romans at Anglon, **ii.25.6–10ff**

Narses (Justinian's treasurer), a Persarmenian, **i.15.31**; sent by Theodora with Marcellus to Rufinianae to discern John the Cappadocian's intentions and, if necessary, kill him, **i.25.24–27**

Narses (Persarmenian defector), he and his brother Aratius defeat Sittas and Belisarius in battle; both men would later desert to the Romans, **i.12.21–22**; deserts along with Aratius and their mother; well received by the emperor's treasurer Narses, a compatriot, **i.15.31**; carries out the destruction of the temples at Philae on Justinian's order, imprisoning the priests and sending the statues to Byzantium, **i.19.37**; gathers soldiers for the planned invasion of Persarmenia; his brother Isaac in command of the army units at Theodosiopolis, **ii.24.12–14**; frustrated that Nabedes had withdrawn his entire force to Anglon; first to engage with the Persians at Anglon; dies in battle, **i.25.11–28**

Nicetas, father of the Roman commander John, **i.13.21; ii.19.36; ii.24.15**

Nonnosus, his *History* in which he recounts his embassy to the Ethiopians, Amerites (Homerites) and Saracens, **§1**; his grandfather sent by Anastasius I on an embassy to al-Harith; his father, Abrames (Abraham) sent by Justin I to rescue two Roman commanders from al-Mundhir, **§2**; despatched to Caïsus (Qays) as an ambassador; his father had previously made a peace treaty with Caïsus, **§4**; instructed to bring Caïsus to the emperor and to meet